T0342315

— AQUINAS AND THE MARKET —

Aquinas and the Market

TOWARD A HUMANE ECONOMY

Mary L. Hirschfeld

Harvard University Press

Cambridge, Massachusetts & London, England / 2018

Second printing

Library of Congress Cataloging-in-Publication Data
Names: Hirschfeld, Mary L. (Mary Lee), author.
Title: Aquinas and the market : toward a humane economy / Mary L. Hirschfeld.
Description: Cambridge, Massachusetts : Harvard University Press, 2018. |
Includes bibliographical references and index.
Identifiers: LCCN 2018007166 | ISBN 9780674986404 (alk. paper)
Subjects: LCSH: Thomas, Aquinas, Saint, 1225?–1274. | Economics—Moral and
ethical aspects. | Thomism. | Happiness—Religious aspects.
Classification: LCC HB72 .H57 2018 | DDC 380.1—dc23
LC record available at https://lccn.loc.gov/2018007166

Contents

Preface

My rather peculiar intellectual journey began with my pursuit of a Ph.D. in economics at Harvard University, granted in 1989, and culminated in a second Ph.D., in theology, from the University of Notre Dame in 2013. Economics and theology are two very different sorts of discourses, and this book is the result of my effort to sort out the resulting cacophony in my own head. When I began my career, I would never have imagined writing such a book. For starters, I was an ordinary somewhat spiritually inclined but definitely not religious type when I began my academic career at Harvard in the fall of 1983.

I went into economics for the same reason many, if not most, economists do. I thought economic flourishing played an important role in the pursuit of happiness. I wanted to make a positive contribution to society. Accordingly, I wanted to work on developing policies that would promote widespread economic prosperity. Also, I was good at economics. Part of what attracted me to economics was the fact that its central insight was counterintuitive: the best way to spread material prosperity is by allowing individuals to pursue their own self-interest. The profit motive gives self-seeking individuals an incentive to provide goods and services that are of value to others. Markets coordinate the choices of individuals far more effectively than any sort of government planning can do. It is therefore a mistake to think that the economic evils we confront are necessarily best solved by some sort of well-intentioned government intervention.

At the same time, the discipline had smart things to say about the limitations of markets and thus could also say something about why government sometimes really can help—so long as it works in a way that respects the fundamental logic of the market. By contrast with the other humanistic disciplines I had dabbled in as an undergraduate, economics felt like a science. There is a rigor to thinking like an economist, and it seems to produce insights into the world that are obscure to others. Being formed in the economic way of thinking is a conversion of sorts; one learns to see the world in a different light. One can even sense a spirit of evangelization among economists. Books like *Freakonomics* by Steven D. Levitt and Stephen J. Dubner and *Discover Your Inner Economist* by Tyler Cowen promise popular audiences a startling and better way to understand the world and even to find a surer path to happiness.[1]

That sense of excited discovery began to falter almost immediately once I began graduate study. To begin with, economics in the 1980s was obsessed with sophisticated mathematical models, often seeming to prize mathematical cleverness over generating insights into how the world actually works.[2] That problem has largely been corrected, as can be seen in the spate of popular books following *Freakonomics.* Although sophisticated theoretical models continue to be produced, the weight of the field has steadily shifted toward empirical work. Indeed, economists have even begun experimenting in labs and allowing the results of those experiments to inform their theoretical reflections.

But my unease was also rooted in a growing sense that there was something off in the economic worldview. I was hardly alone in having difficulty with that view. A cluster of crude complaints has long dogged the discipline, and I was not fully persuaded by economists' ready replies to those critiques. The first of these complaints centered on economists' depiction of human beings as reflected in the rational choice model, which assumes that individuals efficiently allocate their scarce resources (mostly income and time) to acquire the most desirable bundle of goods available to them. It has its roots in the cruder concept of *homo economicus,* or economic man, that developed in the nineteenth-century field of political economy with the aim of focusing on how economic motives would play out in market settings. The vast literature criticizing homo economicus bleeds into modern-day critiques of the rational choice model.[3] Actual humans are not as individualistic and self-seeking as homo economicus. But as economists are quick to point out, most of those critiques are off the mark with respect to the rational choice model, which simply says that people efficiently calculate how best to achieve their desired ends but is silent about the nature of those ends. Rational agents might well simply ruthlessly pursue their narrow self-interest, but the rational choice model can also account for a Mother Teresa, as long as she efficiently deploys her resources to succor the poor as well as possible.

Other standard objections to the rational choice model are also readily addressed by economists. Does the model assume people are omniscient, capable of sorting through piles of information to arrive at the best possible allocation of their limited resources? The rational choice model can easily accommodate problems stemming from the fact that information is limited and costly to acquire and from uncertainty about the future. Is it reasonable to assume that individuals make the sort of complicated mathematical calculations posited by the model? Milton Friedman assures us that as long as the model predicts well, we need not worry about whether it is subjectively true that people solve complicated problems in constrained maximization on the fly. Botanists use complicated calculations to compute how leaves should respond to maximize their exposure to available sunlight, calculations that lead to good predictions but don't entail strong assumptions about "smart" leaves.[4] What about the fact that people sometimes make systematic errors in judgment, say, by being swept up in the euphoria surrounding a financial bubble, leading them to purchase grossly overvalued assets? In the past few decades, economists have become more open to research from the field of behavioral economics that discovers such cognitive "errors" and helps them build models that better capture actual human decision making.[5]

Although economists have good replies to the standard set of critiques aimed at the rational choice model, something about the model nonetheless persistently nagged at me. The strength of the model is its ability to map a wide range of motivations into formally identical mathematical equations. Bernie Madoff might seek his happiness by efficiently getting as many yachts as he can, while Mother Teresa might seek her happiness by efficiently caring for as many of the poor as she can. The math is the same in either case. The economic approach therefore can help us understand the choices of all people, not just those motivated by their own narrow self-interest. Moreover, the mathematical analysis does not preclude a normative assessment. We are free to esteem Mother Teresa more highly than we esteem Bernie Madoff. And yet that normative assessment lies outside of the economic analysis itself. As a result, it comes to seem like a marginal concern.

The impressive mathematical sophistication employed in economic analysis makes it seem more substantive or more "real" than whatever nebulous feelings underlie our normative valuations. It can give an impression that the real truth about Madoff and Mother Teresa is that they both are just calculating how to efficiently achieve their respective goals, with any other moral claims being an optional addition one might wish to make. Not infrequently, I encounter students who walk away with exactly that impression. For them, the fact that all people are "just" pursuing their own desires means that all people are morally equivalent. Luigi Zingales reports the same thing. Students exposed to Nobel laureate economist Gary Becker's analysis of crime as an exercise in weighing out costs and benefits come away thinking that one should commit a "crime" if the expected benefits of doing so outweigh the expected costs (including some probability of jail time).[6]

My unease extended beyond the way economic language masks ethical differences in the goods individuals choose to pursue. The language also seemed to me to obscure differences in the way choices are made. Consider the language Becker employs to describe our marriage choices: "According to the economic approach, a person decides to marry when the utility expected from marriage exceeds that expected from remaining single or from additional search for a more suitable mate. Similarly, a married person terminates his (or her) marriage when the utility anticipated from becoming single or marrying someone else exceeds the loss in utility from separation, including losses due to physical separation from one's children, division of joint assets, legal fees, and so forth."[7]

On the one hand, yes, decisions to marry or to divorce have to be essentially decisions about what makes a person better off in light of the goods that person is pursuing. On the other hand, surely there is a difference between calculating whether ham or turkey will best do for dinner tonight and deciding on a marriage partner. The language of costs and benefits seems appropriate for mundane choices but seems lacking when attached to something as meaningful as marriage. But it is difficult to articulate that difference in a way that can escape the inexorable logic of the claim that people simply act so as to obtain the best outcome measured in terms of whatever goods they think are worthy of pursuit. We may not want to think all of our decisions are calculated efforts to trade off costs and benefits, but economists are good at reducing all of our decisions to just those sorts of trade-offs, arguing that noneconomists simply fail to see how a suitable understanding of the costs and benefits involved in a given decision address the concerns noneconomists might have.

As I struggled with these sorts of questions, I felt like the person viewing the picture that could be an old woman on one take or a young woman on another. Some days it seemed like economic language really was an innocuous way of usefully describing human choice. Other days it seemed like the language was obscuring essential differences in the types of choices we confront.[8] Nor did this seem to me to be purely an academic question. I had gone into the discipline of economics out of a conviction that it had smart things to say about how to promote human flourishing. That hope was undermined by my growing fear that economics rested on a language that obscures the features of human life that give it its richness, meaning, and moral weight. To the extent that economic language influences culture, it could be actively counterproductive in the quest to promote genuine human flourishing.

To compound my problem, I had increasing doubts about the role economic prosperity itself plays in fostering happiness. While it seems clear that economic growth is a real blessing for those mired in poverty, it is less obvious that economic growth helps those who already have the means to meet immediate material needs. Although a field in the economics of happiness has emerged in the last decade, the subject of the relationship between economic prosperity and happiness was not broached in my course work at Harvard. I stumbled on the problem for myself after I got my first job. My income had more than doubled compared with what it had been in graduate school. I went from a cramped studio apartment to a nicely sized one-bedroom apartment. I got my first car. I got a much nicer television. I got better clothes. I was able to eat out more often. Yet I was not only not twice as happy as I had been in graduate school, I was not happier at all. The excitement of the improvement in my standard of living wore off quickly, and I reverted back to a baseline level of happiness that in retrospect depended entirely on relationships and my own personal development. A bit of research revealed that my experience was not an isolated phenomenon. Happiness has at best a dubious connection with economic prosperity once basic needs are met.[9] Insofar as I had been drawn into economics because I thought that promoting widespread economic prosperity was a good way of promoting widespread happiness, this discovery was, to put it mildly, problematic for me.

My response to these qualms was to take a position at Occidental College in Los Angeles, with the aim of teaching undergraduate economics in a liberal arts setting. My plan was to avail myself of opportunities for interdisciplinary teaching, in the hope that I could learn from other disciplines something about the nature of happiness that would allow me to think more clearly about the role economic prosperity does or does not play in promoting it. That hope was largely realized. In teaching these interdisciplinary courses I began to learn enough about history and philosophy to begin to reflect on the provisional nature of the worldview that undergirds modern economic thought. I began teaching a course I called the Development of Capitalism, which used a mix of economic history, economic thought, and intellectual history to trace out the cultural and economic transformations that had to take place to move us from the medieval economy to modern capitalism. As I continued to read and ponder, I launched a course on economics and philosophy that mostly surveyed various challenges to the economic worldview. At the same time, I continued to teach core economic courses—introductory economics, intermediate macroeconomic theory, finance, and econometrics. It was a comfortable mix. I enjoyed teaching the power of economic logic. I enjoyed stepping back and thinking about how that logic fit into the big picture.

And then I converted to Catholicism. I will not recount that story here, but the key point is that it was unexpected. It was not the product of searching philosophical or theological inquiry into the existence of God or the truth of the various world religions. It was more a matter of being knocked off my horse and then dusting myself off with a mysterious but overpowering sense that I needed to go to the local parish and find out what I would need to do to become a Catholic. I was not even particularly sure what that might entail. Given that I was a spiritually inclined person living in Los Angeles, it had been natural to join various pagan groups, and my initial intent in becoming Catholic was simply to translate Catholicism's rather odd set of beliefs into terms I could understand as a pagan. So, for example, purgatory was obviously just a code for reincarnation. That did not last long. Six months later, when I received the sacraments at Easter Vigil in 1998, my intellectual world had entirely upended. St. Augustine and especially St. Thomas Aquinas were my new intellectual and spiritual heroes.[10]

The Catholic tradition I entered into offered a powerful account of the human situation, especially the human project of seeking happiness. It is, however, an account that is radically at odds with the modern take on those questions, especially as embodied in the discipline of economics. The next few years were intellectually exhilarating, as seeing the world afresh usually is. It left me at an impasse, however. It is challenging enough to train students to think like economists when one is fully committed to that project, even more challenging when one has doubts. Yet I was unsure what else I could do. That impasse was overcome through the agency of a woman I know only as Angela, whom I met at a conference on vocation. I had expressed my frustration at having gone through a profound conversion yet finding myself stuck in a job aimed at bolstering a view of life I was no longer committed to. Angela came up to me after our session and asked what I would do if I won the lottery. My answer was unhesitating: I would study theology. She said, "There you go." And so I did. Within a week I had an application in at Notre Dame. I sold my house, gave up tenure (and my corner office), and went back to school.

Although I had expected to end up where I have ended up—working to bring theology and economics into conversation—my first few years at Notre Dame led me to think it might be best to simply be a pure theologian. I loved studying theology. I had the privilege of learning from brilliant and inspiring scholars like Gary Anderson, David Burrell, John Cavadini, Jennifer Herdt, Gerald McKenny, Cyril O'Regan, Joseph Wawrykow, and many others. I especially loved studying Aquinas. But when it came time to start thinking about a dissertation topic, my wonderful adviser, Jean Porter, said to me in her inimitable West Texas accent, "Mary, you have cards to play. The world has plenty of able scholars working on Aquinas. It does not have a lot of people with your background."

I had been resisting working on theological economics. Although I was in some sense bilingual, capable of thinking within the economic paradigm and thinking within a theological paradigm, it was far from obvious to me how to go about making the two disciplines mutually intelligible. On reading works on the economy by theologians, it was easy to see how an economist would respond (usually dismissively). It was harder to see how to respond in a way that would do justice to economics while still taking on board the critical insights offered by the theologians. Moreover, on hearing about my background, people almost always expressed the expectation that I must have some interesting things to say about just wages or economic injustice. Yet for me, beginning with particular economic issues was a nonstarter. The way I would think about them as an economist was radically different from how I would think about them as a theologian, and so I was left with nothing useful to say at all.

The path forward came into focus when I was working on a paper on Aquinas's account of private property. Unlike many of the Christians of his time, Aquinas defends private property, and not merely as a concession to our sinful natures. But his defense of private property seemed to rest on an internal contradiction. On the one hand, he seemed to be saying that private property is lawful because we are more inclined to work when we can enjoy the fruits of our labors, and on the other hand, he argued that we should nonetheless hold private property as if in common, that is, ready to share with others. The first argument read to me like the standard economic argument about the efficaciousness of incentives. But how could those incentives work, if we were to use our property as though it belonged to everyone? I wrestled with this problem for a long time before I realized that the seeming contradiction only emerges if one begins with the assumptions about human nature employed by economists, namely, that our wants are insatiable. Aquinas's anthropology is quite different, and in light of that anthropology there is no contradiction.[11] This was the crucial insight. To do theological economics properly it is best to begin not with economic topics but rather with a theological account of human nature.

In retrospect, this should have been obvious all along. We engage in economic activity to secure the means to pursue the goods we really value. An account of what constitutes a good life is thus crucial to any ethical or theological reflection on economic issues: it provides the standard by which we can judge whether the economy is moving us toward the higher goods we are ultimately seeking. As I pondered further, I found that Aquinas's theological framework provided much-needed traction for working out a full-blown theological economics.

For starters, his *Summa theologica* offers an explicit architecture for thinking about human life in light of the relationship between God and creation.[12] The systematic nature of his thought is not unlike the clarity one finds in economic models. Aquinas lays out his assumptions and explicitly articulates the logic involved in working out the consequences of those assumptions. More importantly, Aquinas begins his account of human nature with the premise that humans are driven by the quest for happiness. That starting point parallels the central premise of the economic approach, namely, that humans seek to maximize utility, where utility stands in for whatever it is that a given agent wants. For both Aquinas and for economists, human desire cannot be satiated by finite goods. Rather, we are driven by the desire for more. The resulting point of contact makes it easier to identify the assumptions that underlie the divergences between Aquinas's account of human choice and that of economists.

As it turns out, the key assumptions rest on metaphysics. How we understand the quest for something more depends crucially on how we understand the relationship between the finite goods of this world and some transcendent good. Economists work within what Charles Taylor would call an immanent frame, bracketing the question of the transcendent good from their account.[13] Aquinas works within an open frame, treating our pursuit of finite goods in light of God, the transcendent source of our ultimate happiness. It might seem that such metaphysical concerns are too arcane to make much difference in how we think about economic life. But as this book shows, attention to the difference in metaphysical assumptions has important ramifications for how we understand human rationality, the role of economic activity, and the relationship between ethics and economic issues. In this light, working out a theological approach to economics based on the thought of Thomas Aquinas is an exercise in demonstrating that economic analysis is not as robust to differing backdrop assumptions regarding metaphysics as economists might think. It also delivers a vision of a humane economy, one that is in service to genuine human flourishing.

At this juncture economists would object that it might be well and good to talk about how economic life should be configured to reflect this different set of metaphysical assumptions, but that has nothing to do with their own project, which involves developing models that offer good predictions about how humans actually behave. As it turns out, Aquinas is also a good resource for meeting this objection. For Aquinas, an objective account of human beings includes not just a description of the way we should order our affairs to achieve the temporal happiness possible in this life but also a description of the ways we fail to do so. In his reflections on temporal happiness, Aquinas draws heavily on Aristotle, who places virtue at the center of his account of human happiness. The cultivation of virtue entails perfecting human nature, that is, fully realizing the potential of being a rational animal. Because we are animals we have powerful emotions—desires and aversions. But because we have reason, we are also capable of guiding those passions in the light of reason's apprehension of the true and the good. As discussed in Chapter 4, most of us have at best mixed success in the project, which means that to a large extent we allow our untutored passions to govern our behavior. This, in turn, leads to the sort of behavior that is well described by the rational choice model. In other words, Aquinas works with a model of human behavior that can explain why economic analysis works as well as it does.

But Aquinas's framework leads us to expect that humans can and at least sometimes do behave in ways that are not captured by the economic models. In addition to being a richer account of human nature, it also provides us with a better understanding of what a well-functioning economy would look like. Thus a Thomistic economist would be able to deploy many of the tools he or she had learned from mainstream economists, but in a more fruitful way. The key question at the heart of this project would be how to balance pragmatic realism about the fact that humans are most often driven by incentives with the need to address humans directly as rational agents capable of discerning what goods are worthy of pursuit, in a form that is better suited to attaining genuine happiness but is not well captured by the rational choice model. The research concerning how to think about this two-tiered account of human behavior would be conducted in light of the richer vision of what an economy that is genuinely in service of human flourishing would look like. My hope for this book is that it might open the door to the possibility of such a line of inquiry, one that I think is necessary if we are to navigate the moral challenges posed by the modern economy.

Audience

The most obvious audience for a book that employs Aquinas as a theological resource for thinking about economics is Christian theologians and Christian economists. One of the primary purposes of the book is to help the Church better appreciate the role of markets in promoting genuine human flourishing. At the same time, it offers an approach that can sharpen the important moral criticisms that need to be brought to bear on modern economic practices. My hope is that the book can help set aside naïve criticisms of both economics and economic life, clearing the ground for the real concerns that should be raised.

The book addresses issues that are important for secular audiences as well. First, it offers a compelling account of how economic activity should be ordered to human flourishing. Much of this account draws on Aristotle, who requires no theological commitment. I do spend much time elaborating on the theological inflection Aquinas gives to Aristotle, because it allows us to see more clearly and more fully the futility of pursuing happiness by trying to maximize a utility function, but the core insights remain available to all. Second, from my perspective, the more important reason this book should be engaged by secular audiences is that it calls attention to the impact metaphysical assumptions have on how we understand the human pursuit of happiness. One of the core arguments of this book is that economics is not value neutral. Mainstream economics is tacitly grounded in its own metaphysics. Because rationality depends on the kind of metaphysical world we inhabit, both the metaphysics itself and its relationship to our concepts of happiness and rationality should be explicitly thought through. If the work encourages secular answers to the questions raised by this approach, one of its missions will have been accomplished. Third, and relatedly, the Thomistic approach demonstrates that we need to begin integrating the various disciplines again. The Thomistic approach can allow for a meaningful conversation between normative-ethical disciplines and positive-scientific disciplines. It sets out a challenge for secular thinkers to find a way to build their own bridges between disciplines—bridges that are essential if we are to address the moral challenges of contemporary capitalism.

— AQUINAS AND THE MARKET —

— 1 —

To Serve God or Mammon?

The Dialogue between Theology and Economics

You cannot serve both God and money (Mt 6:24). The biblical warning points to a paradox underlying Western culture. Rooted in a Judeo-Christian tradition rife with admonitions to avoid excessive materialism and to practice economic justice, the Western world nonetheless has given rise to the set of institutions we might loosely refer to as capitalism.[1] The expanding reach of markets, first within the nation-states of Western Europe and North America and then throughout the world through the process of globalization, has allowed billions of people to enjoy improved standards of living, longer life spans, and better education.[2] Yet capitalism continues to be subject to critiques reflecting the biblical admonitions. Does it promote a culture that is excessively materialistic? Does it depend on or even deepen the problems of poverty and economic injustice? Nor are such critiques the sole province of religious believers. Secular and even atheist voices have raised them.[3] Nonetheless, the tension between the Christian suspicion of excessive wealth and greed and the workings of the global market economy particularly demands a theological response.

Such a response has not been in short supply. Most notably, the magisterium of the Catholic Church has issued a series of encyclicals and pastoral letters on the vexed subject of how to weigh the goods produced by the spread of capitalism against the moral evils that seem to accompany it.[4] Individual theologians across denominations have likewise tackled the subject, with responses ranging from an embrace of capitalism to a radical rejection of it.[5] Haunting these responses, both theological and secular, is the difficulty of finding a language that can bring moral concerns to bear on markets that obey the logic of profit seeking. Without a bridging language, ethical or theological critiques seem to be a matter of imposition on the market—an argument that we should curtail or limit the market's natural functioning.[6]

Charles Taylor offers a good initial description of the situation, suggesting that we live in a secular age in which "as we function within various spheres of activity—economic, political, cultural, educational, professional, recreational—the norms and principles we follow, the deliberations we engage in, generally don't refer to God or to any religious beliefs; the considerations we act on are internal to the 'rationality' of each sphere—maximum gain within the economy, the greatest benefit to the greatest number in the political arena, and so on."[7] The resulting fragmentation undergirds our sense that ethical language is alien to economic thought. Yet there can be no coherence to a society if that fragmentation is complete. And, in point of fact, one can argue that the discourse of economics has come to dominate the public sphere, supplying it with a normative framework.[8] Indeed, as A. M. C. Waterman documents, theology played that role until it was displaced by economics in the early nineteenth century.[9] Economic considerations now decisively shape conversations in the public square. Consider, for example, political rhetoric about education, which seldom touches on its role in forming good citizens but rather dwells on the role of education in promoting economic growth and ensuring that young people gain the skills that will allow them to compete effectively in the economy.

The elevated status of economic concerns in modern culture is at once understandable and problematic. It is understandable that a liberal pluralistic culture would order its public discourse around questions of ordinary human flourishing. The inability to achieve a shared understanding of the higher goods a society might pursue leads naturally to the thought that we should collectively work to ensure that the means for pursuing private understandings of the higher good are broadly and abundantly available.[10] Yet it is problematic because once the public square is shaped around the shared goal of achieving prosperity, the instrumental character of prosperity becomes obscured. We forget to ask what our material wealth is for and often end up sacrificing more important human goods for the sake of greater income. The resilience of critiques about the excessive materialism and injustice of modern market economies reflects the incoherence of a society that de facto treats the instrumental good of economic prosperity as the highest common good.

Because economics itself cannot provide a framework that orders economic flourishing to the higher ends economic flourishing should serve, discourses that directly consider the way goods should be ordered are needed if we are to think intelligently about the ethical implications of market economies.[11] Theology is one such discourse. A theological economics is, of course, of immediate interest for believers who worry about how to reconcile their economic pursuits with their faith commitments. But it is of more general value insofar as it serves as a reminder that some comprehensive framework is necessary if we are to remember that wealth is meant to serve us and not to be our master. Theological economics at least raises the big questions of the proper function of economics in a good society, and thus it should be a useful starting point for broader conversations about how to integrate the various spheres of our lives. Yet theological economics has had difficulty gaining traction.

The Fundamental Dilemma of Theological Economics

For theological ethics to do its job properly, theology would need to be the dominant partner. That is to say, if it is to be the discourse that allows us to think about how the good of economic flourishing is to be related to other goods, such as justice or goods threatened by excessive materialism, it needs to be the discourse that determines how to make sense of economic claims. Yet by almost any measure, economics enjoys greater prestige and correspondingly has a greater impact on public discourse than does theology.

One measure of the relative standing of the two disciplines is that theologians who wish to comment on economic matters need to respond to the discipline of economics, whether to affirm, modify, or reject its claims. The reverse is not true of economists who wish to think about matters touching on religion. In his survey of the subdiscipline of the economics of religion, Lawrence Iannaccone describes the field as consisting of three main branches: the analysis of religious behavior using microeconomic theory; the study of the economic consequences of religion (for example, Max Weber and R. H. Tawney); and religious economics, which is the literature I am calling theological ethics. Because Iannaccone's survey is directed to economists who want a general overview of the field, he focuses on the first branch, briefly discusses the second, and omits the third on the grounds that "its literature is broad and far removed from the research and professional interests of most economists."[12] In other words, the economic study of religion can proceed without any acquaintance with, much less as a response to, theology. Nor do economists in general need to take any note of theological criticisms of economics—it is an ignored branch of a subdiscipline in economics that has only recently emerged and is itself quite marginal to the field as a whole. In sum, theologians have to listen to economists, while most economists do not listen to theologians at all.[13]

There are many reasons, some of them quite good, for the relative status enjoyed by economics. Most obviously, economists are experts in the sort of rationality deemed appropriate for the economic sphere. But the core difficulty in bringing theological reflection to bear on economic matters is the one first articulated by Niccolò Machiavelli in the sixteenth century: "Since my intent is to write something useful to whoever understands it, it has appeared to me more fitting to go directly to the effectual truth of the thing than to the imagination of it. And many have imagined republics and principalities that have never been seen or known to exist in truth; for it is so far from how one lives to how one should live that he who lets go of what is done for what should be done learns his ruin rather than his preservation."[14] We can talk all we want about virtue and what should ideally be the case. But in this world if you want to make things better, it is just more practical to accept humans as they are and go from there.[15] That is the economic project in a nutshell.[16]

Economists see themselves as dealing with the effectual truth of things, which for them takes the form of constructing models that accurately predict human behavior. It is true that economists are widely criticized for their unrealistic model of humans as homo economicus, an individual who rationally weighs up costs and benefits in pursuit of achieving his own ends.[17] Economists have long rebuffed such criticism by relying on Milton Friedman's classic defense of the use of "unrealistic" assumptions. The aim of economic science is to predict human behavior. As long as the models predict well, they are useful models.[18] Indeed, the interest in predictive value can be seen in the fact that economists are happy to incorporate a richer set of assumptions about human behavior into their models, so long as doing so generates better empirical results. The rapid rise in experimental economics in the last few decades, for example, is owing to the fact that models that account for cognitive biases or the impact of norms such as fairness on decision making offer good predictions.[19] Economists thus present themselves simply as pragmatic realists, an appealing stance to take in a pragmatic culture.[20]

Although economic models can incorporate a wide array of motivations, it is true that they often emphasize self-interest. For many, this is just a matter of common sense. It seems self-evident that people prefer high-paying jobs to low-paying jobs, for example. A core corollary of the thought that people pursue their self-interest is that they will respond to incentives in predictable ways. If you want to discourage gasoline consumption, tax it. If you want to encourage investment in education, subsidize it. As Michael Sandel documents, the use of the word *incentivize* has exploded in the past few decades.[21] Yet if economists' primary contribution to human knowledge were their understanding of the way incentives shape behavior, we would still be left with the worry about how to promote social goods in a society of people driven primarily by self-interest. The Machiavellian turn to realism is only pragmatic if it can somehow be turned to good results.

But as it turns out, the real power of economics lies not just in its hardheaded realism about human nature but also in its reassuring insight that markets can channel self-interested or even outright selfish behavior into socially desirable outcomes. This is, of course, just Adam Smith's famous insight that "it is not from the benevolence of the butcher, the brewer, or the baker that we expect our dinner, but from regard to their own interest."[22] The butcher seeks to make money. He does so by offering quality meat at good value. If he fails to do this, his customers will go elsewhere, and he will go bankrupt. Even better, in vying with one another for business, the butcher and his competitors will work to find better and cheaper ways of providing meat. Markets thus spur self-interested people to work hard and to innovate. In addition, the price mechanism turns out to coordinate the behavior of all these self-interested individuals more efficiently than could a benevolent social planner.[23] It is for these reasons that the spread of markets has been associated with a historically unprecedented widespread rise in standards of living. Economists thus present the attractive proposition that realism about human nature "as it is" can actually lead to better outcomes than we could get by simply urging people to be more virtuous.

Nor have economists rested on Adam Smith's crucial insight. They have gone on to rigorously investigate the question of what assumptions need to be in place to secure the claim that markets generate socially beneficial outcomes. In what is known as the first fundamental theorem of welfare economics, the economists Kenneth Arrow and Gerard Debreu have shown that under perfect competition, the market is efficient, where efficiency is taken to be a measure of a socially good result.[24] Chapter 2 takes up the question of whether efficiency is a good measure of social outcomes, but for now it is worth noting the contribution of this sort of work. Because the result rests on some strong assumptions about the nature of perfect competition, it provides a framework for thinking through the conditions in which the market works well and also the conditions in which the market can fail. Although economists have more respect for the workings of markets than do many noneconomists, they have also given us a vocabulary for naming the many forms of market failure: externalities, monopolies, public goods, asymmetric information, and so on. There are lively debates within the profession about the extent of market failures and the ability of the government to intervene to help markets function better. Economists thus have standing because they are positioned to contribute intelligently and pragmatically to some of the key public policy debates of our day, with an apparatus that does not automatically align them with one political viewpoint or another.

In addition to economists' realism about the impact of incentives on human behavior and their pragmatic assessment of the role of institutions and policies in guiding that behavior toward good social outcomes, economics resonates with the culture in important ways. We value individualism and autonomy. Economists model human behavior as individual choice. We associate scientific knowledge with that which can be quantified and empirically tested. Economists use mathematics and statistics extensively in their work. And as noted above, as a result of pluralism we treat economic prosperity as the shared good that should orient our political discourse. That naturally lends prestige to the discipline that studies the economy. Although economists can and do disagree about many things, they maintain a shared commitment to an approach to understanding human nature and the workings of the economy that reflects and amplifies some of the core orientations of our culture.

As appealing as Machiavellian pragmatism is, however, it cannot give us a complete account of the human situation. The moral critiques that have haunted both capitalism and the discipline of economics have persisted over the past few centuries. That sense of misgiving became acute in the wake of the financial crisis of 2008, which issued in a widespread cry for moral engagement with the economy. Indeed, judging from the outpouring of books on the subject by prominent economists, that need is felt even within the profession of economics.

Thus, for example, Thomas Piketty's weighty tome on excessive income inequality became a surprise best seller in 2013 and widely shaped public discourse.[25] Nobel laureate Joseph Stiglitz, a progressive economist, likewise railed against rising income inequality, taking especial aim at the problem of crony capitalism plaguing the United States.[26] Crony capitalism was subject to critique from the right as well, as exemplified by Chicago economist Luigi Zingales's book *A Capitalism for the People*.[27] Noble laureates George Akerlof and Robert Shiller extended the critique of corporate culture, arguing that because manipulation and deceit are rampant, market outcomes are frequently less efficient than economists might think.[28] And Robert Shiller attempted an assessment of the role of finance in the "good society," offering an appraisal of the strengths and weaknesses of financial markets.[29] In all of these works moral questions are central, with particular concerns about the way moral failings cause market failures. Indeed, Jeffrey Sachs opened his contribution to this oeuvre with the claim that "at the root of America's economic crisis lies a moral crisis: the decline of civic virtue among America's political and economic elite."[30]

Although it is good that so many economists recognize the moral dimensions to the economic crisis, they are unable to advance our understanding of the moral problems to which they point. It is not surprising to learn that people who are willing to cheat or use their financial power to secure favorable legislation and regulation from the government undermine the efficiency of the market. But the sense of outrage these economists express cannot be grounded in their own analysis. The whole point of the Machiavellian turn that fundamentally informs economic analysis is to leave aside efforts to exhort individuals to be virtuous in favor of designing institutions and policies that can elicit good outcomes from people as they are.

To the extent that the financial crisis points to systemic weaknesses in our economic and political institutions, it is increasingly difficult to believe that we can rely on institutions and good policy to direct human behavior as it is in socially beneficial ways. It would seem that markets can only deliver their good results to the extent that they can draw on a reservoir of moral sensibilities in the culture. So even if we take economics on its own terms, it needs an assist from some external discourse that is capable of addressing moral questions surrounding economic life. Beyond that lurk the larger questions that lie behind those moral criticisms that have haunted capitalism and the discipline of economics from their inception: What human ends are served by economic prosperity? To what extent do markets serve those ends by supplying the material goods necessary to fulfill them? To what extent do markets thwart those ends by diverting our energy to the pursuit of goods that are not really ordered to genuine human flourishing? How do we relate the pursuit of private ends to our pursuit of the common good? What would constitute justice in a market society? How do we think about balancing the pursuit of economic goods with other goods like environmental sustainability? To think well about these questions we need a framework that can integrate the diverse goods that make up human life. That is to say, we need to find a way to overcome the fragmentation that Charles Taylor associates with the secular age.

Theological economics would be one of the discourses that in principle should be able to play that role. But to do so well, it would need to tackle the challenge posed by Machiavelli. Theology or any other moral discourse is by nature oriented to a discussion of the virtues we should aspire to and the goods we should seek to live fully human lives. Those can be nice conversations to have. But how are they practical? Is there any way to craft a theological economics that can take on board the real insights on offer from the hard-headed pragmatism of economists while still contributing a substantive moral analysis? One of the features of the discipline of theology is its lack of consensus on how to approach its subject. Where economists are essentially unified in their foundational assumptions, their notion of what constitutes proper economic method, and their idea of the content of their field, theologians are fragmented not merely along confessional divides but also with respect to foundational assumptions, theological method, and understanding of the content of their field.[31] That fragmentation is evident in theological discussions of economics, where there is no agreement on the answer to the fundamental question of how to integrate economic understanding with the wisdom of theology.

Strategies for Bringing Theological Reflection to Bear on Economics

Although the literature is quite varied, we can identify three basic approaches to crafting a theological economics. First, economics could be taken as the dominant partner, in which case theological economics is a project in finding theological coherence with economics. Second, the relationship between theology and economics could be viewed as complementary, wherein theology (or any other moral discourse) reflects on what would constitute a good set of outcomes in the political-economic sphere and economists work to craft policies and institutions that would help us achieve those outcomes. Neither of these approaches succeeds in giving a perspective on ethics and economics that is not already addressed within economics itself. The third approach, in which theology is employed as an independent lens for critical evaluation of both economic life and economic discourse could, in principle, expand our perspective on ethics and economics. Unfortunately, works taking this approach are too often subject to the Machiavellian critique—substituting idealistic utopianism for pragmatic reflection on how to promote human flourishing. The aim of this book is to develop a theological economics using this third approach—working out of an explicitly theological framework—but in a way that responds to the Machiavellian challenge by being attentive to pragmatic reflection on humans as they are. To set up the project properly, it is useful to canvass the other approaches, all of which carry important insights, even if they cannot ultimately succeed.

The First Approach: Theology Bends to Economics

In his survey of theological economics, *Divine Economy: Market and Theology,* D. Stephen Long identifies three broad approaches (or traditions, as he calls them) to the question of how to integrate economics and theology. For Long, the crucial dimension for distinguishing approaches to theological economics is the extent to which they conform to market capitalism. Accordingly, he identifies a "dominant tradition" that accepts capitalism and an "emergent tradition" that is rooted in heterodox economics (mostly Marxist) rather than orthodox or modern neoclassical economics.[32] These two traditions share the strategy of developing a theology that coheres with the system of economic thought with which they begin.

Long assigns both conservative and liberal theologians to the dominant tradition.[33] According to Long, these theologians tend to accept global capitalism and the culture it produces, though they disagree about the extent to which markets should be free to operate without government intervention. More importantly, they adopt a worldview that is strongly compatible with that of economists. Like economists, they work out of a framework that distinguishes between facts and values (or positive and normative analysis, as economists would put it). Like economists, theologians in the dominant tradition adopt an anthropology that prioritizes human choice and assumes that it is choice that gives value to things. And finally, like economists they emphasize the role of unintended consequences in dividing human intention from the outcomes thereby produced. Long rejects this tradition on theological grounds, arguing that the set of assumptions adopted by these theologians tends to subordinate Christology and ecclesiology to a doctrine of creation.[34]

I take up the question of whether Long's theological criterion for rejecting this tradition is appropriate below. But leaving that aside, Long's more immediate criticism is that the main thrust of this tradition is to marshal theological arguments in support of one side or the other of contemporary political debates. Thus, for example, Michael Novak can invoke the doctrine of the *imago Dei,* or image of God, in defense of a proentrepreneurial argument for free markets, while Philip Wogaman enlists the same doctrine in arguing for a more Keynesian form of welfare capitalism.[35] As it would be surprising if reflection on the doctrine that we are created in the image of God would independently issue in conclusions that neatly map onto contemporary debates, such theology risks being seen as an effort to adorn prior political commitments with theological dressing. Worse, it is difficult to know how to bring deep theological reflection to bear on policy debates among economists who share foundational assumptions about their own discipline.

Noneconomists often fail to recognize that neoclassical and Keynesian economists jointly make up the field and have done so since Paul Samuelson's classic introductory textbook presented the neoclassical synthesis, which divided the one discipline of economics between a neoclassical conception of microeconomics and a Keynesian conception of macroeconomics.[36] Much has shifted around since Samuelson's original synthesis, but it remains the case that economists share a vocabulary about the types of models and empirical studies that count as evidence in debates about the proper role of government.[37] Because conservatives and liberals are working from the same set of foundational assumptions, theological arguments about those foundational assumptions cannot be used to buttress particular policy arguments within current debates in economics. The dominant tradition aims at relevance but is doomed to remain marginalized because it misconstrues the source of disagreements about the proper role for markets and the government. Could the emergent tradition fare better?

In the field of economics, there is an array of heterodox schools of thought, which would include Marxist, post-Keynesian, and feminist economics. The theologies Long identifies as part of the emergent tradition are likewise quite diverse, ranging from liberation theology to the feminist theology of Rosemary Radford Ruether.[38] According to Long, what these theologians have in common is opposition to the notion that Christian theology can be compatible with capitalism. In addition, they pursue a Marxist strategy for bringing theology into conversation with economics. For Long, this has the virtue of introducing a historical dimension to the analysis that neoclassical economics lacks, but it comes at the expense of acceding to the Marxist idea that "theological production is limited and constrained by its social conditions" thereby reducing the "original gift that makes theology possible" to a "theologically unwarranted materialism."[39] In the end, most of these theologians end up challenging theological orthodoxy insofar as it is seen to be complicit in the oppression they associate with capitalism.

Insofar as the emergent tradition draws on bodies of economic thought that can radically challenge capitalism and the worldview that shapes it, it offers resources for moral reflection on economic life. There are two major limitations, however. First is the one it shares with the dominant tradition. The theological themes are adduced to support the economic analysis offered by heterodox schools of thought, and as such can be seen as mostly serving to extend theological endorsement to existing secular approaches. Second, the underlying heterodox analysis itself does not successfully navigate the Machiavellian challenge. It typically does not address the success mainstream economics has in describing humans as they are and therefore seems to issue in recommendations that seem utopian. Mainstream economists tend to ignore heterodox economics for that reason. Nonetheless, heterodox economics offers valuable reflection on the role of power relations in economic life, and it often draws attention to the important question of what ends economic life should serve. What is needed is a form of theological economics that can learn from those perspectives but also do justice to the insights on offer from mainstream economics.

The fundamental weakness of both the dominant and the emergent traditions is that the theological analysis ends up serving primarily to buttress positions that are already well developed in secular discourse.

An alternative approach would be to argue for an explicit division of labor between theology and economics.

The Second Approach: A Division of Labor between Theology and Economics

A second approach to thinking about a dialogue between theology and economics is to argue that each discipline has its own special sphere of competence. The task of theologians or philosophers is to identify what ends are worthy of pursuit. The task of economists is to determine the best policies or institutions for achieving those ends. Thus, for example, theologians might present an argument that an important goal is to ensure that the working poor are able to make a decent living for themselves. Economists can then take up the task of assessing what sort of policy proposals (such as a minimum wage or an earned income tax credit) might best achieve those ends. Long does not include examples of this sort of approach to theological economics in his survey, perhaps because this way of approaching the subject is one that is more natural to economists.

This proposed division of labor neatly mirrors the self-understanding of economists, who distinguish between positive and normative economics. Normative economics is a discussion of what values we ought to pursue, taking up questions like how much we should weight the often-competing goals of pursuing efficiency or pursuing equity. These are questions economists are generally happy to leave to philosophers (and by extension to theologians). The discipline of economics properly understood focuses on positive analysis, which studies how markets work and evaluates various policy prescriptions in terms of their effectiveness at achieving the goals identified through normative considerations as worthy of pursuit. In other words, economists are experts on evaluating what are the best means for achieving goals identified by others.[40]

An example of theological economics done in this spirit can be found in the pastoral letter *Economic Justice for All*, issued by the U.S. Catholic bishops in 1986.[41] They begin their letter by arguing that their faith impels them to speak out about the economy, insofar as the gospel should be lived out in the world.[42] Their particular aim is to "lift up the human and ethical dimensions of economic life, aspects too often neglected in public discussion," without making any particular political or economic claims.[43] Translating this point into economic language, the bishops are offering theological wisdom about the ends we should strive to achieve in our economy, leaving assessment of the best means to those ends to secular policy makers. Indeed, they go on to say that the pastoral letter "does not embrace any particular economic theory of how the economy works, nor does it attempt to resolve the disputes between different schools of thought."[44] Their intent is plainly to be deferential to the discipline of economics, and they claim to have relied on "wide consultation" in preparation of the document.[45] Nonetheless, in an explicit bid to be relevant, they offer a series of specific policy proposals. In doing so, they reveal the limitations of this approach.

The bishops begin by articulating six basic moral principles that guide their assessment of our economic system. The six basic principles are, first, that we should judge every decision and institution by the impact it has on the dignity of the human person; second, that human dignity can only be realized and protected in community; third, that all people have a right to participate in the economic life of society; fourth, that all members of society have a special obligation to the poor and vulnerable; fifth, that human rights are the minimum condition for life in community; and finally, that society as a whole has the moral responsibility to enhance human dignity and protect human rights.[46] The insistence on recalling that economic activity should be in service of human well-being and reminders that we are to be mindful of the welfare of all members of society present perfectly good Christian principles. Indeed, they are implicit in the central arguments of this book.

The difficulty lies in the fact that the bishops felt the need to push beyond their own area of expertise to offer specific policy proposals. As they argue, "We do not claim to make these prudential judgments with the same kind of authority that marks our declarations of principle. But, we feel obliged to teach by example how Christians can undertake concrete analysis and make specific judgments on economic issues."[47] Their example involves intervening in ongoing debates about the best mix of policies to address unemployment, poverty, and agriculture, offering a set of proposals that parallel the Democratic Party platform of that era.[48] Although the bishops claim to have consulted widely in preparing their letter, they offer no citations of prominent conservative economists, who in the mid-1980s were ascendant in the discipline.[49]

Because the bishops do not claim any economic expertise for themselves, it would seem they favored liberal policy recommendations over conservative policy recommendations on moral grounds. In doing so, they fall into an error that is common to noneconomists, mistaking economic debates about the best means for achieving agreed-upon ends for debates about what ends are worth pursuing. But as Partha Dasgupta writes, the debates in economics are

> rarely about values. It is almost as though the protagonists are embarrassed to air their values because to do so would be to state the obvious and sound grand at the same time. I have yet to read an economic document which does not regard as given that involuntary unemployment should be reduced wherever it is extensive, or that destitution should be a thing of the past, or that it would be a tragedy if the rain forest were to disappear. But there are many disagreements about the most effective ways to reduce involuntary unemployment, destitution, and the extinction of rain forests.[50]

Economists who disagree with the proposition that we should raise the minimum wage, for example, are not arguing that we should be unconcerned about the working poor. On the contrary, they are arguing that out of concern for the working poor we should be cautious about adopting policies that might well result in fewer of them having jobs. The same sort of point can be made about macroeconomic policies, which was the subject of a large section of the bishop's letter. Economists who argue against government policies to boost employment do so on the grounds that such policies are either ineffective or actively counterproductive (that is, will generate more unemployment or instability in the long run). On economists' own understanding these are debates within the realm of positive economics, among economists who broadly share the same set of normative goals.

To be fair to the bishops, economists' self-understanding tends to understate the degree to which prior political commitments shape economic research. As Anthony Randazzo and Jonathan Haidt point out, debates

within economics about questions such as the efficacy of the minimum wage are not purely driven by dispassionate assessment of the
data.[51] Empirical research on economic issues is often mixed, and economists tend to read the evidence in a way that aligns with their political
leanings. Economists on the right are more likely to arrive at promarket
conclusions, and economists on the left are more likely to arrive at conclusions supporting government intervention. Indeed, economists rarely
are forced by their research to change their minds on debated issues.
Moreover, the political cast to intraeconomic debates is rooted in genuine moral disagreement. As Randazzo and Haidt suggest, economists
on the right work out of a moral narrative that sees capitalism as liber-
ating, while economists on the left work out of a moral narrative that
sees capitalism as exploitative. But while it is true that the actual work
of economists is shaped by moral and political concerns, the apparatus
of the discipline is neutral in principle. Economic debates proceed with
the tacit understanding that all parties agree on what counts as a desirable outcome, and with a shared understanding of what sort of economic
research would be useful to settle questions.

We are left with a conundrum. The second approach proposes that
normative goals should be set by a discourse such as theology or philosophy, while leaving the analysis of means for achieving those goals
to economists. But as Dasgupta observes, economists already broadly
share the same sets of goals. It is difficult to imagine finding an economist who does not think economic policy should aim at reducing unemployment, creating more good-paying jobs, eliminating poverty, and
so on. Indeed, there would seem to be a broad social consensus that
these are important aims. The political divisions we have on these
questions center on radically different intuitions about how best to
pursue them. But if that is so, what value is really added by theologians?
How is arguing that combatting excessive unemployment is an urgent
concern different from arguing that finding a cure for cancer is an
urgent concern? Yet no theologians feel compelled to exhort the world
to work harder to cure cancer.

The bishops' pastoral letter reflects a persistent tendency in our culture to imbue technical debates about the best policies for achieving
widely shared goals with a moral valence. Perhaps that tendency issues
from a deeper unease, a sense that seeking to derive good outcomes out

of the baser motives of self-seeking individuals is not an adequate account of human aspiration. Accordingly, the third approach to theological reflection on economics rejects the Machiavellian insistence that we simply accept "the effectual truth" of human nature. To think well about economics, we need to recover a discourse about what humans should be.

The Third Approach: Theological Critique of the Premises of Economics

The third approach corresponds with the body of work Long identifies as the "remnant tradition."[52] It is the tradition that resists economic thought most deeply and thus would seem to be a promising place from which to begin a project in theological economics that has enough independence from economics to be able to fruitfully interact with economics, rather than just rehearse existing economic disputes in a theological key.

Long identifies three writers in this tradition: Bernard Dempsey, Alasdair MacIntyre, and John Milbank. According to Long, what unites these three thinkers is that they draw on Thomas Aquinas to provide a framework for thinking about economics that sees value as objectively embedded in the universe before any human valuation. Aquinas's framework does, indeed, provide resources for integrating economic questions into an overarching moral vision, thereby overcoming the sense that ethical language is somehow alien to economic logic. However, to fully realize this promise, one would have to be able to incorporate the insights on offer from economics. Yet as Long's own categorization of the three approaches suggests, the aim of the residual tradition is to oppose economics. As he puts it, "The three strategies I examine structure the three parts of this work—the dominant, emergent, and residual traditions. Each designation is intended to imply a relationship of theology to the marginalist rationality that orders, and arises from, modern political and economic formations. The dominant tradition is most consistent with marginalism. The emergent tradition is at odds with it, but still seems to maintain some of its vestiges. The residual tradition is in opposition to it."[53]

Of the three writers, MacIntyre and especially Milbank are arguably motivated by a desire to distance themselves from capitalism and the discipline that articulates its principles. The problem is that capitalism is too complex to be either embraced or rejected whole-heartedly. Moreover, economists have a sustained discipline because they base their analysis on aspects of economic activity and the workings of markets that are true, even if the overall framework tends to distort those truths. What is needed is not a theological economics that simply rejects mainstream economics but rather a theological economics confident enough in its own voice, and knowledgeable enough about economics, to offer a more nuanced evaluation about what we can and cannot learn from economists. Long, ironically, ends up ceding too much power to economic thought when he seeks out an approach which is simply in opposition to it. The economic tail is still wagging the theological dog.

To see the difficulties that arise when theological economics is constructed in opposition to capitalism or mainstream economic thought, it is useful to consider the work of one of the most prominent current writers in this vein, Kathryn Tanner. In one of her earliest books, *God and Creation in Christian Theology: Tyranny or Empowerment?*, Tanner tackles the difficulty of theological talk that stems from the strange relationship between God and world. In that work, she argues that the only theological language adequate to the fact that God is neither of this world nor radically apart from this world is "non-contrastive" language.[54] Such language allows us to describe a God who is neither rival to the powers of this world nor wholly aloof from it. On such a view, one might think that theological reflection on a worldly phenomenon like the market economy might be similarly noncontrastive, neither accepting the market on its own terms nor simply talking past worldly understandings.

It is thus with some surprise that one turns to her book *Economy of Grace* in which she deliberately constructs a theological framework with the aim of "[bringing] out the greatest contrast with the economic principles of our experience."[55] Further on she says that the Christian story is "highly malleable" and that her intent is to tell a story that is attentive to the history of Christian thought but "is specifically designed, nonetheless, to be capitalism's contrast case."[56] Tanner thus allows economics to set the agenda, with the only independent exercise of theological reflection being to negate it. In doing so, she concedes too much to economics and misses an opportunity to address the tensions surrounding the Machiavellian challenge directly.

Tanner's starting point is the question of how goods are distributed. She begins by arguing that we should think of the economy and religion as fields wherein goods are pursued and distributed. In the field of economics, the goods are material wealth, and they are pursued in a competitive process because they are scarce. Indeed, all other secular fields are constituted by the competitive pursuit of a scarce good, where the good could be athletic or artistic achievement, physical beauty, or any other metric by which we seek to compare ourselves with one another. Tanner identifies a field of Christianity as a contrasting case, wherein the good, grace, is not scarce and the pursuit of it is noncompetitive. Finally, she asserts the dominance of theological discourse by arguing that we should contest the notion that all fields of human endeavor are inherently competitive.[57] In particular, we should take the principles of the economy of grace and apply them to the material economy to transform it into a field that is likewise noncompetitive to the degree possible.[58]

In making this move, Tanner challenges the notion that economists are just dealing with the effectual truth of human nature. Is it really the case that the best we can do is concede that humans are mostly driven by their narrow self-interest and sit back and hope that a proper mix of markets and government regulation can nonetheless produce socially beneficial results? Tanner offers a vivid portrait of humans as they could be, animated by a spirit of community and self-giving. Nor is it a portrait of human nature that is foreign to our experience. The joy of sharing a meal around a Thanksgiving table is real enough. Insofar as economic logic marginalizes this aspect of human nature, it really is missing something important about the human condition. Moreover, in according economists esteem in part because they present themselves as objective scientists who are simply describing humans as they are, we might lose sight of the way culture can shape human behavior. As Tanner puts it, we need not take our "social worlds of economics and politics" as given, because "as modern people we are aware of their malleability by our own efforts, the way such structures are maintained only by way of our complicity with them."[59] Our adoption of economic logic might actively hinder our ability to live up to the better angels of our nature.

These are valuable reminders. The lost opportunity stems from Tanner's choice to emphasize the contrast between an economy of grace and a competitive economy. Rather than building up a model that begins with human anthropology in relationship to God, Tanner begins with the idea that our experience of God's grace should be the prism through which we consider economic life. The difficulty is that her model deals with spiritual goods, which are therefore not subject to what economists would call rivalry in consumption. A good is subject to rivalry in consumption if my consumption of the good precludes you from consuming that good. Apples, for example, are subject to rivalry if considered as food. If I eat the apple, you cannot also eat that apple.

Tanner acknowledges the question any economist would ask, which is whether the noncompetitiveness that might well be appropriate in a field where the good is spiritual can work in a field where the good is material, but she proceeds to offer no answer to that question. All she says is that "God creates the whole world, in all its aspects—material and spiritual—according to such a noncompetitive economy, so that it should be such a noncompetitive economy to every degree possible; it holds us creatures of body and soul up to its measure."[60] Yet God manifestly did create a world in which some goods are subject to rivalry in consumption. There must, then, be some language that accounts for rivalry and the associated degree of possessiveness that is nonetheless compatible with our call to mirror God's graciousness. But if that is so, it cannot be the case that rivalry or even competitiveness is per se contrary to a spirit of graciousness. On Tanner's own account, it would seem that there is some possibility that some of the structures of capitalism, which are ordered around the rivalry in consumption that is intrinsic to God's creation, are not inherently opposed to the economy of grace. Some interesting theological work could be done on these questions, but Tanner's contrastive approach precludes her from taking them up.

In failing to take up these questions, Tanner ends up simply talking past economists. As economist Julie Nelson puts it,

> Where this book takes a wrong turn, in my opinion, is in assuming that economies are defined by "principles" rather than by actual relations, and then setting up a false dualism with pre-

sumably sinful competition involving exclusive-in-use private goods on one side, and presumably virtuous relations based on public goods on the other. This ignores the fact that various real-world economic relations will be characterized by the existence or nonexistence of exclusivity quite irrespectively of what "principles" we might try to apply. As exclusivity is apparently part of (God's) creation, it seems to me that the appropriate question is not how to get rid of it, but how to deal with it.[61]

Because her main apparatus simply assumes away the core problem of how to allocate goods that are rival in consumption, Tanner's attempt to intervene constructively on specific policy issues in her third chapter ends up recapitulating the naïve instinct that the way to express a concern for the common good necessarily lies in adopting liberal economic policies. In other words, her economy of grace ends up de facto reverting to the second approach to theological economics discussed above.

Tanner avoids many of these problems in her second engagement with theological economics, presented in her Gifford lecture series, "Christianity and the New Spirit of Capitalism."[62] In those lectures, Tanner again adopts a contrastive approach, this time opposing what she calls the spirit of financial capitalism with a proposed retrieval of a new Christian spirit. Her project plays off Max Weber's analysis of the way Christian belief and practices helped to form the spirit of capitalism, arguing that a different reading of Christianity could produce the cultural spirit needed to avoid the dehumanizing effects of the relentless drive to maximize profits fomented by financial capitalism. Tanner's contrastive approach works better in this case, because the contrast she draws lies in the realm of culture, which is more directly amenable to theological analysis. Her lectures provide an illuminating argument that the spirit of capitalism permeates our culture, warping our sense of time, and limiting our sense of the possibilities for genuine human fulfillment. The imperative to maximize profits dehumanizes economic life, and that dehumanization spills out into other spheres of our lives. It is a critique worth attending to.

Unfortunately, the price Tanner pays for shifting the contrast to the question of the spirit that pervades our culture is that she is left with no answer to the Machiavellian challenge that we should avoid utopian thinking. Tanner's critique of the role of finance in our economy omits any account of the function finance could play if it had the right spirit. As a result, there are no tools for pragmatically thinking through what could be done to combat the negative effects she details. Correlatively, Tanner's take on financial capitalism is one sided. There is indeed much to critique. But Tanner gives us no tools for thinking about how to balance the negative effects of modern capitalism with its beneficial role in, say, lifting hundreds of millions of people out of poverty in the past few decades. Tanner thereby leaves herself open to the Machiavellian charge that this is merely utopian thinking.

Each of these three approaches to theological economics has something important to offer. The first works to overcome the fragmentation of the culture, seeking to find harmony between economic logic and discourses like theology that seek for the deeper meaning of our lives. The second explicitly draws on the expertise of economists in discerning which policies and institutions are likely to be most effective in helping us achieve our shared goals. And the third offers the critical perspective on economic life and economics that can give an account of the moral unease that has long haunted capitalism. In this book, I draw on the thought of Thomas Aquinas to offer a theological economics that combines the strengths of all three.

An Approach to Theological Economics Rooted in the Thought of Thomas Aquinas

For theological economics to make a substantive contribution to our reflections on economic life, it has to be premised on independent theological principles. The third approach to theological economics is thus the place to start. The key is to observe that in order for those theological principles to be genuinely independent, there should be no prior commitment to critiquing economics. Instead, the aim would be to evaluate economic life and economic discourse in light of the given theological principles. The writers Long identifies as belonging to the residual tradition all draw on the thought of Thomas Aquinas, who offers a comprehensive theological architecture that can allow us to think through human life as ordered to God. Aquinas is, indeed, an ideal starting point for this sort of project.

There is no shortage of reflection on economics rooted in the thought of Thomas Aquinas. Because Aquinas's thought is so capacious, however, a choice has to be made about where to start one's analysis. One common approach is to begin with his teachings on specific economic topics, namely his arguments about just prices and the problematic character of usury. Bernard Dempsey, for example, takes up the question of whether capitalism is necessarily usurious, arguing that it is.[63] In his subsequent book, *The Functional Economy,* Dempsey tackles a broader spectrum of economic topics ranging from private property to just wages to the role of corporations.[64] Beginning directly with Aquinas's specific teachings on economic issues is a natural move to make, and it can produce useful insights. The challenge of starting with the specifics is that Aquinas developed his economic doctrines in the context of a medieval economy that is distant from modern financial capitalism. As a result, they resist direct application to modern concerns. Moreover, because market logic was not as pervasive in Aquinas's day, he offers us no guidance for dealing with the problem that market logic is not easily brought into conversation with his concerns about justice.

Consider, for example, Aquinas's doctrine on just prices. Although there is considerable controversy on how to apply the doctrine to specific cases, the basic principle is clear enough. In any given trade, there should be a basic equivalence, such that the seller receives a price equal to the worth of the item sold. Our modern habit is to think that the worth of a thing simply is its price, but we retain intuitions that this is not always the case. In the wake of a massive hurricane, the market price for wood will rise dramatically, producing a windfall for sellers who happen to have wood in stock. Their cost of supplying the wood already on hand has not changed, and so the higher prices can be seen as unjust. The sense that sellers should not take advantage of the victims of such natural catastrophes by charging them the price the market will bear has at least some currency.[65] Yet the higher price serves a social function. It signals to distant producers that more wood is needed, and thereby causes wood to move toward areas that have a lot of rebuilding to do. If the price of wood were kept at its normal "just" level, the area trying to recover from a natural catastrophe would experience a shortage of wood.

How to balance out market logic with the sense that it is unjust to profit at the expense of victims of a natural disaster is a complex question. When the subject turns to usury, which is essential to the functioning of modern capitalism, the problem of how to pragmatically apply Aquinas's economic doctrines is even more daunting. To begin to think well about how to sort out these challenges, one would need to begin the analysis further back, with an understanding of Aquinas's fuller account of justice and how that relates to other goods in human life.

In this book, I do just that. Aquinas provides a sweeping architecture for theological reflection in his *Summa theologica*.[66] For Aquinas, the aim of sacred doctrine is to teach about God "not only as He is in Himself, but also as He is the beginning of things and their last end, and especially of rational creatures."[67] Accordingly, he divides the *Summa* into three parts. The first (commonly referred to as the *prima pars*) takes up questions concerning God both as he in himself is and as the source of creation. The second (*secunda pars*) turns to the subject of the movement of rational creatures (that is, humans) toward God, and the third (*tertia pars*) turns to Christ, who is our way back to God. The architecture is obviously theocentric. All questions pertaining to human life are ultimately to be understood in light of our relationship to God. And the heart of our movement toward God is our desire for happiness, as can be seen in the fact that Aquinas opens the *secunda pars* with the five questions commonly referred to as his treatise on happiness.

Aquinas's treatise on happiness serves as a valuable starting point for working out a theological economics. Not only is the topic of happiness the organizing principle of everything Aquinas has to say about human life, the quest for happiness is also central to modern economics. Beginning with the pursuit of happiness thus allows theology and economics to meet on common ground. Of course, because Aquinas sees the world as fundamentally ordered to God, his conception of human happiness is different from the one embodied in the economic worldview. There are two key differences Aquinas's metaphysical assumptions make. First, while Aquinas would agree with economists that the human quest for happiness involves a longing for more, for Aquinas that infinite desire can only be satiated when we rest in the infinite good that is God. Economists, who tacitly adopt what Charles Taylor would call an immanent frame, conceive of our infinite desire as oriented toward acquiring as many finite goods as we can, given the constraints of our scarce resources.[68] Aquinas, of course, acknowledges that even if our ultimate happiness lies in God, there is a meaningful human project in securing the sort of temporal happiness possible in this life. But because he thinks of this temporal happiness as ordered to that ultimate happiness, he argues that our desire for finite goods should properly be finite.

The second key difference is that Aquinas thinks of human happiness as perfection rather than as the satisfaction of desires. Again, this difference turns on the background metaphysical assumptions. God's goodness is manifest in his perfection, the fullness of his act. Insofar as we are created in God's image, our goodness or happiness is likewise manifested by bringing into act all that we are capable of being or doing. As John Paul II writes in *Centesimus annus,* "It is not wrong to want to live better; what is wrong is a style of life which is presumed to be better when it is directed toward 'having' rather than 'being,' and which wants to have more, not in order to be more but in order to spend life in enjoyment as an end in itself."[69] For humans, perfection in being is centered on the project of cultivating virtue. A crucial aspect of cultivating virtue is learning how to discern which goods are worthy of pursuit and ordering one's life in a way that reflects the hierarchy of goods.

These two differences might seem somewhat arcane, but they have a series of important implications for how we should think about economics. The recognition that we cannot find happiness in this life by pursuing a successive string of finite goods calls into question our cultural imperative for indefinite economic growth. That indefinite economic growth, in turn, puts pressure on the environment. As Tanner notes, the uncritical embrace of the idea that profits should always be maximized encourages injustice and the sort of behavior that Stiglitz, Sachs, Zingales, and other economists decried in the wake of the financial crisis. The idea that a key aspect of exercising virtue is learning how to discern goods and order them well serves to remind us that wealth and income are meant to be servants, not masters. That is to say, they are of value insofar as they serve higher ends. On this view it is incoherent to think of economic considerations on the one side and ethical considerations on the other. Any activity that does not move us toward the goods worth desiring is inefficient, full stop.

This book develops these themes at length. The key point for now is that Aquinas's theology can open up an approach to economics that can account for the nagging sense that capitalism is plagued by excessive materialism and is overly prone to generating economic injustice. It provides space for a theological economics in which it is more natural to integrate economic and ethical concerns. And finally, the principle of thinking about how goods are ordered provides us with a framework for evaluating economic institutions and economic practices. In short, this approach to theological economics is well suited to performing the critical role we need from theological economics.

But that leaves us with the other horn of the Machiavellian dilemma. How is it practical? It might well be the case that to secure genuine happiness humans should pursue greater "being" rather than more "having." But the strength of economics is that it does a good job of describing people as they are, and in point of fact, people are well described as pursuing happiness in the form of more having. Aquinas's framework makes possible two distinct ways of speaking to the pragmatic reality that is captured in the economic worldview.

First, even within Aquinas's description of what should be the case if we are to find genuine happiness, Aquinas offers points of contact with the economic view. Most notably, unlike many in the Christian tradition he inherited, Aquinas argues that private property is fitting to human nature and not merely as a concession to sin. It allows us to coordinate our productive activities, and it is congruent with our natural inclination to fend for ourselves and our families.[70] That argument points to the deeper point of contact with modern economic thought. Aquinas does not think that self-interest is inherently sinful. On the contrary, ordinarily speaking, the right thing to do is to secure the immediate needs of oneself and one's family before looking to offer assistance to others.[71] As discussed in Chapter 5, Aquinas's views on this matter are nuanced, and in a theological light self-interest takes on a different set of meanings from the ones that inhere in the modern concept of self-interest. But he avoids the thought that Christian charity should be thought of as a matter of self-denial.[72] From this perspective, economics is premised on real truths, even if its account of those truths is incomplete and distorted.

Second, and perhaps more usefully, Aquinas's view of human nature includes a recognition of the fact that most people, in fact, seek happiness in the way that economists say they do. That is, while he argues that genuine happiness in this life is centered on cultivating virtue, he also acknowledges that few people pursue happiness that way. Indeed, as discussed in Chapter 3, Aquinas identifies two forms of practical reason: the higher form of reason that is cultivated by virtue (most notably by the virtue of prudence) and a lower form of reason that is shared by the animals and is oriented toward pursuing pleasures and avoiding pains. Aquinas's discussion of that lower form of reason has much in common with the form of rationality embedded in the rational choice model. On this view, one would expect that the rational choice model predicts human behavior well.

Furthermore, although Aquinas believes that government should promote the cultivation of virtue, he also argues that legislation needs to meet people where they are.[73] There is thus space in Aquinas's framework to accommodate an approach to policy that is realistic about the impact incentives can have on the choices people make. Indeed, the virtue of Aquinas's approach is that while it accommodates this pragmatism, it does not simply give into it as does the purely Machiavellian strategy. The wise policy maker has to determine how to balance realism about humans as they are, without capitulating to it. Incentives are a valuable tool, so long as they do not underwrite a culture formed around the idea that humans cannot aspire to higher goods.

A Thomistic approach to theological economics thus holds out the promise of capturing the strengths of the three existing approaches to the subject. It provides a framework for finding coherence between economic and theological thought; it has space for drawing on the real expertise of mainstream economics; and it does these two things while retaining a critical purchase on our economic order, possessing the tools to distinguish when economic activity is well ordered to genuine human flourishing from instances when it is not. There remain to be taken up some considerations about the use of a medieval theologian as a resource for thinking about modern economic life.

The first concern is that Aquinas wrote centuries before the emergence of modern capitalism. In particular, he wrote centuries before the crucial insights that markets could produce order out of the uncoordinated choices of millions or billions of people. As already noted, that Aquinas was engaging with a very different economy than ours is a good reason for not appealing to him directly on questions about just wages or the licitness of usury. But the problem runs a bit deeper. Aquinas tends to think that the production of order in a society requires direction from political leaders. It is anachronistic to argue, as I do, that his framework can nonetheless accommodate modern insights about spontaneous order. The aim of this work is thus not to offer a close reading of Aquinas with the aim of determining his specific views on various subjects. It is rather to draw on his overarching principles to construct a theological appraisal of contemporary economic life. I believe the result is faithful to Aquinas's thought, but I do not claim to be offering a definitive reading of Aquinas.

The second question often raised about this project is why not draw on Aristotle as a resource instead? Aristotle is the source of many of Aquinas's doctrines on both happiness and the role of economics.[74] And a project such as this would have a broader appeal if it avoided the faith-based claims Aquinas makes. There are two replies to that question. First, the primary aim of this book is to offer Christians a way of thinking about the relationship between their faith and economics. But second, Aquinas's theological framework offers a richer perspective on the material we could get from drawing on Aristotle. As this project should make clear, all approaches to economics, both secular and faith based, rest on strong metaphysical assumptions. The value of this work is that it calls attention to that fact, thereby opening up space for reflection on important questions about the nature of happiness, and especially the relationship between finite goods and our seemingly infinite desire that are worth exploring in their own right. These are questions worth exploring, even if one wants to reject Aquinas's particular answers to those questions.

A final question could arise concerning the relationship of this project to the body of Catholic social thought. In my survey of the various approaches to theological economics, I pointedly did not take up this body of thought as a whole. Because the encyclicals and letters that constitute that tradition are a complex blend of theological doctrine that carries magisterial weight and practical applications to a series of historically distinct circumstances, it has generated a vast and controversial secondary literature. The complexity of the tradition makes it difficult to categorize easily. I make no attempt to offer a definitive reading of that tradition. The hope is that by working out an approach to economics rooted in Aquinas's thought, I could provide some clarity for thinking about economic life in the Catholic tradition. Aquinas's thought animates the Church, and all of the core doctrines of Catholic social thought (solidarity, subsidiarity, a preferential option for the poor, concern for both human dignity and the common good, and stewardship of creation) fit into the approach to theological economics I lay out in this book. I thus hope that this book could be a resource for reflection on Catholic social thought, but again, my aim here is not to offer up a definitive interpretation of that tradition.

Overview

To begin a conversation between economics and theology, we need a clear picture of modern economic thought. Accordingly, in Chapter 2, I take up the economic model of human behavior as rational choice, taking pains to identify the common misconceptions noneconomists have about that model. I thus argue that homo economicus should not be confused with *homo avidus* (greedy man) and point out that modern economic models incorporate uncertainty, information problems, and even systematic cognitive errors into their best models, all of which are aimed at predicting human behavior. Having cleared out the naïve criticisms one could make of the economic approach, I turn to a discussion of some of its real limitations. First, I take up the problem of dealing with incommensurable goods, using the concerns raised by Amartya Sen as a starting point. The import of this point is that economists have difficulty integrating economic and ethical concerns.

Next I turn to the problematic relationship between preference satisfaction and well-being. The concept of efficiency, which is central to economics, is most commonly measured in terms of preference satisfaction. Yet there is ample reason to believe that preferences are ill formed. These long-standing concerns have been given new life in the burgeoning literature in hedonic economics. At stake in this debate is the question of how much weight we should place on efficiency as a measure of the desirability of a given set of policy choices or institutional arrangements.

Finally, I develop the thought that the treatment of practical reason as an exercise in maximization is problematic. The rational choice model, even when amended to include cognitive limitations, presumes that human desire for finite goods (understood not merely as material goods but as any string of goods or experiences one may pursue in life) is infinite. But insofar as we live in a finite world, it is not obvious that this is a good account of a truly rational pursuit of happiness. Taking these three concerns together, the argument is that we need a better understanding of human beings and the pursuit of happiness than the ones economists can provide.

In Chapters 3 and 4, I turn to Aquinas for that better understanding. Like economists, Aquinas believes that humans act for an end. He calls that end happiness; economists call it utility. But Aquinas's account of the pursuit of human happiness differs in important respects from economists' account of utility maximization. Much of this difference has to do with their disparate metaphysical assumptions. To lay out this argument, I begin in Chapter 3 with a discussion of the formal properties of happiness in Aquinas's thought, contrasting them with the principles embedded in the rational choice model. I then go on to show the metaphysical setting that is necessary in order to fully understand what is at stake in the two competing approaches to understanding human happiness. In Chapter 4, I turn to Aquinas's substantive account of happiness, one that centers on the cultivation of virtue. There I lay out the basic concept of virtue and discuss its relationship to other human goods. That chapter concludes by drawing a contrast between the virtue of prudence and rational choice.

To get a clearer picture of Aquinas's account of happiness, it is helpful to consider his analysis of the role of material goods in a life well lived, the subject taken up in Chapter 5. First and foremost, material goods are instrumental to a good life. Aquinas does reflect the Christian tradition's appreciation for asceticism, as can be seen particularly in his support of the religious counsels of poverty, chastity, and obedience. But Aquinas also values human flourishing and views material goods as genuine goods, insofar as they are well ordered to the purposes they are meant to serve: sustaining human life and providing the material basis for the exercise of virtue, including the quasi virtues of pursuing arts and crafts. Moreover, Aquinas does not think of sustaining human life as a matter of merely maintaining biological life. He sees human life as requiring a standard of living that is socially becoming. Aquinas does not, then, set out an argument that rails against wealth per se. The key distinction is that our desire for material wealth be measured by appropriate ends. In other words, our desire for material goods should be satiable or bounded. This is a core difference between the economic approach and the approach taken in this book, and I explore Aquinas's discussion of the virtue of liberality and its corresponding vices to bring out those differences. The import of the first half of Chapter 5 is that our unbounded desire for material goods turns out to be the root of many of our economic ills.

In the second half of Chapter 5, I turn to the economy itself. Like economists, Aquinas believes that money, what he calls "artificial wealth," is a useful human invention that facilitates trade, which, in turn, facilitates material flourishing. However, Aquinas associates artificial wealth with the temptation to misconceive the proper form of our desire for real wealth by encouraging us to see the pursuit of happiness as a project of climbing a ladder of finite goods rather than ordering goods harmoniously with the aim of reflecting the infinite good. In essence, the quantitative language of money and profits tempts us to see decision making as a matter of calculation rather than deliberation. There are other explanations for the ubiquity of the vice of covetousness, but the approach taken here can help us understand why a capitalist economy is particularly subject to the problem. I conclude the chapter with a discussion of the profit motive, in terms of both its usefulness (as a signal about useful deployments of economic resources and as just compensation for entrepreneurial behavior) and its dangers (the strong temptation to shift from prudential discernment to calculation).

In Chapter 6, I take up one of the core institutions of capitalism, private property. One of the key reasons that Aquinas is a useful interlocutor for modern-day economics is that unlike much of the Christian tradition, Aquinas does not think that the institution of private property is merely a concession to our fallen nature. On the contrary, private property is fitting to our finitude—working both to assign responsibilities and to channel our proper self-interest. The first point provides an opening for the argument that Aquinas's framework can accommodate modern insights about the market's capacity for coordinating economic activity and economizing on information. The second motivates a discussion of the distinction between proper self-interest and greed.

Much of our economic discourse is impoverished by the assumption that behavior is either altruistic or self-seeking (that is, greedy). Aquinas offers a much-needed third way, which affirms the insight that it is appropriate for us to have special concern for the provision of ourselves and our families. The key is that for Aquinas that self-interest should be virtuous, that is, with a bounded measure of what we need to maintain ourselves appropriately. On that view, we should ordinarily have surplus income, and that surplus income is properly due to those in need. In setting up this point there is occasion to talk more about the social component of our material needs, and the way this interacts with our culture's struggle with the vice of covetousness. I then use Aquinas's teachings on private property to argue that to adequately address questions of economic justice we need to first address the question of what it would mean to us today to be in right relationship with material goods. Any discussion of justice that does not challenge the thought that more is always better will fail to do justice to the question of justice.

Chapter 7 takes up the problem that we do not live in a world of virtuous people. Policy makers need to take this into account, but in a way that does not undercut our understanding of what would ideally be the case. A modern economics that understood its own limitations, particularly regarding the normative implications of its positive analysis, would be well suited for helping us understand how to approach policy given how people actually are and to tackle the challenging problem of how to acknowledge the power of incentives without undercutting social norms that are more in alignment with virtuous economic practice.

Fortunately, in the past few decades economists have become more open to approaches that take social norms seriously, and thus there seems to be a prospect for developing economics in a direction that would be more ordered to genuine human flourishing than is currently the case.

Overall, the narrative that follows emerges from this approach to theological economics. Property rights and markets are meant to be in service of our economic activity, which, in turn, is meant to be in service of genuine human flourishing. When they perform their proper roles, they are well suited to human nature and to facilitating meaningful economic progress. The institution of markets is congruent with the profound fact that we are created as finite beings. It allows us to specialize in the areas of our particular expertise and then share the fruits of our labors with others. Through the market, we can achieve a more thoroughgoing and profitable economic coordination than would be possible through planning—an economic model that is not congruent with human finitude.

However, when we forget the instrumental nature of property rights, money, and wealth, the economic system gets distorted. The ability of markets to be manipulated for the sole purpose of making money (as opposed to creating true wealth) resonates with the human temptation to forget that our material wants are finite and to seek to fulfill our insatiable desires. As we succumb to that disorder, a gap emerges between economic logic and moral realities. As the economy distorts, it becomes less efficient in the fullest meaning of the term. It may seem to excel at converting resources into income; but when we ask how much genuine human good we extract from that income, the distorted economy would be seen as far less effective than it might appear. With this diagnosis in hand, it should be possible to think anew about how to move toward a humane economy.

To tell that story, we must first consider whether economists can sustain their claim of a master narrative about human choice that can in principle accommodate the different values individuals might pursue in life. That is the subject of Chapter 2.

2

The Rational Choice Model
and Its Limitations

***

Before constructing a theological economics, it is worth considering the perspectives of economists on their central model of human behavior, the rational choice model. Economists tend to view the rational choice model as a formal framework for analyzing human decision making that is value neutral. Correlatively, they believe they are objective scientists who are merely describing or predicting human behavior, leaving ethical judgments to the domain of normative economics, which is largely the purview of philosophers and theologians. Accordingly, economists are likely to resist any project like mine that would deny that economic activity can be analyzed or evaluated without reference to the overall purpose of human life, which is inherently ethical.

As discussed in Chapter 1, capitalism has come under a wide range of withering ethical critiques. Markets are unjust; greed leads businesspeople to exploit laborers and destroy the environment; the capitalist mentality encourages a radical individualism and denies that we are social creatures oriented toward a common good. Mainstream economics, which Joan Robinson suggests is the discipline that arose to defend capitalism, has likewise been subject to ethical critiques.[1] The discipline of economics falsely promotes a picture of human nature as inherently selfish, obscures the injustice rooted in the system, and celebrates materialism and rampant consumerism. Or so the complaints go. Mainstream economists rarely engage in debates over issues of this sort.[2] For the most part economists assert that they are neutral with respect to ethical issues and are simply pursuing an objective study of human behavior as it is.

Although much of the criticism comes under the heading concern for social justice, such concerns seem peripheral to economic science, which studies human choice under the condition of scarcity. Economists typically use the distinction between positive and normative economics to set aside questions about property rights and income distribution as normative concerns that are properly dealt with by philosophers and political scientists. What economists can do is use their models of economic behavior to explore the consequences of changing institutional frameworks, including assumptions about the assignment of property rights or the consequences of redistributing income. The resulting analysis frequently misses the upshot of critics of capitalism, who tend to have thicker ideas about capitalism and its consequences for social justice than can easily be captured in models. At the same time, those thicker criticisms are not framed in a way that economists can engage with given their tools of analysis. So large swaths of criticism get marginalized and are largely pursued either outside the discipline or at the margins of the discipline, where one finds the "heterodox" economists.[3]

Many of the challenges to economics include challenges to economists' use of the rational choice model, or their related focus on analyzing the behavior of homo economicus. Although many such challenges are naïve in that they are targeted at a caricature of the model of human behavior economists actually use, it is methodological individualism and analysis of unintended consequences that make economic thought distinctive. Because the contrast between Aquinas's conception of the pursuit of happiness and that of economists is central to this book, my discussion of modern economics focuses on the economic model of human behavior.

The aim of this chapter is to explain why economists typically think that ethical challenges to their model of human behavior are off target or are irrelevant and to explore some tensions within economic thought that suggest that the economic model is not as value neutral as economists might think. Essentially, economists argue that their model of human behavior is capacious enough to encompass whatever values economic agents pursue and is therefore itself a value-neutral model. One of the central aims of this book is to challenge the claim that the economic model is value neutral. While the model is indeed neutral with respect to the sorts of goals individuals might pursue, it is not neutral in its description of the *form* of our pursuit of happiness. Economic "rationality" is only rational under a specific set of assumptions about the metaphysical character of our world. The resulting tensions within economic thought open the door to the Thomistic approach I pursue in the remainder of this book.

Key Features of Modern Economic Thought

Mainstream economics is a surprisingly monolithic discipline, with a clear conception of its central models. For my purposes there are three key features of economic thought worth attending to. First, economists have a distinctive conception of practical reason (that is, the form of reason that governs our actions) centered on the model of homo economicus, which is often misunderstood outside of the field. Second, economists sharply distinguish between positive and normative economics, arguing that their models are neutral with respect to philosophical, metaphysical, theological, or any other set of concerns or values a person might have. These two features are related but are worth setting out separately. The third feature is the assumption that wants are unbounded, which is an assumption that directly contradicts Aquinas's account of human nature and needs to be taken into account when doing an inventory of the distortions (from a Thomistic perspective) embodied in economic analysis.[4]

A Few General Observations

Before diving in, a few general observations are in order. First, as a reminder, I'm talking about orthodox economics in particular. There are other forms of economic thought, but they are marginal to the discipline. Accordingly, when I refer to economics or economists I should be understood as referring specifically to mainstream or orthodox economics unless otherwise specified.

Second, economists define their field in terms of their way of thinking rather than in terms of their subject matter. The standard definition of economics identifies it as the science of how to allocate scarce resources, with scarce resources being broadly defined (material wealth, prestige, time, desirable mates).[5] Scarcity results from the observation that our desires tend to outstrip available resources. Sand at a beach is not scarce, because there is more of it than anyone could want, and accordingly the price of sand at a beach is zero. But most goods are not so abundantly available. It is the scarcity of resources that necessitates a science of choice. Insofar as scarcity is an inescapable feature of our world, there is an economics of everything: an economics of the family (supply and demand for children, marriage markets); an economics of political choice; an economics of crime; an economics of religion, and so on. Essentially there is an economics of anything that involves human choice.[6]

Thinking like an economist entails creating models.[7] Models are based on a set of assumptions about human choice and the institutional features in which these choices are enacted. The assumptions are expressed in mathematical language, which allows for a rigorous deduction of the implications of the particular set of assumptions the economist is working with.[8] Alongside the practice of studying models, economists test these models empirically to the degree possible given the limitation that they cannot perform experiments but rather (for the most part) must rely on the data generated about the world as it is.[9]

The emphasis on mathematical precision is the primary reason economists typically model human decision making as an exercise in rational choice. As discussed below, economists are quite versatile in their employment of the notion of rational choice, and homo economicus is not the narrow caricature of human behavior many noneconomists take it for. Indeed, economists are even willing to consider forms of "irrational" behavior. The primary constraint for economists, then, is not so much the insistence that humans are rational as it is that they are only interested in studying human behavior that can be modeled mathematically.[10]

Correlative to economists' definition of their field, economists' primary aim in the classroom is not to teach students facts about how the economy works but rather to train them to think like economists.[11] The emphasis on method is so strong that Alice Rivlin complained that graduate students in economics are required to be familiar with virtually no facts about the actual economy.[12] If you understand about marginal benefits and marginal costs, you are an economist, even if you do not know the current GDP for the United States. Thinking like an economist includes more than just the practice of creating models and testing them empirically. It involves developing an ability to see the world in terms of trade-offs, with a keen eye for the unintended consequences of decisions whether made by individuals or by policy makers, usually by using the basic model of supply and demand. The practice of abstraction is crucial to generating the insights that economists prize. As I discuss at greater length below, economists argue that it does not matter if their assumptions are oversimplified or even flat out not true so long as the prediction of their models can be supported using empirical data.[13]

These general observations combine to create a climate that can make it difficult to critically interrogate economic analysis. Economists rely on models for the bulk of their analysis. For models to produce concrete conclusions or to be capable of being empirically tested, those models require a set of specific assumptions. Very often, those assumptions are questionable. For example, one can argue that not all firms are solely interested in maximizing profits, even though most economists would model firms as being solely interested in maximizing profits. Economists will reply that their apparatus is general enough to handle firms that are interested in things besides the bottom line. Indeed, economists distinguish between pecuniary and nonpecuniary costs and benefits and argue that true profit is the difference between the total of pecuniary and nonpecuniary benefits minus the total of pecuniary and nonpecuniary costs. But, contrary to this theory, the practice is almost always to simply measure profits as the difference between pecuniary benefits and pecuniary costs. The result is that a criticism that has bearing on how economic analysis is actually done will typically be rebutted with an appeal to the general apparatus. I do not believe most economists are aware that they are essentially trying to have it both ways, maintaining a posture of theoretical openness to the variety of human motivations while basing most of their work on a narrower view of human behavior. But the result is that they are frequently deaf to real concerns about the ethical implications of their "neutral" apparatus.

Homo Economicus

If economics is the science of allocation of scarce resources, its model of human choice is central to the economic way of thinking. As with most economic thinking, it is an abstracted model of human behavior. In a nutshell, homo economicus, as some call this simplified version of human nature, seeks to reach his ends as efficiently as possible. He is generally modeled as doing so by maximizing his utility subject to whatever budget or time constraints he faces. According to the standard interpretation, utility is not some entity but rather is modeled by a mathematical function that represents the individuals' preferences. It is assumed that homo economicus has a well-specified set of preferences that meet three criteria. First he must have a complete set of preferences, being able to say of a choice between any two things (or bundles of things), *x* and *y,* either that he is indifferent between them, or that he prefers *x* to *y* or that he prefers *y* to *x.* Second, his preferences must be transitive, such that if he prefers *x* to *y* and if he prefers *y* to *z,* then he must also prefer *x* to *z.* Finally, his preference ordering should be context independent. A preference for *x* over *y* ought not to depend on what other alternatives are available.

We can then represent these well-specified sets of preferences with a utility function, where utility does not refer to any "thing" but rather is just a number available for producing a ranking of options. There is, however, a further set of assumptions that shade the meaning of utility away from simply a ranking of preferences toward some quantitative measure. In particular, economists typically assume that these preferences are continuous, that is, that there are infinite gradations in these preferences. If I have ranked two bundles of commodities, it is possible to imagine some intermediate bundle of commodities that I would rank below the first and above the second. In addition, although for individual goods one can reach a point of satiation, such that further units of that good would reduce one's utility, the utility function itself is treated as unbounded. I may achieve satiation for many categories of goods, but loosening of constraints is nonetheless in practice always viewed as desirable.[14] Under these and a few other technical restrictions, the utility function can be treated as a differentiable function, which allows us to model homo economicus's practical reason as an exercise in utility maximization subject to constraint, where the constraints are usually thought of as budget or time constraints.[15]

As Paul Samuelson concedes in one of his seminal articles, economists have long been engaged in the project of cleansing consumer theory of the discredited psychological concept "utility" as an entity necessary to explain human behavior.[16] Hence the effort to redefine the utility function as merely a representation of preferences. Yet the desiderata of that effort was to reproduce the set of conclusions arrived at based on the idea that there was some entity called "utility" to be maximized.[17] Moreover, the language continues to strongly suggest that utility is a thing to be maximized. Consider, for example, a standard textbook explanation of why an increase in the price of a good tends to cause consumers to reduce their demand for that good.

Utility maximizers will allocate their income such that the marginal utility per dollar is equal across all goods. "Marginal" refers to the incremental unit, in this case the incremental dollar. We assume that consumers have a declining marginal utility for particular goods. In other words, the first slice of pizza is of more value to me than the second slice of pizza. Let us say that given my present allocation of income, the marginal utility I get from an extra slice of pizza is 10, and that the slice of pizza costs one dollar. Let us further assume that the marginal utility I get from a soda is also 10, but the soda costs fifty cents. I can raise my utility if I take a dollar away from the pizza, dropping my utility by 10 and allocating it to soda, raising my utility by 20. I will continue this adjustment process until my dollar yields the same marginal utility no matter where it is spent.

Thus let us say I have shifted my allocation to the point where my marginal utility for pizza is 15 (it rises as I shift money away from it), and my marginal utility for soda is 7.5 (it lowers as I shift money toward it). The dollar's worth of pizza now yields 15 utils whether I spend it on pizza $(15/1=15)$ or soda $(7.5/0.5=15.0)$. I can no longer raise my utility by changing my allocation, and I have thus maximized my utility. Now suppose that the price of soda goes up to one dollar per soda. All of a sudden, my marginal utility per dollar spent on soda drops to 7.5, which means that I can raise my utility by decreasing the amount spent on soda and shifting it toward a good such as pizza, which has a higher marginal utility per dollar. The increase in the price of soda thus causes me to decrease my demand for it (and to increase my demand for other goods).

We can technically translate all of that back into a discussion of consumers' choosing one bundle of goods under one set of prices and a different bundle of goods under a different set of prices, but the intuition here is very much of some quantity, utility, that one wants to have as much of as possible. As seen below, the question of how serious economists are about restricting the meaning of utility maximization to satisfaction of preferences is in dispute in the profession. But let us stipulate for now that technically, "utility maximization" is just a convenient way of discussing the assumption that consumers seek to get the most desirable bundle of goods they can given their budget and price constraints in the market.[18]

Many of the initial objections a lay person would have to the idea of utility maximization can be and are handled by economists. First, there are a cluster of objections one could raise to the claim that individuals actually are rational in this way or have sufficient information to be rational in this way. To the naïve versions of these objections, economists would offer the following sets of replies. First, while we cannot know about the future, we can have preferences over the various probable outcomes, and thus we can talk about expected utility functions. Second, lack of information can be modeled both in terms of models of optimal searching for information and in models documenting the effects of asymmetric information, situations in which the buyer and the seller are not equally well informed about the good being traded. In general economists have been quite creative in finding ways to expand their model of rationality to embrace a wide range of complicating factors. Finally, behavioral economists have studied decision making in laboratory settings and have found that, indeed, humans are not always rational in the way economists assume. There is a rapidly expanding literature on the sorts of biases that can lead to "irrational" choices and thus an attempt to accommodate the rational choice model to various myopias that are known to exist.[19]

Although this last represents a shift away from the standard assumption that humans are rational, it is a rather modest shift. Rationality is still the default assumption, and the modes of irrationality are treated as discrete exceptions to the rule. In any case, the essential idea is that we can rationally approach decision making under uncertainty and can even fold certain persistent "irrationalities" into a general model that treats human decision making as an exercise in utility maximization.[20]

A second set of common misconceptions cluster around the idea that economists falsely assume that human beings are purely self-interested. In point of fact, homo economicus is not identical to homo avidus. Essentially, if the utility function is just a representation of preferences, it is a trivial matter to insert our preference for the well-being of others into the metric. When modeled as a utility function to be maximized, all that is required is to make the well-being of others an argument in the utility function. The content of Bernie Madoff's utility function may well differ from that of Mother Teresa's, but formally there is no difference in the logic of maximizing utility. Indeed, Gary Becker, who is the best-known advocate of using the model of homo economicus to explain all of human behavior, explicitly introduces "altruism" into the utility functions of family members to explain features of household economics.[21] There are limits on how much altruism the model can allow, but these provoke the sorts of paradoxes noneconomists would do well to consider. For example, if two individuals are more concerned about each other than themselves, the result is unstable. If I give to you such that you have more than me, I make you less happy precisely because you do have more than me, and vice versa.[22] But aside from extreme cases, the model of utility maximization can handle altruism.

In summary, the standard model of practical reason employed by economists assumes that individuals have well-defined preferences and systematically strive to attain the highest-ranked choice that is available to them given their budget, time, and information constraints. There are a host of more substantive criticisms that have been made of this basic model, which I briefly canvass below. Before turning to those criticisms, it is necessary to examine the related tenet held by economists that their science is a positive, value-free science.

The Positive / Normative Distinction in Economics

In the first chapter of any introductory economics textbook, a distinction between positive and normative economics will be made. *Positive economics* is the scientific study of the behavior of individuals and markets. *Normative economics* examines the question of what sort of economic policies we should pursue. Thus, for example, positive economics can tell us that an increase in taxes on cigarettes would lead to a decrease in the consumption of cigarettes. Normative economics can tell us that it would be a good thing to set tax policy to reduce cigarette consumption. The positive/normative distinction is routinely invoked to insulate economic practice from ethical critiques.[23] In particular, the assumption that homo economicus is a useful model of human behavior is based on the claim that it successfully generates empirically substantiated predictions about human behavior.

Since economists view themselves as scientists, normative economics tends to be marginalized. As Andrew Yuengert puts it, economists view normative economics as applied ethics and positive economics as "real" economics.[24] The image economists have of themselves as neutral scientists is an important explanation for why economists are particularly deaf to concerns about economic science that are raised by noneconomists, which almost always have an ethical component. As discussed in Chapter 1, many of these concerns fail to grasp what economists are getting at with the positive/normative distinction and thus are rightly dismissed by economists. For example, a noneconomist might think that the most straightforward way to ensure affordable housing would be to cap rents and thus might assume that economists' near-unanimous rejection of rent control means that economists are unconcerned that there be affordable housing. In fact, economic analysis strongly suggests and experience bears out that rent control causes the housing stock to diminish and deteriorate and frequently benefits people who are well-off at the expense of those who are not. The argument about rent control is not about the normative question on society's obligation to provide affordable housing. It is a factual (positive) question about what is the best way to achieve that outcome. And on this question, noneconomists advocating rent control are advocating a policy that runs counter to their own normative concerns.[25]

Indeed, these sorts of mistakes are so common that some economists have swung around to the position that virtually all debates about economic policy are debates about facts rather than debates about values. In his influential article, "The Methodology of Positive Economics," Milton Friedman writes: "I venture the judgment, however, that currently in the Western world, and especially in the United States, differences about economic policy among disinterested citizens derive predominantly from different predictions about the economic consequences of taking action—differences that in principle can be eliminated by the progress of positive economics—rather than from fundamental differences in basic values, differences about which men can ultimately only fight."[26]

Economists have gotten more sophisticated in their arguments about the positive / normative distinction, but those arguments are all directed toward maintaining the claim that the work of economists is primarily scientific. The economist Andrew Yuengert examines these commitments in light of a Thomistic framework. In his book, *The Boundaries of Technique: Ordering Positive and Normative Concerns in Economic Research,* Yuengert argues that most economists are attracted by the simple positive / normative dichotomy because it is persuasive to them; it picks up a real feature of economic practice that is sensible. Yuengert sets himself the task of articulating the relationship between positive and normative economics that preserves the distinction economists rightly (on his account) wish to maintain, while also not marginalizing the normative aspect of all work in economics.

To do so, Yuengert proposes embedding an account of economic practice within a Thomistic account of the moral life. Yuengert focuses attention on the economist as an agent, arguing that economic analysis should be understood on the same footing as any human activity, namely, as done in pursuit of some end or good. He further argues that ends are ordered to other ends, and thus we should understand economic analysis as ordered to higher goods. So, for example, as an economist my aim in using certain techniques is to arrive at the best conclusion I can about a given question, say, the efficacy of using rent controls to guarantee affordable housing to the poor. My question in turn is oriented to some good. Perhaps I have been hired by a think tank to carry out the analysis, and thus my end is to procure an income to support myself and my family. Or perhaps I have a personal interest in contributing to the public dialogue about how best to help the poor. For Yuengert, the next question is what distinguishes the ends an economist pursues qua economist from those the economist pursues qua human being.[27]

Yuengert argues that economics should be understood as technique, a set of methods "that have been formalized in the pursuit of certain ends—explanation and prediction of social phenomena."[28] These techniques are not free of ethical values. As Yuengert argues, the community of economists operates within a milieu that prizes certain values, which, in turn, shapes the development of technique. Thus, for example, economists value statistical measures that are robust or models of human behavior that are parsimonious.[29] For Yuengert, the boundary between positive and normative economics is also permeable in the sense that values external to economic techniques can drive the sorts of questions that are taken up or the concepts that are employed in economic analysis. But there remains an important sense for him that economics is relatively self-contained or autonomous.

Yuengert has gone on to argue that the economic models cannot capture the features of human choice captured in Aristotle's account of prudence.[30] But he stops short of arguing that there is a normative dimension to the inherent limitations of mathematical modeling. Here I want to push into that territory. The values embedded in the sphere of economic technique are not simply related to the scientific qualities that are prized (parsimony and so on). They also reflect strong assumptions about human nature and metaphysics that are shared by practicing economists, who are typically unaware that they have made those strong assumptions. Indeed, economists would claim that their model of practical reason is neutral with respect to theological or philosophical commitments individuals might make. In making that claim, economists implicitly assume that values are on a menu much the way any other goods are on a menu, and that their theory of choice is not affected by the contents of the items on the menu. What they deny is that the very notion that practical reason is an exercise in making choices from a menu is itself inflected with strong metaphysical or theological commitments, or both. To see this we need to return to homo economicus.

Homo Economicus and the Positive / Normative Distinction

As discussed above, the pristine version of homo economicus simply chooses from among the possibilities available to him given his various constraints. That model is said to be purely neutral because economists place no restrictions on what sorts of goods individuals might pursue, or even the manner in which those goods are pursued. Suppose I am deciding whether to buy a shirt made in a sweat shop in Cambodia. If I am simply concerned with my own well-being, I buy the shirt if its value to me is greater than the price. If, on the other hand, I find sweat shops to be repugnant, the shirt has no value to me and I do not buy it regardless of the price. The model is indifferent to the question of whether my valuation of the shirt is based merely on my own desires, or on my social concerns.

Now it is true that economists typically assume that people choose according to their narrow self-interest. Thus, for example, a series of articles appeared in the *American Economic Review* debating the question of whether the practice of gift giving creates a deadweight loss (inefficiency).[31] The question arises because in surveys the value individuals assign to gifts they have received tends to be lower than the cost of the gift to the giver. It would be more efficient on that account for the giver to simply give cash rather than an item that is worth less than the cash value of the item to the recipient. The failure of givers to shift to cash gifts (or gift cards) thus creates inefficiency in the market.[32] The logic of rational choice theory in its most pristine form would suggest that there is, in fact, no deadweight loss but rather some nonpecuniary value attached to gift giving that compensates for the deadweight loss that appears when only pecuniary factors (cost of gift, estimate of value of gift to recipient) are taken into account. In a move in that direction, Joel Waldfogel "solves" the puzzle of the apparent irrationality by positing that givers attach a stigma to cash, that is, that the preference ordering of the giver includes not just the satisfaction of giving a gift of a certain value to a loved one but also the form in which that gift is given.[33] He justifies this move by saying that consumer choice must be rational by tautology and therefore it would be a mistake to call such patterns irrational. That economists had to do some groping to arrive at the social nature of gift giving as an explanation for the phenomenon is a measure of the way their values do shape the questions they ask and the presuppositions they bring to those questions, as Yuengert argues. But the model itself would seem to be capable of neutrally handling a situation where gift giving involves more than pecuniary matters.

But even if economists worked to remain mindful of the impact of nonpecuniary elements of decisions, the model still is not value neutral. As I argue in Chapters 3 and 4, the formal structure of decision making employed by economists reflects strong philosophical claims about both human nature and metaphysics. But even if we bracket that question, there is a problem with economists' effort to claim neutrality for their model. In particular, their notion of efficiency draws directly on the idea that utility should be maximized and thus carries with it a stronger philosophical claim about the nature of the good than most economists would concede they are making. Efficiency, in turn, is central to economic analysis. Indeed, the primary justification for markets is that they are efficient. The intuition, loosely, is that in a market a trade will only occur if it is beneficial to both parties to the trade. The buyer has a maximum price she is willing to pay, and the seller has a minimum price at which he is willing to sell. If her maximum price is above his minimum price, there is a net gain from the transfer because we have moved the good from a person who values it less to a person who values it more. Assuming that a price has been struck in between the two valuations, both parties gain. The buyer pays less for the good than it is worth to her, and the seller receives more for the good than it is worth to him. Inefficiencies occur when something prevents such mutually beneficial transactions from occurring. Thus, for example, if we impose a sales tax on the good, the buyers' willingness to pay will drop by the amount of the tax. That reduces the effective demand for the good, causing a contraction in sales. Insofar as those lost sales all would have represented transactions that were mutually beneficial, the tax creates a deadweight loss.[34]

The analysis of the impact of policy on the buyers and consumers is called welfare economics, which is not to be confused with welfare programs. It is simply the analysis of the net welfare (gain to buyers and gain to sellers) created in the markets. In a perfect market, the equilibrium price also tends to maximize welfare (by causing every mutually beneficial transaction to take place). Sometimes the market itself is imperfect, as when there are externalities. If, for example, my widget factory generates pollution, there are social costs stemming from my production that do not figure into the transaction between me and those who buy my products. In those cases a tax to producers that causes them to internalize that social cost can restore efficiency to the market. But when there is no reason to think that the market itself is inefficient, government intervention nearly always generates deadweight losses. These are quite large in the case of price ceilings and price floors (hence the near-unanimous opposition by economists to rent control laws). But they also occur with any tax or subsidy.[35]

Welfare economics is the bread and butter of the discipline. It is the analysis economists sell to policy makers about the expected impact of various policies, and it is an analysis that is sold as a matter of neutral observed fact. But the concept of efficiency is value laden because the analysis depends on the equation of a consumer's willingness to pay with her marginal benefit and the seller's willingness to sell with his marginal cost. The problem of what the utility function represents enters into the question of efficiency because it is from the utility function that we get the measure of the marginal benefit to the consumer. Utility thus figures into every calculation made about the efficiency of a given market. As the name of this sort of analysis is welfare economics, utility begins to sound a lot like welfare or well-being rather than just a representation of a consumer's preferences. A fundamental argument in favor of markets is that they maximize welfare. Is that argument as powerful if we pause and remind ourselves that technically all that means is that markets meet consumers' preferences as well as possible?[36]

There are many, many reasons to think that consumer preferences are an imperfect measure of a consumer's well-being. To what extent is it good to fulfill preferences that are shaped by advertising or social influences?[37] What if people adjust their preferences to accommodate the reality of what is possible, declaring that they do not want what they cannot have?[38] If the aim of public policy is to satisfy preferences as fully as possible, how do we do the analysis when the policy itself is likely to change preferences?[39] The standard argument about why we should expect firms to be good at calculating the effect of their choices on their profits is that if there is sufficient competition, firms that fail to maximize profits will be driven out of business. But there is no equivalent argument for the household. A household that fails to figure out how to maximize its well-being simply lives less well than it otherwise might.[40] The lack of a clear link between preference satisfaction and any particular measure of well-being is an important problem in economic philosophy.[41] Although these critiques are most commonly generated from outside the discipline or from figures on the margin of the discipline, two recent debates within economics go directly to the question of what utility actually is and what the attendant implications are for how we understand the nature of welfare economics.

Two Debates on the Normative Content of Homo Economicus

The two debates center on questions of interpretation and use of the term *utility*. The first we will take up is actually the more recent, and it is about the question of whether economists ought to be more interested in well-being (however defined) than in preference satisfaction. The debate plays off the shading of the meaning of *utility* toward actual well-being and is primarily concerned with the question of how to measure well-being, along with a general sense that the aim of policy makers is to maximize well-being rather than preference satisfaction. The second surrounds Amartya Sen's challenge to the model of homo economicus, which argues that serious distortions are done to actual human behavior if we collapse all distinctions between different levels of motivation. For Sen, the primary concern is whether the model properly treats nonegoistic motives. The defensive posture in both debates seeks to maintain the neutral model of rational choice as an exercise in satisfying preferences as well as possible.

Well-Being versus Preference Satisfaction

Early this century, interest arose in the question of how to measure well-being, suggesting that economists are uncomfortable with the perceived gap between preference satisfaction and well-being and that some, at least, think that well-being is at least as relevant a goal as preference satisfaction in assessing the performance of markets or the efficacy of policy.[42] In part this is in response to studies that reveal that the simple assumptions required by the preference satisfaction model, such as the assumption that preferences are consistent, are often violated.[43] The resulting field of hedonic economics focuses on measures of subjective well-being and its determinants.[44]

Over the same period that studies in hedonic economics became more common, the field of neuroeconomics emerged, using the techniques of neuroscience to determine the impact psychological variables like affect, risk aversion, or cognitive load have on choice.[45] Although these studies are more focused on discussing the ways in which psychological variables can lead people to make choices which deviate from the rational choice, they are also used as an argument against relying on the choices people make as an objective measure of the satisfaction of the actual underlying preferences.[46] Like those advocating hedonic economics, those advocating neuroeconomics believe that their studies can help improve our assessment of the impact of various policies on people's well-being. These two lines of research are premised on the idea that welfare economics ought to have at least as much to do with well-being as it does with preference satisfaction.

These developments have generated a response from more conventional economists defending the use of choice as the measure to use in welfare economics. In their paper "The Case for Mindless Economics," Faruk Gul and Wolfgang Pesendorfer argue against these two developments, in part by arguing that the effort to associate utility with any measure of happiness undermines the neutrality of the rational choice model.[47] They further argue that economists pushing in the direction of hedonic economics and neuroeconomics are guilty of misunderstanding the role of welfare analysis in economics. Instead, Gul and Pesendorfer argue, welfare economics should be understood in the following manner: "Standard economics identifies welfare with choice; that is, a change (in consumption) is defined to be welfare improving if and only if, given the opportunity, the individual would choose to make that change. The neuroeconomics critique of standard welfare analysis mistakes the economic definition of welfare for a theory of happiness and proceeds to find evidence against that theory. The standard definition of welfare is appropriate because standard economics has *no therapeutic ambition;* it does not try to improve the decision maker but *tries to evaluate how economic institutions mediate (perhaps psychologically unhealthy) behavior of agents.*"[48] They go on to observe that standard welfare economics is a part of positive economics and that economists primarily use that analysis to explain the persistence of efficient institutions and the problems and anomalies that arise in inefficient institutions.

The attempt to disassociate welfare economics from a theory of happiness preserves the sense that economic analysis is scientific in character. In addition it serves to excuse economists from entering into debates about the nature of happiness and immunizes the basic model from theoretical arguments and empirical findings, which suggests that people do not always choose what is in their best interest. And as the telling phrase "no therapeutic ambition" adverts to, it wards off impulses toward paternalistic legislation. The latter concern is frequently the first reaction people (and not just economists) have to arguments that choice can be distinct from well-being. Although it does not logically follow that one should design policy to force people to maximize their welfare, the concern reflects the presumption that economic analysis should issue in policy recommendations. And, indeed, hedonic economists often do move in that direction, though they tend to limit their prescriptions to a so-called light paternalism.[49]

Were it the case that a primary question in economics concerns the persistence of institutions and their ability to mediate the behavior of agents, one could plausibly argue that economics is value neutral, or at least as close to that as any effort at social science can be. The problem, of course, is that economic analysis is not prized because of its ability to explain the persistence of institutions. For starters, we can observe that "efficiency" is invariably used in an evaluative sense. Policies and institutions are better or worse to the extent that they are more or less efficient. To take the example of most relevance to theological economics, economists typically urge us to recognize that many policies that might promote economic equality or alleviate poverty also generate economic inefficiencies. And while economists would not say that the resulting inefficiencies are sufficient to conclude that we ought not to pursue economic equality, they insist that we recognize the loss of efficiency associated with many such policies. Textbooks present this problem as the trade-off between equity and efficiency.

The intuitive sense that efficiency is a good is related to the intuition that greater economic wealth or income is a good. If more of something is better, then it is desirable to get as much of it as possible from a given set of resources. In other words, efficiency is desirable because it would seem to be in service of something we value as good. And as the name of the field suggests, that good presumably has something to do with human welfare or well-being. To put this all as directly as possible, economic analysis is taken seriously by policy makers and the public at large because economics is thought of as the science of improving well-being, at least in a material sense. If that is so, then the problem that the preferences or choices of individuals do not always promote their well-being comes into play, which is exactly why hedonic economics has come into being. Were economists to seriously adopt the view of standard welfare economics defined by Gul and Pesendorfer, it would seem that economics could no longer command the public attention it currently enjoys. Yet most economists do, in fact, want to influence public policy.

Is there a way to acknowledge the reliance of welfare economics on some notion of well-being without making strong philosophical commitments as to its nature? Daniel Hausman succinctly argues against Gul and Pesendorfer, positing that the impossibility of talking about welfare economics (or efficiency) without invoking terms like "better," "benefit," "advantage," or "welfare" tells us that welfare economics is concerned with more than preference satisfaction and its mediation by institutions.[50] He does not go on to endorse hedonic economics, particularly in the dominant form represented by Daniel Kahneman and his collaborators, which defines happiness as the sum of net momentary pleasures. As he points out, it is a view of happiness that no contemporary philosopher would adopt.[51] Instead, he appeals to the argument he developed with Michael McPherson in their paper, "Preference Satisfaction and Welfare Economics."[52]

Hausman and McPherson argue that welfare economics is a tool for assessing the effect of policy on well-being. However, given the many difficulties of drawing a direct connection between choice and well-being, they argue, the standard interpretation of welfare economics, which presumes that preference satisfaction is per se welfare enhancing, cannot be maintained. Instead, they suggest, welfare economics can be defended on the grounds that there is an "evidential connection" between preferences and well-being. In particular, in circumstances where people are choosing with respect to their own well-being, we assume that people are choosing what they believe will be best for them and that, insofar as individuals are better judges of what will benefit them, we can take their preferences as evidence of welfare, without thereby mistaking preference satisfaction for welfare itself.

Their proposal would still modify the use of welfare economics. In particular, it would only be of value in cases where we have no reason to think there might be systematic misjudgments or where people are not considering factors other than their own well-being. Moreover, it would require judgment to discern which cases meet those criteria. Although Hausman and McPherson do not explore the possibility, it is conceivable that hedonic economics and neuroeconomics could provide findings that would help in making those discernments. Hausman and McPherson see their proposal as offering a way of retaining welfare economics as a tool of scientific analysis, which is cleansed of any particular philosophical commitments to the nature of what constitutes well-being. However, for their proposal to work, Hausman and McPherson still require the assumption that it is normally the case that individuals are the best judge of their own welfare. Thus, although they challenge some of the philosophical presuppositions latent in standard economic analysis, they continue to adhere to the larger notion that basically people know what will make them happy. As Chapters 3 and 4 show, that position itself requires some strong philosophical commitments.[53]

In arguing that satisfaction of preference is not itself indicative of welfare, Hausman and McPherson argue that there are two wedges between preference satisfaction and welfare. Thus far we have considered the wedge that occurs because individuals may make mistakes about what makes them well off, since that is the principle concern of hedonic economics. The second wedge is that individuals may make choices based on something other than their own well-being. They might well have altruistic, moral, or aesthetic motivations that are not directly related to their personal well-being. The question that arises in light of these considerations is whether it matters that different sorts of motivations impact choice. The issues involved can best be seen in light of Amartya Sen's challenge to rational choice theory.

Can All Motivations be Collapsed into a Single Metric of Preference?

The debate about neuroeconomics highlights the difficulty of really valuing economic research if one defines efficiency solely in terms of satisfaction of preferences. The second main challenge shifts focus from the question of whether we ought not to be more concerned with well-being to the question of whether collapsing preference into a univariate measure distorts our understanding of practical reason in important ways. The classic form of this challenge comes from Amartya Sen, in his seminal article, "Rational Fools."[54] In that article, Sen argues against the claim that rationality is simply a matter of choosing the best available option.

Sen's argument challenges the neutrality of the model of homo economicus not so much on the question of how to interpret the nature of the utility that is to be maximized but rather by challenging the structure of decision making implied by that model. In particular, it collapses all motives into one scale or vector and reduces rationality to the task of determining how to get as far out along that one vector as possible. Sen's argument is that there are qualitatively different sorts of motivations and that a theory of decision making that obliterates those distinctions is distorted in various concrete ways.

In his first formulation of the argument in "Rational Fools," Sen argues that we can distinguish between three sorts of motivations. At one extreme, we can be motivated by our own well-being. At the other extreme, we can be motivated by purely nonegoistic concerns, wherein we choose things that do not make us personally better off (say, the choice of a rich person to fight for a more progressive tax structure because she thinks it is more just, even though the adoption of that policy would make her personally worse off). Sen calls this sort of nonegoistic motivation "commitment." He then goes on to identify an intermediary case wherein we are motivated out of concern for others because we take personal pleasure in their well-being, which he calls "sympathy."[55]

The basic argument then goes as follows. Sympathy causes trouble to some conclusions in economics, in that it functions like an externality. But those difficulties can be accommodated. Gary Becker's account of the economics of the family, discussed earlier in this chapter, is an example of how readily the framework of utility maximizing can capture the case where a person derives happiness from the well-being of another. Commitment, on the other hand, drives a wedge between personal choice and personal welfare. On this account, once again, welfare economics, which can only address the satisfaction of personal choice, cannot be used to make claims about well-being. Sen documents a variety of economic questions that could benefit from the recognition that individuals can operate out of commitment rather than either of the variants of egoism. For example, on the standard economic account, it is difficult to explain why rational people would bother to vote. A single ballot is vanishingly unlikely to determine an outcome, but there are real costs to going down to the polls and standing in line to cast a vote. Commitment can serve as an explanation for why so many people nonetheless do take the time to go and vote.[56]

The rejoinder, however, would be to say that rational choice still functions, in that it simply traces out the consequences of individuals pursuing their own goals—and can thus handle cases wherein the person's goals are based on principles of disinterested commitment. Sen has thus since reformulated his distinctions, pushing in the yet more radical direction of arguing that individuals can operate out of goals that are not their own.[57] He identifies three varieties of self-interest, or privateness. Individuals can pursue a self-centered concept of welfare, which depends only on their private well-being without reference to the welfare of others. Or they can pursue a self-welfare goal, where they are interested in pursuing their own welfare where their welfare may or may not depend on the welfare of others. Thus far, this is just a reformulation of the distinction between egoism and sympathy. But Sen's third form of self-interested choice offers up a different way of being private, the violation of which cannot be subsumed into the individual's "all things considered" preferences. Rational choice at its broadest would seem to require that individuals at least pursue their goals as they define them, and Sen's argument is that there are modes of reason that can transcend even this broad definition of rational choice.

Economists and philosophers of economics have struggled to parse Sen's arguments. All agree that Sen wants to pose a radical challenge to conventional rational choice theory, arguing that it cannot account for all forms of rational choice. The difficulty is that there is enough fluidity in understanding what rational choice theory actually entails for there to be dispute about exactly what form of rational choice theory Sen is trying to undermine. In particular, as we have seen, there is a question of whether maximizing utility is to be understood as picking the best option, based on whatever considerations the agent deems relevant, or whether it asserts stronger claims about what constitutes preference, namely, that it be connected with personal welfare or something of that sort.

Philip Pettit and Daniel Hausman both are sympathetic to Sen's critique of economics in ways to be discussed below, but both reject the strongest charge, namely, that the rational choice model on its broadest construal cannot accommodate elements of genuine rationality.[58] As Philip Pettit frames the argument, if we understand rational choice as the basic folk psychology wherein individuals pursue goals, then it would be hard to count as rational a choice that was aimed at something the person was not aiming at.[59] Pettit proceeds to go through an exercise of trying to construe what Sen is aiming at with the claim that it can sometimes be rational to pursue goals that are not one's own. He offers three hypotheses about how Sen is construing rational choice theory to make the claim that it cannot accommodate instances where individuals pursue goals other than their own. The first two he concedes are not likely to be what Sen has in mind. The third, which he thinks could plausibly be Sen's view, is the argument that there might be a time lag between the time individuals confront and act on goals that are not their own and the time when they have integrated them into their overall set of preferences so that the goals can truly be called their own.

In point of fact, Sen is engaging a problem about the prisoner's dilemma that has nothing to do with the integration of goals into one's own set of preferences over time. Instead, Sen is concerned with the prisoner's dilemma and economists' efforts to understand why people often choose to cooperate despite the fact that it apparently violates rationality.

The prisoner's dilemma is a well-known problem in game theory that runs as follows. There are two players who are not allowed to communicate with each other. They are presented with the following sets of op-

Table 1   Payoff matrix for the prisoner's dilemma

	Person B	
	Cooperate	Confess
Person A		
Cooperate	3,3	1,4
Confess	4,1	2,2

tions. If they cooperate with each other, they receive an outcome they each value at, say 3. If one confesses while the other cooperates, the confessor gets an outcome he values at 4, while the cooperator gets an outcome she values at 1. Finally, if they both confess, they get an outcome they each value at 2.[60] We can arrange the situation as in Table 1, with A's payout listed first and B's payout listed second.

Consider the problem from A's perspective. If A assumes that B will cooperate, then she does better by confessing, raising her payoff from 3 to 4. If A assumes that B will confess, then she does better by confessing, raising her payoff from 1 to 2. Thus the dominant strategy, regardless of what B does, is for A to confess. B's situation is identical, such that he makes himself better off by confessing regardless of what A chooses. Both, therefore, have incentive to confess and thereby end up with a lower payoff (2,2) than they could have gotten had they found some way to cooperate (3,3).[61]

There is a twofold problem for economic theory here. First, economists find it hard to find a way for players to rationally get to the optimal solution.[62] Second, in experimental settings, individuals choose cooperation frequently enough to make it impossible to claim that one can safely predict a person's choice by assuming they will follow the rational strategy.[63] Sen's argument is that the dilemma exposes a problem with the narrowness of rationality as conceived by economists. In particular, the dilemma arises if players focus only on their own goals. If, instead, the players appeal to a rationality that accepts norms of behavior, the norm of fairness can steer the players to a better solution, one that helps them better achieve their personal goals than if they simply pursued their own goals directly. This is what motivates Sen to argue that the model of rational choice as the pursuit of our goals, however broadly we define those goals, is not sufficient to capture the full range of rationality. The move allows him to escape the argument that "commitment" as he defined it earlier can be subsumed under this broader notion of rationality and therefore does not pose an insurmountable problem for the rational choice model.

To see why Pettit swerves around this logic and gropes for other ways of understanding Sen's claim that it is sometimes rational to *not* be committed to one's own goals, consider Hausman's appraisal of Sen's argument, which does directly engage the example of the prisoner's dilemma. Hausman appeals to Ken Binmore in making the argument that for players who factor in fairness or commitment it is unlikely that they are actually playing a true prisoner's dilemma if we actually see them cooperate. If we start off with a matrix of outcomes that measure personal advantage (see Table 2), then we have to adjust that matrix to reflect the value of fairness, which would cause the payouts in the cooperation category to rise. If they rise enough, it would no longer be the case that cheating is the dominant strategy.[64]

The move is to factor the other value into the preference ranking. It is this sort of move that allows economists to see their model of rationality as value neutral. But the problem can be seen in the question neither Binmore nor Hausman takes up: whether people amenable to Sen's sort of rationality could ever play a true prisoner's dilemma. As Sen stresses, and as Hausman acknowledges, Sen is assuming that the matrix of values has already factored in values—whether they be of altruism or fairness or whatever. The matrix represents the comprehensive value of the outcomes to the players. If that is the case, and the payoff values still lay out the way the prisoner's dilemma does, it is still the case that the players can do better with respect to their own goals (however broadly conceived) by declining to pursue their own goals directly and instead pursuing a communal commitment to fairness.

The point Sen has in mind is that commitment in this case has no independent value (beyond what is already factored into the payoff matrix) but is rather instrumentally useful. A community that has a norm of fairness will arrive at better outcomes whenever the prisoner's dilemma crops up than would a community that lacked such a norm. Moreover, members of such a community would clearly be rational in

Table 2 Payoff matrix for the prisoner's dilemma, adjusted for valuing fairness

	Person B	
	Cooperate	Confess
Person A		
Cooperate	3 + F, 3 + F	1 + F, 4
Confess	4, 1 + F	2, 2

pursuing the goal marked out by commitment, even if it meant re-nouncing a direct pursuit of their own goals. If that argument goes through, rational choice, which requires direct pursuit of one's own goals, is not the only possible mode of rationality. A rules-based ratio-nality succeeds better in the case of the prisoner's dilemma than does a rationality based on pure utility maximization.

Hausman concedes that it is possible for people to rationally cooperate even if their own internal goals are represented by a matrix of payouts as configured in the prisoner's dilemma. His response, though, would be to continue to insist that rational choice is simply the claim that people pursue their preferences, broadly defined in the "all things considered" sense, and that the sort of rational cooperation described by Sen simply means that game theorists need to think harder about how strategies are conceived and beliefs are constructed. In other words, if people coop-erate and are assumed to be rational, then it must be the case that they are confronting a matrix of payoffs that are not configured as they are in a true prisoner's dilemma.

The question can seem like a semantic one, but what is at stake is whether rational choice is at root an all-encompassing formalism. Both Pettit and Hausman are sympathetic to Sen's concern that economists are too quick to assume they understand the content of individual's pref-erences "all things considered" and that this can lead to faulty analysis, like the one we saw above, where economists struggled to account for the "inefficient" practice of gift giving. On the other hand, if there is no theoretical content limiting what can constitute all-things-considered preferences, we are left with a tautology: when people act purposively they do so in a way that seems best to them. So even if we conclude that Sen does not, in the end, resist the rational choice theorist's argument about whether it is possible to rationally cooperate in a true prisoner's dilemma, we can still question whether the implementation of rational choice theory does not inevitably sneak a thicker conception of rationality into the supposedly formal apparatus of rational choice theory. As seen in the debate over hedonic economics, Hausman and McPherson are arguably too quick to assert that there are many cases where it is reasonable to take expression of preference as a measure of actual welfare. It is similarly possible that Hausman is too optimistic in assuming that economists and game theorists are going to spend much time thinking about strategic modes that may include communal elements or other nonstandard considerations.

Perhaps a way of giving a snapshot of the problem is to consider Ken Binmore's characterization of individuals who would choose to cooperate in a prisoner's dilemma. Binmore asks us to consider Adam and Eve, who are rational and who therefore both correctly choose to confess (that is, not cooperate) in a prisoner's dilemma game involving monetary payouts. Their neighbors, Ichabod and Olive, irrationally choose to cooperate. Of course, Ichabod and Olive end up richer than do Adam and Eve. Binmore continues: "So what makes Adam and Eve so smart? The answer is that they have made the best of the opportunities that life has offered them, while Ichabod and Olive have not."[65] If they had switched around so that Adam played Olive and Eve played Ichabod, Olive and Ichabod would have ended up worse off.

Binmore's example is not couched in terms of all-things-considered preferences, and he is therefore leaping past all the considerations of communal identity or commitments to fairness that he himself has argued would require that we understand that the true payout matrix to Ichabod and Olive is not given by the monetary rewards. In his abstract consideration of the problem, Binmore acknowledges that we have to be careful about how to specify the payout matrix. But in practice his gut instinct is to look at two people cooperating when confronted by cash payouts configured in a prisoner's dilemma and call them irrational. To put it another way, both Binmore and Hausman are too quick to assume that for people like Ichabod and Olive it may be impossible to construct any all-things-considered matrix that conforms to the prisoner's dilemma because they are always going to see the possibility of rationally cooperating.

To summarize the story thus far, we have seen that economists understand their model of human behavior, the rational choice model, as being in principle a formal construct. Because of its formalism, economists deny that there is normative content in what they do. The formalism is achieved by focusing on preferences, conceding that individuals can base their preferences on any belief systems. Efficiency, which is a central concept in the "positive" evaluation of markets and various government policies, measures the degree to which preferences are satisfied.

However, in practice, efficiency seems to be desirable not because it is a measure of preference satisfaction but rather because it is a measure of well-being. The disjuncture between the two concepts has become more visible in the wake of the development of hedonic economics, which suggests that individuals fail to efficiently pursue well-being for a variety of reasons. Although many economists argue that findings that consumers are not efficient at pursuing their own well-being are irrelevant because the task of economics is to measure the ability of institutions to mediate individual behavior, pace Gul and Pesendorfer, the interest in hedonic economics suggests that economists recognize that the value in their research lies in the perception that economics is the science of well-being.

The formalism of rational choice theory has also come under pressure with respect to questions about the nature of rationality, and in particular the question of whether an understanding of preferences as all things considered is sufficient to capture all forms of rational behavior. Does it inhibit our ability to understand human decision making if we collapse all considerations into the formal category of preferences? The model of rational choice seems to import a bias toward associating rationality with self-seeking behavior of some variety. In principle we can define *self-seeking* so broadly that it includes the pursuit of goals to which one is committed even at the expense of one's own well-being. But it seems that there are two weaknesses with this approach. First, it might be too easy to relapse to an association between preferences and personal well-being. Second, it may be that by the time we have stretched the concept of preference so broadly as to include the instrumental use of commitment to address problems like the prisoner's dilemma we are left with a theory that is void of any content at all.

In the latter case, economists can reply that they are still insisting that rationality requires that preferences meet the formal criteria of completeness, transitivity, and context independence. But as noted, part of the impetus for developing the field of hedonic economics has been findings in behavioral economics that suggest that even these criteria may not be satisfied. One could further argue that one might expect incompleteness and intransitivity if one takes into account what is really entailed in maximizing utility in a metaphysical world such as the one characterized by Thomas Aquinas. Before getting to that, it will be helpful to briefly set out the features of consumption economics that raise the issues a Thomistic approach to economics is designed to address.

Consumption, Scarcity, and the Nature of Maximization

Although interest in it has expanded in recent years, the consumption side of the economy has traditionally received less attention than the production side. In the current set of course listings for the graduate program in economics at Harvard, of the twenty-five courses offered just one is directly related to consumer behavior (psychology and economics). Consumption figures as an important element in both microeconomics and macroeconomics, but it is all premised on the basic assumption that individuals are interested in maximizing utility and do so subject to price and income constraints. There is an open research interest within that basic framework about how to handle cases of apparent irrationality (addiction, self-control issues, and the like), and that field of inquiry will only expand as the field of behavioral economics continues to grow. So the field is not static, and it is possible that some of these issues will be or, at least in principle, could be addressed by mainstream economists.

That said, there is one maxim that is universal: individuals have unbounded desires. Economists frequently object to this claim, arguing that the rational choice model does not require an assumption that desires are unbounded. But the assumption that desires are unbounded undergirds most of economic thought. This can best be seen in the widespread assumption that, ceteris paribus (all else being equal), more economic growth is to be preferred to less. Because individuals have infinite desires, growth in wealth is to be desired since it will allow consumers to achieve higher levels of utility. In his best-selling undergraduate intermediate macroeconomics text, Greg Mankiw introduces the chapter on national income accounting with a quote from Jane Austen: "A large income is the best recipe for happiness I ever heard of."[66] The unstated premise of macroeconomics and development economics is that economic growth is always desirable. The notion that unlimited growth in income is desirable is what makes it difficult to struggle with the question of how to achieve environmental sustainability, and it is why concerns about efficiency are taken to be a reason to be reserved about embracing policies that promote income equality.

The foundational nature of this assumption can be seen in the most commonly adopted definition of economic science as the science of the allocation of scarce resources between competing ends. Scarcity is inevitable because human desires are infinite while our resources are finite. To be sure, we can have enough of individual goods. But there are always bundles of goods that are preferable to whatever bundle it is that we can currently afford. The fact that there will never be enough means that we need to think in terms of trade-offs and costs and benefits so that we can use our finite resources as well as possible. Because human wants are considered to be insatiable, the economic problem of how to allocate scarce resources will never disappear. Notice that the conjunction of the intuition that economic growth is always desirable and that scarcity is insurmountable produces something of a paradox. We will always be infinitely far from satiety, so what sort of good does economic growth actually achieve? But the paradox is never really addressed. The picture economists have is of a range of preferences extending ever further out such that we can reach higher and higher levels of preference satisfaction as our income levels rise.[67]

In the discipline today, it is mostly taken for granted that economic growth is desirable ceteris paribus. This has not, however, always been the case. Most notably, John Maynard Keynes worried about the problem that would arise as the "economic problem" neared solution.[68] In particular, he worried about what would occupy the masses when it was no longer necessary to work long hours to achieve a decent standard of living. Vestiges of that concern can be found in the modern literature.

Tibor Scitovsky argues that patterns of saving across money, time, and energy do not form a consistent whole and suggests that we are obsessed with economizing resources quite apart from our use of those resources to achieve genuine welfare.[69] Juliet Schor has expanded that insight with empirical work on pressures that cause Americans to overwork and overspend.[70] Stephen Marglin argues that while scarcity might always be with us, its meaning has shifted over time. In particular, in premodern times, scarcity manifested itself as difficulty in meeting basic needs or an established standard of living, whereas in modern times scarcity manifests itself as a chronic sense that relative wants always outstrip resources.[71] He uses that notion to reconcile Keynes's prediction of the end of the economic problem with Schor's empirical work, which suggests that households feel as economically constrained as ever despite economic growth having unfolded at the rate Keynes predicted.

It is also arguable that as a matter of economic history, endless economic striving is not a universal feature of human nature. In particular, there is the phenomenon of "backward bending labor supply curves," wherein populations with low levels of economic development respond to rising incomes by reducing their labor supply, a phenomenon that can be explained as the rational response of those who are working with a fixed output in mind and who are happy to switch from labor to leisure as soon as that output is achieved. E. P. Thompson argues that in the early stages of the Industrial Revolution, one of the key tasks was to retrain a generation of workers to refrain from leaving work once they had met a basic income requirement.[72] Finally, in the late nineteenth century, social workers consciously strove to raise immigrants' ideas about appropriate standards of living to mold them into good industrious Americans.

Arguably, globalization has succeeded in advertising the desirability of economic growth to all cultures. Economic development has been on the global agenda for at least a half century. In the past few decades, economic development took off in many parts of the world—most notably in India and China—lifting billions of people out of poverty. The amelioration of poverty and want is a genuine good. At the same time, it is not clear how much economic growth beyond a certain level genuinely contributes to human well-being. If one follows the practice of hedonic economics and uses subjective reports of well-being as a measure of well-being, it appears to be the case that the correlation between income and well-being is positive when income levels are low but then drops close to zero when income levels rise beyond a certain level.

Richard Easterlin first documented the difficulty of establishing a strong correlation between income and well-being, and the phenomenon is known as the Easterlin paradox.[73] Recent studies using newer global surveys have found evidence that there is a positive correlation between income and happiness.[74] However, studies of the body of statistical studies suggest that those results might be driven by the dramatic decline in quality of life in the very poor countries in sub-Saharan Africa and that the results one gets are very sensitive to the underlying model employed or the sort of data one studies.[75] The upshot is that at best the relationship between economic growth and genuine well-being is complicated and almost certainly is mediated by institutional and cultural factors which have an independent effect on well-being.

Given that there are both historical and empirical reasons to think that it is doubtful that unlimited economic growth should be the principal goal in economic life, it is worth asking why economists take its desirability as a self-evident proposition.[76] In part, it is presumably just a reflection of the presumption in modern life that progress is best seen in terms of an advance in standards of living. Political-economic discourse is premised on the notion that governments should be judged by their ability to foster a climate of economic growth. But the rational choice model seems to invite language that supports a conception of desire as insatiable.

To be fair, the formal structure of rational choice need not entail the idea that maximization means more. It is often construed as having the minimalist sense of "not worse"—that is, the choice made is not worse than any other available. If rational choice really just reflected the truism from folk psychology that people do what appears to them to be best to do, it is a framework that could accommodate individuals who had satiable desires. However, there are features of the thought, particularly the notion that preferences can be mapped onto a utility function, that invite the shift to the idea that more is always better.

For starters, the model of rational choice assumes that we can order our various options in a clear set of rankings that can be mapped onto a utility function that is to be maximized. Recall that we assume that preferences are complete, such that we can consider all possible options and know how we would choose when presented with any possible set of choices. If we are truly thinking about all possible choices, that would seem to imply an infinite set of possible choices. And if they can be rank-ordered, that would further imply basically a wish list that likewise extends out indefinitely. Once we do that mapping, it is natural to think of each possible choice as having an assigned value on an open-ended scale. Because there is no point of arrival on that scale, it becomes necessary to think of the consumer's problem as being one not of maximization but rather of maximization under constraint. If that is so, anything that relaxes that constraint must be welfare enhancing. It is a short step to identify income as the relevant constraint and to conclude that, ceteris paribus, an increase in wealth is welfare enhancing.[77]

In addition to inviting us to think of preferences as an ever-ascending scale of value, the rational choice model also invites us to collapse all goods into a single metric. Insofar as economists simply intend the scale as a measure of order, they are not guilty of arguing that people maximize some entity of goodness called utility. Nonetheless, the single scale invites us to think of all goods as sharing broadly similar qualities. In particular, if economists are mostly focused on material goods, their native thought is to think about resource constraints as the limiting factor in the production of material goods. But if we then step back and say that preference orderings can include values assigned to abstractions like fairness, or the virtue embodied in our choices or acts, we might fail to notice that it is not the case that such values are limited by resource constraints. Put another way, the rational choice model is not, in fact, applied as a merely formal structure. It is conceptualized in terms of one type of good—material goods—and that conceptualization is then applied to all goods. As a result, the model ends up being nonneutral.

Finally, the model takes preferences as given and focuses our attention on attaining the most desirable option. In doing so it helps us avoid asking real questions about whether human desire is properly characterized as insatiable. As discussed in further chapters, there are many reasons to think that humans might be tempted to think of desire as insatiable but that such desires are likely to be misdirected. In addition to failing to challenge us to think about ill-conceived preferences, the rational choice model focuses our attention on the means of attaining our desires. If we unhinge the question of the pursuit of income from the question of what we wish to use that income for, we are more likely to falsely conclude that more income is, ceteris paribus, always to be preferred.

These features of economic analysis are premised on strong ethical and metaphysical commitments. The rational choice model and the correlative distinction between positive and normative economics are both invoked to ward off ethical critiques of the economic approach. Yet such defenses do not address the concerns I raise here. To see the import of the concern, an alternative model is needed. Accordingly, Chapter 3 begins an account of Aquinas's conception of human happiness and his related discussion of the form of practical reason best suited to achieving it.

3

Happiness and the Distinctively Human Exercise of Practical Reason

The Metaphysical Backdrop

As we have seen, economists present the rational choice model as a value-neutral framework, which can be employed to describe or predict all human choice. Chapter 2 explores some tensions within the discipline about whether that claim can be sustained. In this chapter and Chapter 4, I challenge that claim by developing Aquinas's account of happiness and the form of practical reason, prudence, suitable for guiding us toward it. Like economists, Aquinas believes that humans act for an end. Thomas calls that end happiness, while economists call it utility, but insofar as both Aquinas and economists believe that human action is teleological, Aquinas's economics does not simply talk past modern-day economists. That said, Aquinas's understanding of that end differs substantially from the one envisioned by economists. In particular, Aquinas's conception of happiness is centered on the notion of perfection of our beings. An economist might naïvely suppose that all Aquinas is doing is specifying a particular utility function, which would leave the rational choice model unchallenged as a universal model of practical reason.

However, it turns out that the sort of practical reason one would have to adopt to direct oneself toward the substantive end described by Aquinas differs substantially from the account of practical reason embodied in the rational choice model. To put the matter simply, individuals directing their lives toward the sort of happiness Aquinas describes would be systematically thwarted from their goal were they to adopt the model of practical reason described by economists. The rational choice model is not, therefore, value free. It is a choice among philosophical options even if few economists are aware of having made it. When I paint my living room blue because there are eighty gallons of blue paint in my garage, I am still making a choice among colors. The claim that the behavior described by economists is rational rests on a controvertible concept of happiness, which, in turn, rests on a set of assumptions about the metaphysical structure of the world that is not shared by all.

Aquinas's views on happiness offer more than a simple counterexample to the claim that the rational choice model is value neutral. They are of value in their own right. Aquinas's approach offers a way of integrating economic and ethical concerns, allowing us to distinguish between the sorts of desires the fulfillment of which actually moves us toward genuine flourishing and those that do not. In addition, Aquinas's approach allows us to better understand the creative and aesthetic aspects of decision making, which are ill captured by the calculating form of practical reason studied by economists. As I hope to show, it is an attractive model of human nature and practical reason. But this would leave economists with the argument that however attractive one might find Aquinas's account of happiness and practical reason, the fact of the matter is that the actual behavior of actual humans is reasonably well described by the rational choice model. As it happens, Aquinas's view of human nature is capacious enough to accommodate that fact. Although humans are capable of aspiring to the more fully human and multidimensional form of practical reason Aquinas describes, they very often operate out of a lower form of reason that parallels the rational choice model in important ways. He thus offers an approach that can allow us to deal with the pragmatic reality that humans most often act on the lower form of reason that responds to incentives, while also accommodating the equally important reality that we sometimes act on a higher form of reason.

Chapter 4 develops Aquinas's substantive account of happiness, but it is helpful to begin in this chapter with Aquinas's discussion of the formal properties of happiness. As it turns out, Aquinas opens his treatise on happiness with a discussion that includes a response *avant la lettre* to the formal properties of happiness embedded in the rational choice model. The resulting contrast serves to secure the point that the rational choice model is not value neutral.

Before beginning a close reading of Aquinas himself, it is worth pointing out that one could fill a good-sized library with the secondary literature on Aquinas. Within that literature there are lively debates on how Aquinas should be interpreted. Because this book is oriented toward an engagement with the discipline of economics, I do not engage competing interpretations of Aquinas. The reading offered here is my best understanding of Aquinas.

The Formal Properties of Happiness

Aquinas sets out the formal properties of happiness in the opening question of his "Treatise on Happiness," which concerns our "last end."[1] In other words, Aquinas's basic presupposition is that humans act purposively, working to achieve some ultimate goal or end.[2] That ultimate end is happiness; but as the first question lays out, Aquinas's formal conception of happiness differs in three ways from the notion of maximizing utility subject to constraint that undergirds the economic approach.

First, Aquinas distinguishes between human purposiveness and the motives and impulses that guide other animals, whereas economists tend to blur the distinction. Second and correlatively, a crucial aspect of a fully human purposiveness is that human actions are ordered toward some sort of completion or perfection. Aquinas specifically rejects any account of the fully human pursuit of happiness as the pursuit of an indefinite series of ends in which more is better, such as the one that underlies the rational choice model. Third, although Aquinas recognizes that different people will have different ideas about what constitutes happiness, he does not believe that our true end is subjectively determined. Jointly the three points converge on an understanding of human action as oriented toward achieving our perfection in a characteristically human manner in a cosmos that is suffused with order. On this account, human actions are also always moral actions. As a result, there can be no essential quarrel between ethical and economic values. An action that does not move us toward our own perfection is a morally bad act, but it would also be inefficient in that it is incoherent to think of an efficient movement away from our proper end.

The Distinctively Human Character of Our Last End

The human situation is complicated. We are animals, endowed like other animals with a set of biological drives and an ability to navigate the world so as to pursue ends largely determined by those drives. To the extent that rationality involves deliberation about how best to pursue those ends, we share a form of reason with animals. My dog calculates how best to chase the rabbit in the backyard. Presumably my calculations about how best to make a living are more sophisticated. But we are both thinking about how to get what we want. Aquinas begins his "Treatise on Happiness," however, by arguing that there is nonetheless a form of reason that is distinctive to humans. This form of rationality gives us a freedom that the other animals do not enjoy. Indeed, it is because we enjoy this special form of reason that human actions always have a moral character. Because there are two modes of reason, Aquinas is at pains to distinguish them so that we can think clearly about the character of human rationality.

Aquinas begins by taking up the question of what makes a given act properly human. We differ from nonrational animals insofar as we are "masters" of our own actions.[3] The essence of the human act is that it is an exercise of our reason and our rational appetite, that is, our will. They are actions undertaken for a reason. Thus any actions that do not proceed from the deliberations of reason, such as absent-mindedly scratching one's nose, are actions done by humans but are not properly human acts.[4] But what does Aquinas mean by this? How does human choice differ from the choice of an animal?

We get some answer to this in Aquinas's next article, which asks whether it is proper to the rational nature to act for an end, that is, whether it is only humans who act for a purpose. The answer is no. All creatures, even inanimate beings, act for a purpose. This seems like an odd conclusion, since some beings are "altogether without knowledge as insensible creatures, or because they do not apprehend the idea of an end as such, as in irrational animals."[5] Against this view, Aquinas argues that all created beings move toward an end, the crucial distinction being that humans move themselves toward their end, while other beings are led by their natural inclinations or appetites. Their end is fixed by another (the Creator), who implants in them the natural inclinations that move them toward their end.[6] Thus trees naturally grow up to find the most light to sustain themselves through photosynthesis as a result of natural tendencies built into their beings.

Turning to the contrast between humans and nonrational animals, Aquinas argues that animals do apprehend their immediate ends—my dog sees a rabbit and is attracted to it. What animals lack is the ability to "know the nature of the end as such," and therefore they are unable to "ordain anything to the end."[7] In other words, my dog is attracted to the rabbit but does not understand that the rabbit is ordered to her nutrition. She is responding to a natural appetite but is not directing herself. As Aquinas elaborates in his reply to the first objection, a person acting for an end knows the end—knows what the purpose of the action is. But we can imagine a person in an army, for example, who is ordered to do something without knowing its purpose. Just so the animals.[8] They follow their inclinations the way a soldier obeys a commander, but they do not know what purposes those inclinations serve.[9]

We might be tempted to ask here whether Aquinas is overstating the difference between animals and humans. Since his day we have learned more about animals and the capacities of the higher animals, leading many to challenge the sharp distinctions Aquinas seems to be making. For example, in his book *Dependent Rational Animals: Why Human Beings Need the Virtues*, Alasdair MacIntyre argues that not all species of animals are merely following their natural appetites without any sense of purpose.[10] In particular, dolphins seem to be able to respond to a given object sometimes as food and sometimes as an object of play, which would seem to require that they be able to order objects to some purpose much as humans do.[11] MacIntyre's point that animals are on a continuum, with some animals showing more intelligence and likeness to us than others, is well taken, though I would observe that my cat also can treat a mouse as an object of food or an object of play without implying anything more than that the mouse interests her differently when she is already sated. It is not clear from what MacIntyre reports why we should view the same behavior differently in the case of dolphins. Nonetheless, MacIntyre raises the question of how we can square the evidently intelligent behavior of the highest species of animals with Aquinas's insistence that there is a special distinction to human reason. There are clearly differences in the degree to which various animals can discern their environments, adjust their behaviors accordingly, and work together in social groups. The highest animals, such as gorillas, chimpanzees, and dolphins, exhibit behaviors that seem purposive in the same sense that we would describe human actions as purposive.

MacIntyre is not alone in arguing that animals can act rationally. Economists would make the stronger claim that the rational choice model can predict animal behavior just as it can predict human behavior. For example, they have found that pigeons and rats observe the law of demand and respond to price and wealth shocks in a way that is consistent with the rational choice model.[12] More recently, economists have used higher animals in laboratory experiments to discern whether animals are subject to the same limitations in rational choice as humans (such as reference dependence and loss aversion), concluding that, indeed, capuchin monkeys replicate human choice both when it comes to basic consumer demand behaviors and in exhibiting specific forms of irrationality.[13] It may seem ironic that economists see their model as applicable to animals, given that one criticism frequently launched at neoclassical economics is that the mathematical calculations posited in the rational choice framework are complex and are likely to be beyond the capacities of an ordinary person.[14] However, as mentioned in Chapter 2, the standard rejoinder, following Milton Friedman, has always been that all that matters is that individuals act as if they make such calculations, not that they actually do make such calculations. The comparison Friedman invokes is instructive: we can use mathematical methods of optimizing to calculate the density of leaves on a tree if we use the assumption that the leaves deliberately seek to maximize the amount of sunlight they receive. That the model works does not imply that the leaves actually did any optimizing.[15] And thus economists are unsurprised when their experiments can demonstrate that pigeons and rats are likely to respond to "price" shocks much as do humans.

Aquinas would be overstating the distinction, then, if he did not acknowledge that animals exhibit behavior that suggests some sort of rationality. But in fact, Aquinas does acknowledge that animals are quasi-rational. He makes this point in the *Summa theologica* in his discussion of voluntary acts. An act is voluntary if the agent is acting for an end.[16] Insofar as Aquinas has suggested that the distinctively human character of reason consists in our ability to act purposively or for an end, it would seem that animals ought not be able to do that. Yet Aquinas rebuts this concern, arguing that animals are capable of "imperfectly" voluntary acts. A "perfectly" voluntary act entails that an agent move himself with "perfect" knowledge of the end. By that, Aquinas means that we not only recognize the end but also understand it as an end, in addition to understanding the relationship between the means and the end. But as we have already seen, for Aquinas animals can apprehend an end but not apprehend the end as an end. I choose to eat knowing that food is ordered to sustaining my life, while my dog just chases the rabbit. Yet if we take on board the scientific observations MacIntyre cites, this is not sufficient to demarcate human rationality from animal rationality.

To dig deeper into Aquinas's meaning, we can turn to his lengthier treatment of the question of whether irrational animals are capable of voluntary actions in his *De veritate*.[17] Here we find that the crucial distinction is that humans can judge their own judgment. In particular, we are able to consider the finite good that our appetites present to us under the aspect of more universal considerations. So, for example, I can judge that the apple before me is good to eat but determine to not eat the apple because it is an hour before mass and I judge it is more important to follow the Church's strictures about fasting before mass. Or to use the example Aquinas invokes, a man can ignore his knowledge that fornication is evil and choose to fornicate because his appetite sees it as an act that is good for him here and now. It is our capacity to judge the judgment of our appetites that makes us free (and therefore subject to moral judgment). Aquinas's argument is that animals are not free in the same way. They can discern what a thing is, and that it is good, but having made that discernment, they are then impelled to act on it. They cannot judge whether it is good to act on their judgment.[18] For dolphins to pass this threshold, they would have to be able to see a school of fish, judge that it would be worthwhile to hunt and eat them, yet not act on that judgment in light of a higher judgment that for some other reason it would be better to refrain from the appealing choice to hunt the fish. In short, they would have to be able to second-guess their initial assessment.

What seems to be important here is that we are able to discern qualitatively distinct finite goods in light of the universal good and make judgments regarding which of those finite goods we will pursue. What Aquinas would deny is that there is a metric by which we can reduce these various goods to a single measure of value such that reason is just an exercise in determining what delivers the highest value. If I see the act of eating now as something that should be curbed because of liturgical practice, I will make one choice with respect to the apple. If I see the apple as food, I will make a different choice with respect to the apple. It is my judgment about how to see the apple that determines whether I eat it or not. The dolphin has no comparable choice (so far as we know). The fish are food. If it is worth hunting them, they will be eaten. If the dolphin is already full, the fish might be played with. But a hungry dolphin seems unlikely to face a choice about whether to see the fish as food or as an occasion for play, whereas a hungry human does seem to have a choice in such matters.

Aquinas goes on to argue that humans and brutes alike are capable of being guided in their actions by changes in the costs and benefits presented before them. We can induce a dog to get off the couch by scolding it; and we can induce healthy young persons to buy health insurance they do not need by taxing them if they fail to do so.[19] This is exactly the behavior economists find in humans and pigeons alike. But there is a crucial difference. Humans do not have to respond to the incentives. A healthy young person could choose to buy the health insurance that costs more than the benefits she can expect to derive from it even without a tax on noncompliance on the grounds that as a part of society it is proper for the healthy to support those who are less healthy.

On this view, economists have a good model of the aspects of human behavior that are similar to that of animals. What economists lack is an account of the distinctively human ability to judge our own judgments, to refrain from taking an action that on first blush seems like a good action to take, because we choose to see the object in a different light. An economist might ask at this juncture whether this second-order judgment is different in kind from the first-order judgment. If I choose to defer eating an apple that is otherwise attractive because I make a judgment that it would be better to wait until after mass, how is that not simply a revelation that I prefer following the rules about fasting before mass to satisfying my hunger more immediately?

The reply is that the way economists frame the problem collapses two distinct sorts of judgments into one. On the one hand, there is the choice to be made on how to see the good embodied in the apple. It is either a way of satisfying hunger or it is an impediment to good liturgical practice. On the other hand, there are choices between instruments that deliver different levels of a comparable good. The former judgment is a moral judgment. It is the choice of what good to pursue, whereas the latter is a more economic judgment about how best to pursue a good one has already decided on. Why might this matter? There are at least three different ways economists' use of the rational choice model can lead them to a faulty understanding of actual human choice.

First, consider economists' sense that incentives are the best way to mold human behavior in desirable directions. Much policy analysis is about how to best structure incentives to achieve desirable outcomes, and this is frequently preferred to simply trying to persuade people about what ends might be desirable to be pursued. In many instances, incentives are an effective way of shaping behavior. There is a reason that the criminal code is not simply a moral exhortation but rather also includes penalties for malfeasance. But incentives are not always helpful and can indeed backfire if the process of imposing them causes people to alter their higher-order judgment about the nature of the good in question. Michael Sandel cites several examples of this in his book, *What Money Can't Buy: The Moral Limits of Markets.* To take one example, an experiment was conducted at Israeli day care centers involving a change in policy to try to encourage parents to pick up their children on time. A fine was imposed on parents who came late. The result was that more parents ended up coming late because the imposition of the fine apparently caused many parents to shift from seeing timely pick-ups as a civic obligation toward seeing it as a commodity, opting to pay the price required to have the day care center look after their children a bit longer.[20]

A second effect of focusing on lower-order judgments would be the difficulty economists have explaining why people might cooperate when confronted with prisoner's-dilemma style problems as discussed in Chapter 2. The rational choice to not cooperate is the lower-order judgment about what is directly in our best interest, but there might be a higher-order judgment that allows one to rationally cooperate because one can see that by doing so we can jointly secure a better outcome than would be available if we followed our first-order judgment. Add in a judgment that it would be better to be the sort of person who can see the rationality of cooperating and an expectation that the human being with whom one is playing the game is capable of similar sorts of higher reasoning, and it becomes reasonable to at least start the game by cooperating. And, in fact, the strategy of starting out a prisoner's dilemma game by cooperating and then following up with a tit-for-tat strategy has been found to be the most successful approach to playing multiple games of the prisoner's dilemma.[21]

The third effect is to notice the long-standing critique that the rational choice model cannot account for the creativity involved in entrepreneurship, as the Austrian school of economics has long argued.[22] Creativity would seem to be a component of our capacity for higher-order judgment. In choosing our own ends, we are allowed to determine ourselves in a way that is not possible for animals. A human can choose what to work at, how hard to work at it, whether to spend spare time reading or rock climbing, and so on. Dolphins do not have that sort of freedom because they lack the reflexive capacity of reason. They have a fixed sense of what is good for them, and however intelligently they go about pursuing that good, they are constrained to act according to that fixed sense of the good, very much like homo economicus. But entrepreneurship seems to be nearer this sort of self-creation than a model of profit maximization would suggest. On this view, the rational choice model precludes economists from investigating a phenomenon that is an important driver of economic growth. Granting that the model cannot extend to account for the phenomenon, one could at least say that the fact of entrepreneurship should make economists wary about identifying reason so narrowly with the calculations of a particular sort of instrumental reason.

With this material behind us, we can see what Aquinas means when he goes on to say that all properly human acts are also moral acts. Unlike other creatures, we have been given the capacity to be provident for ourselves.[23] Indeed, that we choose our ends is what confers an essentially moral characteristic on all acts that are properly human.[24] We choose the light in which we view a given good, and we are accountable for our judgments. This moral quality means that a given act can take on different moral characteristics depending on the intention. The act of killing a man could be a virtue if it is a means of safeguarding justice or a vice if done to satisfy an angry impulse.[25] By contrast, we do not affix a moral character to a cat's act of killing a mouse, even if in a given instance the cat does not need to kill the mouse to satisfy her hunger. The cat is responding to a natural inclination and does not order its acts to a given end. It has no choice but to respond as it does, however much intelligence is involved in hunting and killing the mouse.

By drawing out the distinctive aspect of human reason, Aquinas locates the essential exercise of reason precisely in our moral discernments, our determination of what ends are worthy of pursuit. As discussed in Chapter 2, Amartya Sen suggests that the rational choice approach simply cannot do justice to the distinctive exercise of reason involved in these sorts of judgments. Indeed, economists tend to collapse the distinction altogether, seeking to treat the higher exercise of reason as having no formal properties distinct from the lower exercise of reason that we have in common with nonrational animals. This flattening is not merely a matter of deflecting attention away from the role of reason in determining which goods are worth pursuing.[26] The economic approach also fails to do justice to the distinctly human mode of reason that allows us to order our various decisions into a coherent whole.

Human Action as Ordered to One Last End

After establishing the unique way in which humans act for an end, Aquinas goes on to argue that properly human action is ordered to one final end.[27] In other words, we are able to structure our lives into a coherent, purposive whole. Aquinas makes this point by arguing that there cannot be an infinite regress in intentions. We act for a reason. Most of our actions are for reasons that point to yet other reasons. Thus, for example, in the morning I put the kettle on the stove. The reason I want to do that is because I want to heat water for some hot tea. The hot tea, in turn, is desirable because caffeine in the morning helps get my day off to a good start, and so on, and so on. According to Aquinas, if we never arrive at a good that is desired for its own sake, we would never begin to act at all.[28] Human action has a purpose or a point, which suggests that it is directed toward something that in principle would constitute a stopping point were we to arrive at it. Without having some ultimate aim toward which our other intermediate ends are directed, we would have no reason to get started at all.

A great deal is implied by this position, as we can begin to see by asking what economists would make of this argument. They agree that we act for an end—but why does Thomas insist that this requires that we act for a specific good as a final end? As we saw in Chapter 2, the rational choice model postulates that humans choose the best bundle of goods available to them, with an underlying tendency to imagine that there is an infinite sequence of possible goods and that we try to get as far along that vector of goodness as is possible given our resource and time constraints. Aquinas explicitly considers this possibility, taking up the question whether man's last end is such an end. He formulates the objection as follows: "Further, things pertaining to the reason can be multiplied to infinity: thus mathematical quantities have no limit. For the same reason the species of numbers are infinite, since, given any number, the reason can think of one yet greater. But desire of the end is consequent on the apprehension of the reason. Therefore it seems that there is also an infinite series of ends."[29] In other words, shouldn't we think of the pursuit of happiness as a journey up a ladder of greater and greater goods?

Aquinas rejects this characterization of the last end, arguing instead that happiness carries with it a sense of arrival. In the *Sed contra,* he appeals to Aristotle's argument in the *Metaphysics* that "to suppose a thing to be indefinite is to deny that it is good" and observes that "it is contrary to the nature of an end to proceed indefinitely."[30] An economist could concede that we must have an ultimate purpose to act at all but might ask why that final end could not still be indefinite in the sense that one could act for the purpose of moving as far out along a vector representing levels of happiness as is possible. The exercise of maximizing utility subject to constraint is, after all, a well-defined mathematical problem. The key point of contention, then, centers on the question of whether happiness entails having a sense of "arrival." Aquinas's conception of happiness involves coming to a rest in our ultimate good. Economists model happiness as an unbounded quest for more.

From a Thomistic point of view, there actually is good reason why the economic view of happiness might seem plausible. As discussed further below, Aquinas believes that our perfect happiness is to be found in the beatific vision, which is an enjoyment of the infinite good, which is God.[31] So economists are not wrong to think of happiness as an orientation toward an infinite good. The difference lies in whether we think of that infinitude in quantitative rather than in qualitative terms. To think of infinitude in quantitative terms is to think of it as extension. To think of it qualitatively is to think of it more as a fullness or completion. Although it will take a fuller account of Aquinas's metaphysics to see what is entailed in thinking of approaching the infinite through perfection rather than extension, we can begin to get a sense of Aquinas's point by considering the way he addresses the objection in more detail.

The force of the objection is that reason can always think of just one more thing, and therefore our desire is really to move as far along a vector of good as we can. Aquinas replies by arguing that reason is not inherently quantitative in nature. When, for example, we seek a demonstration, we are not looking for an indefinite string of arguments. We expect to come to a conclusion. The string of arguments leading us to the conclusion is finite because the arguments have an essential ordered connection to one another. It is only when things are accidentally related that we can imagine an indefinite string; it is not essential to the number 8 that we can add 1 to it and arrive at 9.[32] The essence of reason is in the way arguments are connected such that they come to a point. The feature of reason that can identify an indefinite string exists, but that is not really the point, so to speak.

It might seem curious that Aquinas replies to an argument about our ability to imagine an indefinite string of goods with an argument about the nature of speculative reason. What bearing does the argument that speculative reason aims at coming to a conclusion have on the claim that we can always think of yet another bundle of goods that would be even more desirable than the one we are currently contemplating? Aquinas makes the connection as follows: "[It is not] possible to go to infinity since if there were no last end, nothing would be desired, nor would any action have its term, nor would the intention of the agent be at rest. . . . On the other hand nothing hinders infinity from being in things that are ordained to one another not essentially but accidentally; for accidental causes are indeterminate. And in this way it happens that there is an accidental infinity of ends, and of things ordained to the end."[33] I take Thomas to be making the following argument: For properly purposive action, we need a final end to which all other ends are ordered, connecting the various goods we pursue in an essential way. That does not prevent us from having an infinite number of ends, as rational choice theorists might conceive, but we can only do so on pain of having ends that are not ordered to one another, that is, are only accidentally related. In other words, a proper exercise of reason involves making a cohesive whole out of one's life, or at least trying to. The successive points of more and more happiness (or utility) that economists might conceive just involve moving from one end to another, without really going anywhere.

It is something of an illusion to call this indefinite movement from one end to another an exercise in achieving more happiness, as becomes clearer below, when we take up Aquinas's substantive account of happiness. But for now the key point made at this formal level is simply that the only way we can imagine an infinity of ends is if we are thinking of ends that are accidentally, but not essentially, connected with one another. It is the difference between accumulating indefinitely and working to achieve a particular vision of a good life. The former is a simulacrum of the purposiveness that is proper to human beings, which fails to fully exercise our higher powers of judgment by failing to order our ends in a coherent way. Although the rational choice model need not rule out such purposiveness, it lacks a vocabulary for distinguishing between the pursuit of a comprehensive good and pursuit of a string of ends with no essential connection between them.[34] Once again, the economic view of rationality entails substituting a lower form of reasoning (calculating how to move out along a vector of an unconsidered string of goods) for the proper exercise of human reason that lies not only in discerning what goods are worthy of pursuit but also in thinking of how to order the finite goods in our lives into a meaningful whole.

That a Thomistic framework requires that we identify some conceptions of the pursuit of happiness as illusory brings us to the final formal characteristic of his thought, which differs from modern economic thought—namely, his willingness to identify the comprehensive good we should seek rather than thinking of happiness primarily in terms of the satisfaction of whatever subjective desires we happen to have.

The Objective Nature of Our Last End

In a pluralistic culture, there is an aversion to arguing that there is an objective character to the good we seek. That is to say, we can all agree that we want to be happy, but we have wildly differing ideas about would we would need to call ourselves happy. Aquinas is hardly unaware of the diversity of opinion about what constitutes happiness. After his discussion of the formal properties of happiness, Aquinas immediately moves to consider a catalogue of possible candidates for the good in which we can find happiness: wealth, fame or glory, honor, power, health, pleasure, spiritual goods, or any created good in general.[35] But he does hold that we can have a rational discussion about what good or goods constitute happiness and that, indeed, there is an objective answer to the question. Before turning to his argument on that question, it is helpful to take up some final points Aquinas makes about the formal character of our last end.

First, having argued that happiness cannot be achieved by pursuing an indefinite string of goods, Aquinas argues that neither can happiness be found by pursuing a finite cluster of distinct goods. People might say they are seeking happiness both in wealth and in virtue, but Aquinas denies that this is really possible. One reason he offers for this position is that because we desire our own perfection, the final end is our "perfect and crowning good."[36] It represents our complete fulfillment and by definition one cannot want more once one is completely fulfilled. The idea of perfection or completion is central for Aquinas and will be taken up more fully in the next section. But here, the key point is that happiness involves resting in a comprehensive good that leaves nothing to be desired. We can still ask why that comprehensive good cannot be a composite good, such as desiring to be both wealthy and virtuous.

The problem with the composite good is that it resists the idea of perfection or completion in other ways. In particular, for Aquinas whatever we take to be our idea of the comprehensive good shapes our entire set of desires. As he puts it in his *Sed contra,* "That in which a man rests as in his last end, is master of his affections, since he takes therefrom his entire rule of life."[37] In other words, having identified something as our crowning perfection, we frame our other choices in light of that overarching idea of the good. We may think we desire both wealth and virtue, but we find out what it is that matters when the two come into conflict. Even if we are not consciously thinking of our ultimate purpose in each and every choice we make, our conception of the ultimate good shades our perception of the goods we confront and thus is reflected in each choice, much as a traveler does not think of the end of a journey during each and every step taken.[38] Even if we do not all reflect deeply on our ultimate purpose and order our various ends to that ultimate purpose, it is part of human nature that our will, which directs our activities, is aimed at a good it perceives as constituting our crowning good. This fundamental orientation of the will is what gives our lives the distinctive casts that they have.

That our lives have these distinctive casts raises the big question. How can we say there is one and only one comprehensive good for all humans given that we have just observed that people shape their lives quite differently depending on which good they pursue as their comprehensive good? Aquinas first argues that in a formal sense, all individuals agree about the last end—namely, that all desire fulfillment. However, there is not agreement about what good would be fulfilling. Some desire wealth, others power, others pleasure, and so on. But Aquinas asserts that this is not just a question of *de gustibus non est disputandum:* "All men are not agreed as to their last end: since some desire riches as their consummate good; some pleasure; others, something else. Thus to every taste the sweet is pleasant but to some, the sweetness of wine is most pleasant, to others, the sweetness of honey, or of something similar. Yet that sweet is absolutely the best of all pleasant things, in which he who has the best taste takes most pleasure. That good is most complete which the man with well-disposed affections desires for his last end."[39] In other words, we all take pleasure in the fulfillment of our subjective desires, but we are not the source of value. Instead, we are measured according to the quality of our desires.

Of course, Aquinas's assertion that there is an objective answer to the question of what constitutes our last end grates against modern sensibilities. We have some work to do before we can fully enter into Aquinas's perspective on this matter. But before moving on it is worth pausing to summarize the story thus far. That we do not all desire the "consummate good" follows from the uniquely human freedom with which we began this section. The essence of human reason is the capacity to think about our ends and guide ourselves accordingly. That is why human choices are inescapably also moral. We all share an intention of seeking fulfillment, and however much or little we think about it, that intention permeates our decision making and therefore gives a shape to our lives.

However, we have the capacity to think about our judgment of what would make us happy, and if we find that we are aiming at an incomplete form of happiness, we can attempt to retrain our affections so that we can pursue that more complete good. Moral life for Aquinas is not about disregarding our desires in favor of doing what is right; it is rather a matter of exercising our higher judgment about what actually constitutes a fulfilling end and then training ourselves (to the extent possible) to desire that end. For Aquinas, human choice is not about efficiently getting what we want so much as it is about learning how to want what is genuinely good. That is the essence of a life of virtue, which, in turn, is bound up with the idea of happiness as perfection, to which I now turn.

The Metaphysical Setting that Underlies Aquinas's Account of Happiness

Aquinas's assertion that there is an objective order of good may be jarring to modern sensibilities, but it flows directly from his understanding of the metaphysical structure of the world in which we find ourselves.[40] To put the matter crudely, if one believes that God created the world, it is more natural to think there is an objective order of goods than it would be if one thought of the universe as an inanimate given. Indeed, all of the points of formal contrast identified in the previous section flow from differences between Aquinas's metaphysics and the metaphysics that tacitly informs modern beliefs.[41] Thus to understand Aquinas's approach to happiness, both in terms of its formal properties and its substantive content, it is necessary to have a sense of the metaphysical framework he is using. What follows is a sketch that focuses on two key features of Aquinas's metaphysics that are essential to the theological economics that follows: first, that God's relationship to the world is strange and can only be understood analogically, and second, that God is both the highest perfection and the source of all perfections. These two features inform Aquinas's substantive approach to happiness, a subject that will be taken up in Chapter 4.

The Analogical Relationship between God and World

An essential aspect of the Christian God is that he created the world ex nihilo and therefore transcends it.[42] Creation is not to be confused with making—we are not talking about some sort of Platonic demiurge who crafts the world out of inchoate but preexisting matter.[43] Such a god would not transcend the universe but rather would be a part of it. The difficulty is that while we can understand what would be involved in making the world out of preexisting matter, we have no experience of what it would mean to create out of nothing. The relationship between God and the world he made is thus rooted in the strangeness of creation.

As Robert Sokolowski suggests, a distinguishing feature of Christian thought is the distinction it makes "between the world understood as possibly not having existed and God understood as possibly being all that there is, with no diminution of goodness or greatness."[44] One of the fundamental questions Christians bring to the world is why it exists at all—that is to say, they begin with a sense that the world is contingent. It obviously exists, but it is not obvious that it had to exist. One of Aquinas's five proofs for the existence of God works from the contingency of the world to the conclusion that there must be some being that had to exist—a necessary being—and this is what we call God.[45] Leaving aside the question of whether this proof is such as to compel a skeptic to affirm the existence of God, the concept of a necessary being lies at the root of Aquinas's metaphysics of creation.[46]

To say that God is the necessary being is to say that God's essence is his existence.[47] That is a statement that needs to be unpacked some. Essence refers to what a being is, while existence refers to the fact that a being is. God's uniqueness lies in the fact that what God is is identical with the fact that God is. It is difficult for us to penetrate what that really means, since for all created beings, what they are is distinct from the fact that they are. I could tell you about an old cat named Simon who has tan and black stripes and who used to be a great hunter. Nothing in describing Simon requires that Simon actually exists, though, in fact, he does.[48] It lies beyond our power to describe a being who cannot be thought of apart from his existence. God is thus radically strange, and that strangeness extends to the relationship between God and creation.

Since creation does not have being of itself (or by its own essence, to use Aquinas's vocabulary), it depends on God to be sustained in being. Aquinas refers to this as our "participation" in divine being.[49] Notice that on this view, creation does not refer specifically to the moment the world began (in the Big Bang, perhaps) but rather its ongoing existence.[50] We are being created at every single moment in time.[51] The core truth about the temporal world, then, is that it is absolutely dependent on God. There is no aspect of creation that could subsist on its own, since that property belongs to God alone. There is literally nothing that could exist apart from God, since God is the unique being whose essence is to exist.

On this view God and the world are neither side by side nor contained within the same category. Rather, in some mysterious way, creation participates in God's being and is related to God through the ongoing act of creation. The challenge is to craft a theology that captures the strangeness of that conception. Aquinas does this in his discussion of the way human language is inadequate to the strangeness that is God. Ordinary human language allows us to speak of created beings whose essences are distinct from the fact that they exist. To use Aquinas's terminology, created beings are composite. In the sentence "Socrates is a man," we identify Socrates's essence (humanity) as something that is predicated of the existent being we call Socrates. God, by contrast, is "simple"—because His essence is his existence, there is no attribute we could ascribe to him that is really distinguishable from him.[52]

We have a twofold problem, then, when it comes to talking about God. First, we only know created beings in which essence and existence are distinct. We simply cannot comprehend an essence that is existence. Aquinas thus affirms the traditional claim that we cannot know God as he is.[53] Second, the structure of our language cannot capture God's simplicity. If we say "God is a being whose essence is to exist," we are not speaking truly. To predicate the term *being* of God is to grammatically ascribe composition to him, when in fact he is not aptly thus described.[54] Thus both our concept of God and the very grammar with which we speak of God must necessarily fail to capture the truth of who and what God is.

The impossibility of speaking about God in a way that does not simultaneously mislead about God's strangeness leads to much theological reflection on exactly what theological language means. Aquinas frames this as the question of whether the names we apply to God should be thought of as univocal or equivocal.[55] Consider, for example, the sentence "God is good." If we think of the names associated with God as univocal, that means we think that the word "good" in that sentence has the same meaning as does the word "good" in the sentence "My dog is good." By contrast, if we think of the names of God as equivocal terms, then the meaning of the word "good" in the first sentence is unrelated to the meaning of the world "good" in the second sentence. This may seem like an arcane theological concern. But a great deal turns on how we answer the question of the sort of language we are using when we speak about God.

To think of the names of God as univocal is perhaps the most natural starting point. If one has not begun with the understanding that God is radically strange, there would be no obvious reason to think that the language that works to describe everything else we encounter cannot be extended unproblematically to talk about God. The problem is that such language treats God as one being alongside all the other beings we encounter. My dog is good. God is very good. It implies a continuity between the things of the created world and the Creator, thereby occluding

God's transcendence.[56] Any god that could be unproblematically named by univocal terms would be a being who is but one part of creation. Even if we wanted to assign to that being superlatives, claiming that such a god is the most desirable being, or the most knowledgeable, those claims would still put that god on a continuum with the other goods we encounter. This is a view that resonates with the notion that our pursuit of happiness is an effort to get as far as possible along a vector of ever more desirable goods. Getting more goods would move one closer to the ultimate good. So a theology rooted in univocal language would cohere with the view inherent in the economic approach.

It is, however, a view that is incompatible with Christian doctrine. For starters, it subordinates God conceptually to whatever categories we assign him to. If God is good and my dog is good, then "good" is logically prior to either my dog or God. Such a subordination is problematic if God is, as St. Anselm puts it, "that than which nothing greater can be thought."[57] More directly, univocal language simply cannot do justice to the strangeness of God that we have been discussing. If God is the being whose essence is to exist, we cannot expect that his goodness is to be understood the way we understand the goodness of created beings. The traditions of Christianity, Judaism, and Islam have all rejected univocal language as being inadequate to the mysterious transcendent God who created out of nothing.

Indeed, the traditions' concern on this point has been sufficiently strong that they all have emphasized the need to speak of God negatively or apophatically. Thus, for example, Maimonides argues that any positive quality we assign to God should be understood as a negation. For example, when we say God is good, what we really mean is that God has no property that could be regarded as bad.[58] On this view, names we attach to God should be understood as being equivocal: the meaning of the word "good" in the sentence "God is good" is entirely different from the meaning of the word "good" in the sentence "My dog is good." Indeed, one could say that if one adopts equivocal language, that the sentence "God is good" should read "I have no idea what God is, but whatever it is it is not evil." The apophatic tradition, with its use of equivocal language, has the virtue of persistently reminding us of God's mysterious transcendence, his radical strangeness. But in practical terms it creates a cleavage between God and the world. God is linguistically left outside of all intelligible human discourse, and it is not a far step from that to the idea that we might as well just focus on what we can understand. Thomas Hobbes may or may not have been an atheist. But if he was a believer, he believed in this equivocal God, the one who is so beyond our ability to comprehend we can safely ignore him when thinking about how the world works.

As mentioned above, Aquinas affirms that apophaticism is the primary mode in which we undertake theological discourse. As he puts it, "Now, because we cannot know what God is, but rather what He is not, we have no means for considering how God is, but rather how He is not."[59] The next series of questions takes up attributes of God, all under the rubric of discussing what God is not. But when Aquinas turns to the question of how we should talk about God, he denies that all theological language should be read as purely apophatic. To construe theological language that way fails to do justice to the fullness of the theological talk handed down by the tradition. As Aquinas puts it, when people say things like "God lives" they mean more than just "God causes life in us" or that "God is different from inanimate bodies."[60] In other words, there are positive or kataphatic moments in theological talk. Although the negative moment is primary for Aquinas, that second moment of kataphatic speech is nonetheless crucial because without it theological concerns would have no clear connection to the temporal world.

Aquinas carves out room for kataphatic speech by emphasizing creation's dependence on the Creator.[61] If God created the world ex nihilo, then everything in creation reflects something of God. There is nothing apart from God from which created beings can draw either form or substance. Aquinas gets at this through the notion of God's perfection.[62] As discussed more fully below, for Aquinas, perfection means being fully in act, or having no potency (no unrealized potential). Only that which is fully in act (God) can draw others into act, where being itself is understood as an action. From this, it follows that all perfections found in creation are representations of God's divine perfection, albeit necessarily imperfect ones. That is to say to the extent that we more fully realize whatever potential exists in our nature, we become more like God. As

Aquinas puts it, "When we say, *God is good,* the meaning is not, *God is the cause of goodness,* or *God is not evil;* but the meaning is, *Whatever good we attribute to creatures, pre-exists in God,* and in a more excellent and higher way."[63] There is thus a connection between goodness in creation and the goodness that is God, and that connection is grounded in the nature of the relationship between creature and Creation.

The next question asks what sort of speech we can use to capture both the dissimilarity and the similarity between creatures and Creator. Aquinas's answer is that it is analogical language that can perform this function.[64] If we were to imagine that we were using terms like "being" or "goodness" univocally in their predication of both God and creature, we would be failing to capture God's dissimilarity. By the same token, were we to imagine that terms like "being" or "goodness" are entirely equivocal when predicated of creatures or of God, we would be denying the element of similarity between God and creation. We must, therefore, say that our language for talking about God is analogical, which is some sort of mean between univocal speech and equivocal speech.[65] In particular, we need to use the Aristotelian form of analogy called *pros hen* analogy. The idea refers to a cluster of meanings of a given term that are neither equivocal nor univocal, but rather reflect a set of relationships.

The classic example employed by both Aristotle and Aquinas runs as follows. Consider the word *healthy.* It does not mean quite the same thing when predicated of food as it does when it is predicated of body. Yet though the term *healthy* does not have a univocal meaning in these two predications, there is nonetheless a relationship between them. In particular, we call food healthy if we think that it is wholesome and likely to contribute to our physical health. There is a community of ideas expressed in the various predications of the term *healthy.* Likewise, there is a community of ideas involved in the predication of terms like *being* or *good* to both God and creation. In particular God is the principle and cause of creation and as such it is in God that perfections like being and goodness "preexist excellently."[66] There is no prior notion of being that takes one form when applied to God and another when applied to creatures, but rather creatures have being insofar as they participate in God's perfect being. Although analogy is a sort of mean between univocal and equivocal language, it lists toward equivocal language insofar as it is more important to maintain God's radical dissimilarity to creation than it is to acknowledge the similarities between God and creation.

Because creation is completely dependent on God, the proper meaning of the words *being* or *goodness* is the meaning they have when predicated of God.[67] This is true despite the fact that we first predicate those words of God based on our encounter of being and goodness in creation. Although we come to know that God is good because we see that creation is good, the goodness we see in creation is but an analogical reflection of the ultimate goodness that is God. On this account, our need to use analogy in our talk about God is directly related to the way creation depends on and reflects God. In other words, analogy is not just a description of theological talk; rather, it is an essential aspect of the relationship between the created world and God.[68]

As we will see below, the conception of the created world as analogically related to and dependent on its Creator has profound implications for how we view happiness, and on this view, it would not be rational to pursue happiness as an exercise in constrained maximization. There are two other technical implications of this view that need to be briefly touched on, since they likewise suggest that a rational pursuit of happiness cannot be adequately described by the rational choice model. These implications stem from reflection on what it would mean for a finite creation to analogically reflect the superabundant good which is God.

An essential element of Aquinas's doctrine of creation is that God is sufficient to himself in his superabundant being and goodness, and as a result his decision to create is entirely gratuitous. There is nothing about creation that demands that it had to be. God's decision to create was not, however, entirely random. That God did not create out of necessity does not mean that God did not have a purpose in choosing to create. According to Aquinas, God's intention in creating is to "communicate His perfection, which is His goodness."[69] In other words, creation should be seen as a reflection or mirror of God. That raises the question of how God can reflect his infinite perfection in a creation which is finite.

As already discussed, a central feature of created beings is that their essence is not their existence. God, whose essence is his existence, is "uncircumscribed." By contrast, created beings are determined, through their essence or form, to be one thing or another.[70] The thought here is that God, in his simplicity, contains all things, and he creates by setting forth one aspect or another of this superabundance in finite forms. As a result, created beings or the effects of God cannot imitate him perfectly "but only as they are able." The defect of their ability to imitate or represent God is that "what is simple and one can only be represented by divers things."[71] If we think of God as infinite superabundance, no one thing can represent him. But a plurality of created beings can represent God by having each one pick up some aspect or reflection of God's simple superabundant goodness. As Aquinas puts it, "God produced many and diverse creatures, that what was wanting to one in the representation of divine goodness might be supplied by another. For goodness, which in God is simple and uniform, in creatures is manifold and divided; and hence the whole universe together participates in the divine goodness more perfectly, and represents it better than any single creature whatever."[72]

The notion that God's goodness requires a multiplicity of beings to be represented in finite terms reminds us of the superabundant fullness of divine being. One implication of Aquinas's view is that for us to see the representation of divine goodness in creation, we need to be able to see goods as heterogeneous. It is in their particularity that we catch glimpses, like shards, of God's glorious goodness.

At the same time, the essential heterogeneity of created beings does not imply that the world is hopelessly fragmented. God may need a multiplicity of created beings to represent the fullness of his being, but as the quote above suggests, it is the whole universe together that serves as an analogical mirror for God. Thus there must also be a unity to creation if creation is to give witness to the fact that God is one. God communicates this unity by ordering created beings to one another and all things to him.[73] The concept of ordering is simply the idea that creation is a web of relationship. Bees, for example, are ordered to the pollination of flowers. These two features—the heterogeneity of created beings and their ordering to one another (and ultimately to God)—need to be respected if we are to pursue happiness in a truly rational manner. The final feature of Aquinas's metaphysical views that requires a shift in how we think about the pursuit of happiness is his conception of happiness as a matter of perfection rather than extensive accumulation (of material goods or experiences).

The Perfection of Being

Although the goods we find in the created world are objects of desire, happiness is not a matter of possession or acquisition. If we are reflections of the Creator, then by analogy our own happiness or fulfillment is a reflection of God's happiness. God's happiness can perhaps best be understood in terms of his perfection. So what does it mean to say that God is perfect? For Aquinas, perfection is found in being or in act. God is the perfect being, because God is sheer act. That is to say, there is nothing potential in God, nothing that needs development. This is part and parcel of God's status as the one necessary being that brings creation into existence ex nihilo.

Since all creation comes from God, God is never passive in relation to created beings. As Aquinas puts it, "The first active principle must needs be most actual, and therefore most perfect; for a thing is perfect in proportion to its state of actuality, because we call that perfect which lacks nothing of the mode of its perfection."[74] God is the fullness of being, and as such contains all created perfections within himself.[75] There is nothing that any created being can become that is not already present in God. That is what it means to say that God is sheer act or fullness of being.

Perfection, then, is coming to the fullness of being that is possible. And for Aquinas, this has the quality of being desirable. Indeed, goodness and being are really the same, differing only in the way we understand them. In particular, goodness conveys the sense that being is desirable. Thus all creatures desire their own perfection, or the fullness of being that is possible for them. On this account, the U.S. Army's invitation to be all you can be is on to something. Like all creatures, we want to actualize our potential to the extent possible, that is, realize as fully as possible the way in which we reflect God's goodness.

Indeed, this desire for our own perfection is just a reflection of our desire for God, the perfect being in whom all perfections can be found. As Aquinas puts it, "All things, by desiring their own perfection, desire

God Himself, inasmuch as the perfections of all things are so many similitudes of the divine being."[76] The vision here is of creatures being made such that they desire their own perfection, which, in turn, amounts to realizing their place in the universe. Aquinas describes the perfection of creatures as having a threefold quality. First, there is perfection "according to the constitution" of the creature's own being. In other words, creatures desire to fully realize the potential inherent in their nature. A cat desires to be a cat, and more importantly a "good" cat, that is, one that is healthy, a good hunter, and so on. Second, creatures desire the perfection of any accidents added that are necessary for their perfect operation. By "accident," Aquinas means a quality that attaches to a being, but which is not part of its essential nature.

The fact that I am a Caucasian, for example, is part of who I am but not essential to my nature as a human being and is therefore an accident. An accident that perfects my operation would be something like the fact that I am a professor. Being a professor is the mode through which I perfect my nature. Finally, creatures desire "attaining to something else as the end," which entails resting in the creature's own place, fulfilling its role in the ordered universe.[77] In other words, creatures desire the perfection of being what God created them to be, operating in the way God created them to operate, and playing the role in the ordered universe God created them to fulfill. So what does that mean for a human being? Chapter 4 takes up that question.

4

Happiness and the Distinctively Human Exercise of Practical Reason

Virtue and Prudence

Having laid out the metaphysical backdrop, we now turn to Aquinas's substantive account of human happiness. Like all creatures, we find our happiness by perfecting our nature, that is, by fully realizing our potential. But human nature is complicated. Like all animals we have material bodies and natural instincts. But unlike nonrational animals, we are rational, endowed with the capacity to seek the true and the good. As we will see in this chapter, the essence of human happiness in this life is the cultivation of virtue, or excellence. But to fully understand that account, we need to begin with some preliminary considerations.

Setting the Stage for Aquinas's Account of Earthly Happiness as a Life of Virtue

Before turning to Aquinas's account of virtue, we need to think first about the relationship between virtue and the other goods we might pursue in this life. In addition, because Aquinas thinks of happiness in light of some final end, or *telos,* we need to think about the relationship between happiness in this life and the happiness we hope to enjoy in the next.

The Ordering of Goods in This Life

Aquinas's exploration of the various goods we might construe as being the ultimate good we seek can help us understand the centrality of perfection and also the way it relates to our more conventional understandings of happiness.[1] The first question Aquinas takes up is whether any of the so-called external goods—wealth, honor, fame or glory, and power—might constitute the highest good for humans. All of them are related to happiness, but none of them constitutes happiness in itself. Wealth is instrumental to happiness, in that we use material goods to sustain or perfect our natures, but it is not an end in itself.[2] Honor is a sign of excellence or perfection, and therefore is not an end in itself, likewise fame or glory.[3] Finally, power is what allows us to act, but it is not the perfection of our acts; happiness requires not that we have more power to act but rather that we are able to act well.[4]

Three further goods are part of happiness, though not constitutive of it. First, there are bodily goods such as health and vitality. Insofar as our bodies are part of our natures, bodily goods are part of our perfection. But our ultimate perfection also entails seeking something else as an end, and thus bodily goods cannot themselves be the ultimate good. Moreover, human nature is body and soul, not just body, so bodily goods cannot even constitute perfection of our beings.[5] A second good, pleasure, does indeed belong to happiness. This would be the end economists postulate in assuming that humans seek subjective happiness through the satisfaction of their desires. Aquinas argues that delight in attaining an end naturally follows on reaching one's end, but it is the end itself that constitutes happiness. We do not seek what we want in order to take pleasure in it; rather, we take pleasure in getting what we want.[6]

One might expect that Aquinas would argue that the third good, goods of the soul (virtue, knowledge, love), might constitute our final end. After all, they constitute the perfection of our being and the perfection of our operations. The goods of the soul are, indeed, closely bound up with happiness. But to the extent that we think of the goods of the soul as the capacity to act, they are not themselves our ultimate happiness, since happiness lies essentially in act, not in potential to act. The ultimate acts of the soul, knowing and loving, are part of our ultimate end. But they are actions that are directed towards some object. The acts themselves, then, are only part of our ultimate happiness.[7]

That leaves the question of what the object of our knowing and loving might be, and after considering whether it might be higher beings like angels, or perhaps the cosmos taken as a whole, Thomas argues that the something else is God.[8] This, of course, is no denouement. God is the ultimate good, and our souls desire that ultimate good. In knowing and loving God, we know and love the object that fully satisfies our boundless desire to know and love. Taken together, the picture Aquinas has sketched runs as follows. We find our happiness in our perfection, which we desire as a reflection of the ultimate perfection, which is God. Our perfection consists in our being, body and soul, but even more importantly in acting. As rational creatures, our ultimate acts are to know and to love. And our ultimate end is to know and to love the ultimate good, which is God. Material goods are, indeed, good. But they are purely instrumental. It is not enough to be wealthy. Happiness requires that we deploy our wealth toward the worthy end of realizing our nature as fully as possible in lives ordered to God. This is the happiness we are built for, and it is the only sustainable or lasting happiness that is possible for creatures such as ourselves. Some questions are raised at this juncture, however. God seems to be quite distant in this life. So what sort of happiness is possible in this life? And how does it relate to our ultimate happiness?

The Analogy between Perfect and Imperfect Happiness

The implications of Aquinas's metaphysics for his account of happiness are encapsulated in his claim that our ultimate happiness is to be found in knowing and loving God as God knows and loves himself.[9] However, it is an end that is beyond our natural capacities, because God transcends nature.[10] Should we reach that end, it will be through God's grace, and even so it cannot happen in this life.[11] Given that, we have to ask how the temporal happiness that is possible in this life is related to that ultimate end. The possibilities correspond to the three ways of understanding theological language discussed in Chapter 3. The first approach would be to think of temporal happiness as lying on a continuum with our ultimate happiness. We could thus think about happiness in this life as something to maximize, with the tacit background assumption that such maximization would move us closer to the ultimate good. It is good to feast in this life. Heaven will be an infinite feast. More feasts in this life are therefore better than fewer feasts. This view entails seeing the relationship between happiness in this life and happiness in the next in univocal terms, and as such it is ruled out by Aquinas's metaphysics.

The second approach would be to argue that insofar as our ultimate happiness is entirely beyond our powers and unavailable in this life in any case, temporal happiness should be understood as being unrelated to the ultimate happiness we hope for. Any thoughts we might have about our eternal end offer no particular guidance for the pursuit of happiness in this life. Such an approach would lead to a sort of compartmentalization in life. Go to church on Sunday and pursue your ordinary ends the rest of the week. But as we have already seen, creation itself, while radically other than God, is not radically separate from God. The language we use to talk about God is not equivocal, as it would be if God and creation were two entirely separate things. It would thus be strange if the happiness we can enjoy in this life is likewise entirely separate from the happiness we hope for in the next. If God and creation are analogically related, then it would seem that our temporal happiness should have an analogical relationship to the beatitude we hope to obtain.

Although there is some controversy about how Aquinas understands the relationship between our temporal and eternal ends, a plausible argument can be made that the two ends are related analogically.[12] Aquinas argues that happiness has diverse meanings, but they form a cluster of related terms. That is, they should be understood as a *pros hen* analogy, like the one offered in Chapter 3 about the multiple meanings of the word "healthy." "Happiness" means some final perfection, but various things attain various degrees of perfection, and so the term *happiness* is not univocal. Thus, for example, God is "happiness essentially," whereas angels are happy "in respect of some operation, by which they are united to the uncreated good."[13] More to the point, for humans there is a twofold form of happiness, one perfect and the other imperfect. Perfect happiness represents the "true" notion of happiness, whereas imperfect happiness is that which doesn't reach perfect happiness "but partakes of some particular likeness of happiness."[14] On this account, happiness in this life reflects the perfect happiness we hope for in the life to come.

To get a fuller picture of what this happiness entails, it helps to examine Aquinas's treatment of the doctrine of the *imago Dei,* the belief that humans are created in the likeness of God. As already discussed, all creatures reflect God, so we might ask why this is a distinctive claim to make about human beings.[15] The answer lies in the gradations of perfection. All created things reflect God insofar as they exist; all living creatures are even more like God insofar as they live; and humans have a special likeness to God insofar as we are rational beings capable of knowing and loving.[16] As discussed in Chapter 3, it is rationality that endows us with the free will and control of our actions that distinguish us from animals. As Aquinas puts it, like God we are the "principle" of our actions.[17]

The essence of our happiness, the perfection of our capacities, is realized when we direct ourselves to know and love God, who is the infinite good. Insofar as God knows and loves himself, our fulfillment of the capacity to know and love him represents both our own fulfillment and the perfection of the image of God. However, we remain finite creatures, so this image is only analogically related to God. Because God is simple, his happiness is essential to his very being.[18] By contrast, we are not simple, so the fact that we exist does not necessarily entail that we achieve happiness. For humans there is a dynamic quality to the way we image God. As Aquinas argues, the preposition "to" in the phrase "to the image and likeness of God" is meant to suggest a quality of motion.[19] As we perfect our capacity as rational animals we approach or perfect the image of God we carry in our beings.

Aquinas thus identifies gradations of the perfection possible to us, three successively better ways in which we are able to mirror God. First, by nature as rational creatures we have the raw capacity to know and love God. In this sense, all humans are made in the image of God. Second, that capacity can begin to be imperfectly exercised insofar as we come to "habitually know and love God," something that is possible in this life through grace. By this, Aquinas means we are able to order ourselves to God, even though we do not know him as he is. Finally, in glory we can perfectly exercise our capacity to know and love God. In other words, we perfect the image in the beatific vision.[20] The perfection of the image we bear in glory is nothing but our perfect happiness.[21] Just so, the imperfect exercise of our capacity to habitually know and love God corresponds to the imperfect happiness that is possible in this life.

But what does it mean to know and love God imperfectly as is possible in this life? For believers, this would involve consciously pursuing the good in this life in light of our final end. In the terms we have been using so far, it would, in particular, mean pursuing perfection rather than maximization, as is consistent with an understanding that the world is analogically related to God. It is the sacramental vision that sees created goods as reflecting or pointing to the ultimate good that is God. And it is a language that naturally leads to an understanding of happiness as the pursuit of perfection rather than the pursuit of maximization. What this means in practice is developed further in the remainder of this chapter and in Chapter 5.

But does this formulation leave out unbelievers, perhaps suggesting that they are simply off track in their pursuit of happiness? As it turns out the analogical view is helpful on this point. Unbelievers pursue goods. But on Aquinas's account, all the goods of the world are but a reflection of God. Accordingly, we exercise our capacity to know and love God when we exercise our capacity to know and love the goods of this life, which reflect God's goodness.

Nonbelievers are thus capable of meaningfully pursuing happiness in this life. As we will see, Aquinas has distinct accounts of the pursuit of virtue in the manner that is possible, in principle, apart from grace and that which is possible with grace. The latter is a higher form of perfection and thus a more perfect form of virtue, largely because grace allows us to direct ourselves more consciously toward our end in God. But the former remains a real perfection, and as such represents an implicit movement towards God.

Indeed, the beauty of the teaching about the *imago Dei* is that it helps us see the twofold nature of happiness. In perfecting ourselves to the degree possible, we become more like God. And we perfect ourselves by knowing and loving God as well as possible given our capacities. To put it another way, we become good by seeking the good, and the more clearly we understand and love the good we seek, the better we become. As humans we have the special gift of consciously choosing this path, and we do so by cultivating virtue.[22]

Virtue as the Center of Human Happiness in This Life

In contrast to the notion that happiness should be understood as the satisfaction of desire, Aquinas builds on the Aristotelian tradition that the fullest happiness available to humans lies in the cultivation of our character, thereby perfecting our beings. As we have seen, for Aquinas, this view of happiness follows directly from his metaphysics. The ultimate good is God: in perfecting our natures we become more like God and therefore participate more fully in his happiness. The more fully we realize our potential, the more "being" we have.

Aristotle refers to this project as the pursuit of virtue. The Greek word for virtue, *arête,* is best understood as "excellence." That is, it means being good at what one does. A virtuous cat is a cat that hunts well. A virtuous human is one who acts in an excellent way. One might worry that an economic life that centers on the cultivation of virtue is too high minded to be applicable to ordinary humans who just want to provide a decent standard of living for themselves and their families. But the pursuit of virtue need not be seen as something we do as opposed to seeking a good life. On the contrary, virtue can perhaps be best understood as seeking the good life in a distinctively human manner. To see this point, it helps to first set out Aquinas's account of virtue, followed by a reflection on the relationship between virtue and ordinary human flourishing or well-being.

What is Virtue?

If virtue is a matter of perfection, then we need to begin with an account of the human nature that we are striving to perfect. The essence of human nature is that we are rational animals. Like animals, we are endowed with bodies and are moved by passions—raw desires and aversions. Unlike animals, we are able to discern what goods are worthy of pursuit and are therefore able to direct our passions, at least to some degree. Because we develop through time, we cannot think of human nature as static. There is the nature we are born with, the raw set of possibilities that are part of being human. But there is also the nature we acquire through time on the basis of the choices we make.

For Aquinas, these habits are the "intrinsic principles or internal source of our actions."[23] They consist in the abilities and predispositions we acquire through time, based on our choices. So, for example, the abilities to speak a language or play a piano are habits. Habits principally work to shape our actions, and they help us navigate a complex world in which we are confronted with an almost unbounded set of choices.[24] In essence, habits are a sort of second nature; they represent the development of stable patterns of response to the world, whether for good or for ill.[25] They therefore have a great deal to do with molding our passions in accordance with what our rational nature has determined to pursue. We can develop habits through repeated acts, and they can increase through use or diminish through disuse.[26] Habits can also be infused by God, who is the source of the theological virtues, and the related set of infused cardinal virtues.[27]

Virtues are good habits, insofar as the word *virtue* "denotes a certain perfection of a power."[28] In other words, they are habits that help us reach the full potential of our nature, which as has been noted already, is the essence of what all creatures naturally desire. As Aquinas goes on to explain, we can understand power in reference to being and power in reference to act, and the perfection of either would be called virtue. If we think about virtues of the body, strong muscles and the like, these are things we share with the animals. So for Aquinas, the essence of human virtue lies in the soul, that is, in our rational powers, which are the powers through which we act.[29] Again, note Aquinas's emphasis on what distinguishes humans from irrational animals. More importantly, he goes on to argue that it is in the perfection of our acts that we are most like God, whose "substance is His act."[30]

We begin to see why virtues are central to Aquinas's account of human happiness. We are created for the purpose of being in the image and likeness of God.[31] We are in the image and likeness of God insofar as we are the "principle of our own actions."[32] Virtues are the interior principle that perfects our actions. The more perfect we are in virtue, the more perfect (completely actualized) are our actions, and the more like God we are. Furthermore, virtues or good habits are the means by which we train the passions, desires, and aversions we share with irrational animals to be directed toward the ends we have freely determined are good to pursue. They are instrumental in helping us achieve the freedom that is proper to humans.

To see this, consider the project of raising a child. A two-year-old is a good picture of human nature before the project of acquiring virtue has gotten fully under way. Small children are dominated by their passions and have no control over them. As children grow up, they learn to curb those desires, so that they are able to act appropriately in various settings. We can feel the vestiges of that training. When I bump my head unexpectedly, part of me wants to wail with a mighty cry. But I have the habit of not making an undue fuss, and that feeling of outrage at the unexpected injury quickly subsides. And most often, the appropriate reactions really are second nature. As a child I wanted all the candy for myself. As an adult I really could not enjoy the candy if I did not offer to share some with those around me. To the extent that we have acquired virtue, we have mastered ourselves and are thereby able to act well or even excellently.

The virtues should not be understood as simply subordinating our raw passions to the dictates of reason. I have not achieved full mastery if I can offer the candy to others because I know that is what is socially expected while still secretly wishing I could have it all. If that were our understanding of virtue, it would seem to be opposed to true happiness. We might have mastery of ourselves, but we would have it at the expense of what we really wanted. For both Aquinas and Aristotle, true virtue lies in actively wanting that which reason has discerned is worthy of wanting. That is to say, it is fully realized when we have trained our passions to respond as we would wish—through the cultivation of the relevant habits. That element of self-creation is why it is the exercise of virtue itself that constitutes the highest human fulfillment. The achievement of virtue is the achievement of the freedom that is proper to rational animals like ourselves. On this view, vice is a defect or weakness. It is a failure to order our desires according to the goods discovered through reason, which results in an inability to exercise the freedom we are made for.[33]

It is not a freedom that is easily achieved. In the wake of the Fall, the grace required to keep the passions ordered to reason was lost.[34] We start out life, then, without a taste or emotional desire for virtue. As virtue develops we train our passions to genuinely desire what is good and right, but that leaves the question of how the process can get started. In an analysis of this problem as it is found in Aristotle, M. F. Burnyeat argues that the process begins with young people as they seek to emulate those whom they admire. In the process of mimicking virtue, they gradually develop a taste for it.[35]

But this is a process that is difficult to start if one has not had a good upbringing while young. And even under auspicious circumstances it is unlikely to be complete. That is to say that most people have some taste for virtue but also a taste for following their untutored passions. Perfect virtue is achieved when the passions are brought into alignment with reason. Thus the person who determines by reason that it would be good to get up early to go to the gym, and who likes getting up early to go to the gym, has achieved virtue. Those who have not achieved that alignment are either continent or incontinent. The continent person sets the alarm. When the alarm goes off, her passions urge her to hit the snooze bar, but she forces herself to get out of bed anyway. She does what she intends but is not fully happy about it. The incontinent person hits the snooze bar and does not get to the gym. He did what he wanted to do in the moment, but his failure to follow up on his better intentions leaves him feeling regretful, and again, not fully happy.

Most people oscillate between continence and incontinence. For the majority of people who fall into this camp, there is something like two orders of reason—the virtuous exercise of reason and a more distorted reason that bends to the passions, rationalizing instead of reasoning. This lower form of reason, because it is in service of untutored passions, is well described as responding to immediate calculations about marginal benefits and marginal costs, and it is the form of reason that can be influenced by incentives.

The upshot of this point is that virtue requires that we train up our passions so that we have a full unity of being, reason and passion both wanting to do the right thing; and that failure to train up our passions can leave us subject to disregarding the discernment of our higher reason in favor of giving way to what our passions desire. We thus have two sets of desires—one based on reason's discernment of what is worthy of pursuit and the other based on our untutored passions. We also have two forms of reason—the sort of reason that discerns what is worthy of pursuit and the form that is in service of the untutored passions. The latter is the form of reason modeled by economists. Thus on Aquinas's own account we should expect that the economic model would predict well. The quarrel is mainly with how we interpret that behavior. In particular, it is subrational behavior that has displaced the fully human exercise of reason we are capable of. Nor should the higher form of reason be understood as being in tension with desires. It is in tension with the untutored desires; but as we grow in virtue, our desires come into alignment with our judgment of what is good. As discussed in Chapter 7, economists do have models that can handle the fact that we have different sets of desires.[36] What they lack is an account that can accommodate the two forms of reason Aquinas identifies.

To round out this account of Aquinas's basic understanding of virtue, it helps to sketch out his discussion of the core virtues. All human virtues perfect either our intellect or our will.[37] Virtues of the intellect, such as our ability to reason well, certainly perfect our nature. But for Aquinas these are not essential to happiness in the same way as are moral virtues, which perfect the will. The reason for this distinction is that as previously discussed, the realization of our perfection as human beings consists in our acts as human beings, and it is the will that is central to our acting. Thus I am not a good or just person if I merely see that it is good to act justly. I need to actually act justly to be a good or just person.[38]

Accordingly, Aquinas devotes an entire volume to cataloguing the various moral virtues, organizing them around seven core virtues: faith, hope, charity, prudence, justice, fortitude, and temperance.[39] The first three are the theological virtues, which can only be had through infusion and which order us to our supernatural beatitude, namely, our end of knowing and loving God as God knows and loves himself.[40] The last four are the cardinal virtues, which dispose us to act well in this life. These four virtues each play a distinctive role in helping us realize our end of acting well as human beings. All of them are aimed at the good as defined by reason.

Fortitude and temperance are the virtues that respectively bring our aversions and desires into alignment with the judgments of reason. Both have the quality of seeking the mean. Thus fortitude allows us to act despite our fears when challenges are worth meeting but also to respect our fears when it would be rash to ignore them. Temperance allows us to enjoy the pleasures of life without being controlled by them. There is no guidebook for how to make these judgments. It is temperate for the Olympic swimmer Michael Phelps to eat ginormous breakfasts because he needs the fuel to sustain his training regimen. The same breakfast would be intemperate for someone like me, whose lifestyle is more sedentary. Justice perfects our will with respects to others. It is a feature of human nature that is essential to us because of our social nature. It is the virtue that allows one to readily give to others their just due and to see the exercise of justice as part of one's own well-being. And prudence is the master virtue, which allows us to discern what goods are worthy of pursuit and to order them into a coherent pattern of life. It is the very act of discerning what is good to be done here and now. It is both an intellectual and a moral virtue, with an emphasis on the latter insofar as prudence is fulfilled when we act on what we judge is best to do.[41] Prudence is Aquinas's alternative to the rational choice theory of economists as an account of the type of reason that can guide us toward genuine happiness.

A person possessed of the cardinal virtues is a person who has self-mastery. Self-mastery gives us a twofold freedom. First, we are free from slavish desire to our raw passions. But perhaps more importantly, we are free to creatively interact with the myriad goods around us constructing purposeful and coherent lives. Because the virtues are the habits that allow us to deal with the particularities of our situations, no two virtuous people will have identical lives. But it is through the virtues that we can recognize excellence in forms of life that differ from our own.

To achieve this full self-mastery, the virtues must be jointly developed. Aquinas's emphasis on the connection of the virtues is in keeping with his emphasis on order. Although we can imagine imperfect instantiations of virtue occurring apart from the other virtues—as in the case of the brave Nazi—perfect moral virtue requires that the virtues be connected.[42] There are two reasons for this. First, if we see the virtues as distinguished by properties—that is, discretion as a property of prudence, or rectitude as a property of justice—we can see that a moral act done well requires all of them. If, for example, I have rectitude but not discretion, I would want to do right by others but would be unable to do so wisely. A lack of fortitude might make me quail when confronted with evidence that a given act, though challenging, is also the right thing to do, and so on. Second, if we see the virtues as distinguished by "matter"—that is, the aspect of the human being that they govern—we can again see that they are more perfect when they are connected. In particular, the moral virtues (justice, temperance, and fortitude) incline us to a fitting end, while prudence reasons about the right thing to do. Prudence has nothing to reason about if the ends are not before it, and we will not see how to move toward those ends without prudence. On either view, we realize our perfection by ordering distinct goods in a coherent way.

With a basic sketch of virtue established, the next question to be addressed is whether this account can have any purchase with a modern audience that believes that economic and political life should be oriented toward the promotion of ordinary human flourishing or well-being. But as it turns out, the virtues properly understood are not opposed to human flourishing. On the contrary, they promote it, and a full conception of happiness includes a good life that should be recognizable as such to modern audiences.

Virtue and Well-Being

In her book *Nature as Reason: A Thomistic Theory of the Natural Law,* Jean Porter offers a compelling and close analysis of the relationship between virtue and well-being in Thomas's thought.[43] Her basic argument is that our exercise of the virtues entails the perfection of our appetites as directed toward the proper flourishing of the kinds of creatures we are. That flourishing, in turn, centers on the basic features of a recognizably desirable mode of human life: physical and mental health, a family, an occupation that exercises one's capacities and provides a material basis for living, community ties, and so forth.[44] We can see the basis of this formulation by considering two sets of texts from the *Summa*.

The first can be found in Aquinas's discussion of natural law.[45] For Aquinas the universe is governed by eternal law, and humans participate in that law in a special way through natural law.[46] In essence this is a restatement of the thought that God has ordered the universe and that humans have the special capacity to direct themselves to their own end within that ordered universe. Because that end entails the fulfillment of our nature, it is unsurprising to learn that all virtuous acts belong to the natural law.[47] The fundamental precept of the natural law is that good is to be done and evil is to be avoided, which, in turn, entails pursuing our natural inclinations. For creatures like us, there are three basic inclinations. First, we seek the preservation of our own being, an inclination we share with all created beings. Second, we have the inclination we share with all animals, namely, the inclination to propagate the species. Finally, we have the inclinations specific to rational animals, namely, the inclination to know the truth about God and live in society.[48] But these are just a set of inclinations that would incline us to something like ordinary human flourishing: making a living, raising a family, and pursuing communal goods. Prudence thus will discern goods that constitute a recognizably desirable life.

One might be erroneously tempted here by the notion that the virtues are virtues *because* they help lead us to these sorts of goods. That would make those goods themselves the end of human action, with virtue as an instrumental good. But the whole point of identifying a natural law as distinct from the eternal law that orders the universe is that humans have the special role of directing themselves. It is our act of becoming beings who can pursue these goods in an excellent way that constitutes the full realization of our nature. The pursuit of the goods, then, is the material on which we exercise that excellence. That is to say, while a life filled with goods is desirable, our truest happiness lies in the agency we exercise in obtaining them.

A second take on the relationship between virtue and well-being surfaces in Aquinas's treatise on happiness. In his discussion of whether the body is necessary for perfect happiness, Aquinas argues that in this life, the body is essential because our happiness in this life consists in an operation of the intellect, which in this life is only possible if we have bodies. This might give us the false impression, that material well-being, as represented by a healthy body, is necessary because it enables us to exercise our intellects, which in this life takes the form of the exercise of virtue. But as Aquinas goes on to argue, even in the perfect happiness possible to us in the next life, the body will contribute to our happiness—not as essential to that happiness but rather as a contributor to our well-being.[49] The full complement of happiness, then, is a life of virtue, but one that is sustained by and that sustains well-being, which of itself is a secondary contributor to happiness. Aquinas is thus very far from the view that virtue alone is what matters. We should not call a man happy who is suffering the rack with courage.[50]

The cultivation of virtue perfects our appetites, which are directed toward a life well lived as a human being. But because we are human, there are myriad ways in which we could direct ourselves toward fulfilling lives. The essence of reason is our ability to discern among finite goods. That freedom is what gives us the capacity to sin, which nonrational animals lack. But it is also the freedom that undergirds our creativity and the enormous diversity one finds in instantiating a good human life. The language of rational choice does not do justice to this sort of exercise of reason. To pursue Aquinas's vision, we need a different model of practical reason, and for that we need to turn to Aquinas's account of the virtue of prudence, or practical wisdom.

Prudence versus Rational Choice

To modern ears, the word *prudence* carries a sense of smallness—the prudent person is careful and cautious, anxious for the future. It can carry an economic connotation—prudence is attention to the bottom line, restraining the impetus to be carried away by other pursuits. Indeed, Deirdre McCloskey associates the virtue of prudence with straightforward utility maximization, faulting economists for treating it as the only virtue but praising it as nonetheless a genuine virtue.[51] But this is not what Aquinas means by the term. For Aquinas, prudence is not an exercise in constrained maximization. Nor should it be regarded as one of four virtues. Rather, it is the "virtue most necessary for life." It is the virtue that perfects all of our decision making, not just those decisions taken in light of our own narrow self-interest. Insofar as a good life consists in good actions, the virtue that assists us in making good choices about what to do is essential. Good choice, in turn, has two aspects—first, there is a matter of choosing the end, and second, there is the matter of choosing suitably with respect to that end. The former requires a good will, but the latter requires good habits of reason, which is the role prudence plays.[52]

Although prudence is largely concerned with choosing suitably with respect to a given end, it should not be seen as a species of purely instrumental reason. Prudence directs the moral virtues not only with respect to choosing the means but also with respect to choosing the end.[53] According to James Keenan, there are two ways in which prudence's role in determining ends can be understood. One way of understanding the role of prudence is to argue that the will determines on achieving virtues like temperance or fortitude, but prudence determines what constitutes temperance or fortitude in a given situation. Temperance, for example, is not a matter of simply restraining desire but rather one of cultivating a desire for goods in the right proportion—something that is referred to as finding the mean. Fortitude is likewise a matter of finding the right degree of aversion to bad things. Prudence thus plays a role in determining the appropriate ends to which temperance and fortitude should be directed.

The second way to understand prudence is to see it as directing us to the overarching good that we seek. Insofar as there are myriad finite goods that can be ordered to our ultimate good, prudence plays a role in exercising the resulting freedom we have, choosing and ordering the particular goods into the unique form of excellence we choose to pursue. In other words, prudence should be thought of as wisdom in human affairs.[54] As Keenan writes, "Prudence has a privileged place among the cardinal virtues: it recognizes the ends to which a person is naturally inclined, it establishes the agenda by which one can pursue those ends, it directs the agent's own performance of the pursued activity, and finally it measures the rightness of the actions taken. Prudence, in short, guides the agent to living a self-directed life that seeks integration."[55]

Prudence is not simply the virtue that directs individuals to their respective ends. Because we are social creatures, there is a species of prudence related to governance, or the choices we make in common. There is room for disagreement about how to parse the relationship between prudence and the other moral virtues, but the general view I take of prudence's role is as follows: If we have good wills, we have an end of pursuing the human good. We do so as part of society since we are social creatures. Accordingly, one species of prudence directs the individual qua individual, and another species directs the individual qua governing (or governed) member of society.[56] Prudence in either case discerns how we move to that general end. Because human life is capable of so much diversity, prudence is necessary to identify how to instantiate a good life or a good society in a given set of circumstances. To do this well requires an exercise of practical reason that is qualitatively different from that described by the rational choice model. Before contrasting the two models of practical reason, it will help to take a closer look at the set of skills one must develop in order to cultivate prudence.

The Parts of Prudence

An essential feature of practical reason understood as prudence is that we have to deal with the contingencies of life, in all their particularities. General principles can help us to order our thoughts, but the circumstances we confront are too complex and varied to be easily categorized. Accordingly, the exercise of prudence requires a good deal of mental agility. Aquinas identifies eight "parts" or features that contribute to the exercise of prudence: memory, understanding or intelligence, docility, shrewdness, reason, foresight, circumspection, and caution. Each of these skills serves to help us navigate the complexity of the world.

Memory is necessary because while there are not fixed regularities that we could capture by simple formulas, we can find patterns or general trends of behavior. To do this, it helps to have a lot of experience. Our memories of those experience can be used to find similar cases to the one we confront now.[57] An example of this would be Machiavelli's pattern of reasoning in *The Prince,* wherein he canvasses history for examples of successful governance in a variety of circumstances to formulate general principles that might be helpful. To compare a current situation with the patterns one has experienced, it is necessary to be able to identify the particular. Hence understanding, or the ability to know what something is, belongs to prudence, specifically with respect to recognizing particulars.[58] The skill of understanding is what fits prudence to a universe in which God's goodness is reflected through the heterogeneity of created goods.

Because there are an infinite variety of particulars to consider, it would take too long were we to try to sort everything out from scratch. It is, therefore, useful to learn from the wisdom of others, and hence docility is an integral part of virtue. It is particularly helpful to listen to older people who have more experience.[59] But one must also rely on one's own judgment, and shrewdness is the capacity to discern well for oneself. It is the ability to weigh a variety of factors together in a sensible way.[60] Some part of this process will involve making deductions and connections, and so reason is also part of prudence.[61]

We act into the future and thus need to develop foresight, which helps us anticipate the effects of our actions and also future contingencies that should be weighed in the moment. In some sense this is the essence of prudence, since all acts necessarily open out into a contingent future.[62] To have good foresight, one needs to be alert to things that can work against us, or bad consequences of our action, and so caution is part of prudence.[63] Finally, because matters are complex, we need to look at the whole set of circumstances in play rather than focusing too narrowly on one aspect of a choice. The circumstances in which a choice is made might alter the way that choice will work, and hence circumspection is a part of prudence.[64]

Taken together, this is just an exploration of what wisdom requires. Note also that Aquinas's account conveys an underlying sense of humility. Because of the vast array of particularities that are the subject of practical reason, we can never be certain of our conclusions. Humans act out into the future and thereby shape it, but there are limitations on the control we can exercise. The freedom we enjoy as rational creatures is a reflection of God, but only a reflection.

As Aquinas says in the prologue to the *Secunda pars,* humans are made in God's image, in that we are the principle of our actions, by virtue of having free will and control of our actions. Prudence is the virtue that directs those actions, and accordingly it should have an analogue in God, and providence would seem to be that analogue. Providence refers to the fact that all created things are ordered to an end, and specifically to the end of divine goodness. In his discussion of providence, Aquinas specifically connects prudence and providence, arguing that it belongs to prudence to order things to an end.[65] Because this is an analogical connection, there are important differences. God does not require counsel, and His judgments are certain. But the essence of prudence is to command an act, and this God does supremely in his providential ordering of the universe he created.[66] We can see a further connection between prudence and providence in Aquinas's claim that rational creatures are subject to divine providence in a "most excellent way," in that we "partake of a share of providence, by being provident" both for ourselves and others.[67]

If we grant an analogy between providence and prudence, then we have an invitation to see human decision making as a reflection of God's creative activity—one of the ways we reflect God's goodness. Ours is a responsive creativity. Our invitation is not to institute our own order but rather to partake of the order God has set forth. A model of practical reason that emphasizes the satisfaction of subjective preferences will not do here. Instead, we need a model of practical reason that has to do with discerning the order in the world around us, so that our acts can creatively participate in the unfolding of that order through time. In other words, it would take something like prudence, which allows us to discern order in a world of myriad particulars, so that we can order our acts toward our end (which is also God's end) wisely.

This might raise the worry that prudence is a matter of discerning God's will, in a way that curtails the exercise of anything we might understand as freedom. But on Aquinas's view, our ability to consciously direct our own part in creation is part of human excellence—the essential way in which we are the image of God. Furthermore, that we are doing this imaging as finite creatures gives us another sort of freedom. Recall that the infinite is reflected in the finite by an array of distinct heterogeneous goods that are well ordered. It takes myriad diverse goods to reflect the infinite fullness of being (goodness) that is God. Just so, there is not just one way of ordering human goods into a pattern of life we could call virtuous. If our prudence reflects God's providence, it should require a diverse array of human lives to reflect that providence. Each virtuous life shows us something of God, but for those lives to be fully reflective of God there should be an array of them. Thus saints all have distinctive stories, distinctive paths. Prudence countenances neither an attitude that says all choices are equal nor an attitude that says there must be one right way. It is rather like art. We can tell good art from bad art. But the greatness of Bach does not dictate the form of greatness that Miles Davis can pursue.

Prudence thus suits Aquinas's framework. It is set up as an analogical reflection of divine providence, one that conceives of practical reason as an exercise of wisdom that suits an account of a creation in which myriad diverse goods are ordered to one another and ultimately to divine goodness. It is the form of practical reasoning that is suitable to the pursuit of happiness as perfection. At this juncture, many economists would protest that their strength lies in modeling and that just as it is possible to construct models of choice that can accommodate uncertainty, altruism, and even cognitive biases, so too it should be possible to construct a model of choice that captures the set of skills that constitute prudence. That claim would hold only if the pursuit of perfection can meaningfully be thought of as a variant of constrained maximization. Can prudence be modeled? And more importantly, can it be modeled as a form of constrained maximization?

Can Prudence be Modeled as a Form of Constrained Maximization?

In his book, *Approximating Prudence,* Andrew Yuengert explores the question of whether economic models can be extended to capture prudence.[68] As he formulates the problem, the economic approach to human decision making is always meant to capture the salient features of a given set of choices. Parsimony dictates that an economist should abstract from complexity in building his models to the degree possible. All models are then approximations, and the question is whether they are good approximations. But as Yuengert argues, to know whether economic models are good approximations we need some account of what it is that they are approximating. He adopts Aristotle's account of prudence as a good starting point for thinking about what goes into actual human decision making and argues that not only are economic models not good approximations of such decision making, but also in principle they cannot be good approximations. That is to say, complicating economic models of choice will not move them closer to prudence.

Yuengert cites four features of Aristotle's account that "cannot be captured in a quantitative optimization model of choice."[69] First, prudential reasoning requires that we reflect on the ends we pursue, with no sure guide about how to compare those ends. Second, although economic models can capture the problems posed by risk using probabilities, they cannot capture genuine uncertainty where the probability distributions are unknown and we are not even certain about our own preferences. Indeed, many of the other virtues are virtues precisely because they help us navigate the radical contingency of the world in which we find ourselves. Third, although economists do have models that can handle the problems of self-management that call forth the need to develop the virtues of fortitude and temperance, those models cannot adequately account for the value of freedom, or self-mastery, as a good in itself. And finally, economic models cannot account for the social embeddedness of practical reason, the way we learn from others things that cannot be learned from books of instruction. In short, the complexity of the world defies easy capture by mathematical models. The quantification does not do justice to the project of ordering diverse goods coherently in a radically uncertain world.

Aquinas's account of prudence is rooted in Aristotle's approach, so the concerns Yuengert explores all obtain. But Aquinas's own understanding of prudence is rooted in his metaphysics, suited to a world that analogically reflects the God who created it. As a result, there are reasons to argue that economic models of choice as quantitative constrained optimization not only fail to approximate prudence but also represent a mode of choice that would actively prevent the agent from moving toward happiness. First, to optimize, the diverse goods that we pursue need to be collapsed into a single function to be maximized. The problem is not just that it is difficult to compare diverse goods to make rational trade-offs. It is that the move to see diverse goods as fungible positively invites us to minimize the heterogeneous character of the diverse goods we find in this life.

But it is through that heterogeneity that God's goodness is reflected in the world. The goodness of the apple is most fully realized in its appleness. To see the apple as a vehicle for delivering nutritional inputs that can be traded off against oranges with a different configuration of nutritional inputs is to miss the deepest good of the apple. Optimization requires that we blind ourselves to an essential source of the goodness available in this life, instead flattening out the qualitative distinctiveness of goods in favor of the thin quantitative dimensions that would allow us to view them as directly comparable. In the field of economics it most notably does this by inviting us to see goods primarily in terms of their prices rather than in terms of what they actually are in themselves.

Second, the world reflects God's goodness not only through the diversity of created goods but also through the way those goods are ordered. The essence of prudence is to think about how to order diverse goods into a coherent whole. To make choices in this light is not a matter of calculation; it is a matter of discernment. The prudent person is less an applied mathematician than an artist working to arrange the distinctive goods in her life into a harmony that brings out an underlying unity of vision. Economists might argue that this is not a problem for their mathematical models. As long as I can rank one form of ordering as better or worse than another form of ordering, I am still optimizing—choosing one arrangement of goods as preferable to another.

But that leads to the third and most fundamental problem. Perfection is different from maximization. For starters, the notion that practical reason is an exercise in constrained optimization carries with it the idea that the aim is to get "more" good, with an implicit sense that by getting more we are moving closer to the ultimate good. But the analogical character of a universe created by God rules out such a notion. We approach happiness in this life by perfecting a mirror of that ultimate good, a mirror that respects our essential finitude and that therefore eschews any attempt to stretch out to the ultimate good through an expansion of finite goods. Moreover, while it is true that we can think of better or worse achievements of perfection, it is not the case that what keeps us from achieving greater perfection is resource constraints in the form of either time or money (or even knowledge, if by knowledge we mean better technology). The painter does not improve his painting by adding more paint. The poet does not improve her poem by adding more words. The constraints that the artist faces have to do with wisdom and aesthetic discernment, not a limitation of the materials. Nor is it the case that the only thing preventing me from becoming the next Picasso is a limitation of time. Whatever it is that constrains our efforts at perfection, it is not the set of constraints modeled by a rational choice model.

As discussed more fully in Chapter 7 of this book, it remains the case that economic models of human choice can play a useful role insofar as they do work as good approximations of human behavior as it actually is. On Aquinas's own account, we would expect much human behavior to be well described by the sort of constrained optimization economists describe—because humans very often if not mostly act out of the lower form of reason that we share with animals and that does look like a series of optimization problems. The problem with the economic approach is that it identifies such decision making as rational. And with that comes a normative implication that permeates economic science, and indeed the public square. To wit, insofar as we think of the pursuit of happiness as an exercise in constrained maximization, it seems natural to focus one's attention on loosening those restraints. Economic growth and technological progress are embraced as ultimate goods, because they allow us to reach to more desirable bundles of goods. Collectively, we seem to think that what it would take to have better paintings is more paint.

If the Thomistic approach simply issued in a rejection of economic and scientific progress, it would be rightly dismissed. But Aquinas's account of ordering finite goods toward perfection offers us a vocabulary for thinking about the genuine goods that are served by progress. To see this, we need to move on to the subject of the role material goods play in a life well lived, the subject of Chapter 5.

5

Economic Life as Ordered to Happiness

With Aquinas's metaphysics and his correlative account of happiness es-tablished, we are finally in a position to develop an account of economic life faithful to Aquinas's broad principles. His essential insight into eco-nomic life is that it is ordered toward the pursuit of happiness. The re-sulting framework gives us conceptual tools that can help us distinguish between economic activity that is of genuine value from economic ac-tivity that is disordered and properly subject to critique. Although the framework Aquinas develops diverges from the economic view in its willingness to make such distinctions, Aquinas has instincts about eco-nomics that are compatible with the economic view. Among these is his recognition (following Aristotle) that there is a distinction between the actual goods and services produced by the economy and the money used to facilitate economic exchanges. Aquinas refers to this as the distinc-tion between natural and artificial wealth; economists refer to it as the distinction between the real and the nominal or monetary economy. Aquinas invokes the concept of ordering to articulate the relationship between the two. Natural wealth is ordered to genuine human flour-ishing; artificial wealth, in turn, is ordered to the acquisition of natural wealth.[1]

Although economists differ from Aquinas on the subject of how natural wealth is ordered to happiness, they share his sense that money and related financial instruments are ordered to the "real" economy. Money's principal function is to serve as a medium of exchange, allowing us to avoid the cumbersome process of bartering.[2] Because money is simply the medium of exchange, transactions should essentially be understood in terms of the underlying exchange of real goods or services. Accordingly, most economic analysis is done in terms of the real economy, though the values are expressed in dollar amounts. Thus, for example, "real income" is measured in inflation-adjusted dollars but is meant to represent the command over real goods and services one earns. Because money as the medium of exchange is simply meant to facilitate transactions, it should not have a direct impact on the real economy. Yet both Aquinas and economists recognize that the division between the real and the nominal economies is not so neat. Although Aquinas and economists share this basic framework, not surprisingly their accounts of both the real economy and the nonneutrality of money diverge. This chapter takes up the real economy and the monetary economy, in turn, and concludes with some reflections on what a widespread adoption of Aquinas's ideas about the role of wealth in a life well lived would mean for the economy as a whole.

Natural Wealth as Ordered to Virtue

For Aquinas, the term *natural wealth* refers to material goods like food, shelter, and clothing along with implements that humans use in their sundry activities.[3] The first thing to be said about natural wealth is that it is an instrumental good. That is, it is a good that is desired for the sake of something else. The car in your driveway is valuable in terms of the higher goods it provides. Perhaps it is reliable transportation. Perhaps it is a way to signal status. Perhaps it is aesthetically pleasing. Nobody would want material goods if those goods did not serve some higher end. The thought here is not unlike the one captured by Gary Becker's household production function, wherein households convert material goods and time into the ultimate goods desired, a list that includes things like health, prestige, and comfort.[4] For Aquinas, the most obvious good served by natural wealth is the support of physical life. But he goes on to argue that external goods like natural wealth are necessary as "instruments to happiness, which consists in an operation of virtue." Those goods serve both as supports of bodily life and the "operation of active virtue, for which . . . [humans need] also many other things by means of which to perform [virtue's] operations."[5] On this account, natural wealth cannot be our ultimate aim—it is always desired for the sake of something else.

Thus far, Aquinas's position is in accord with modern sensibilities. His next move is not. Because our physical needs (including our need for implements to carry out our various activities) are finite, our rational desire for natural wealth is also finite.[6] As explained below, when we take up the question of artificial wealth, Aquinas recognizes that for many people the desire for material goods is unbounded, just as economists assume. The difference is that Aquinas calls such desires "disordered." Aquinas's view that the rational desire for natural wealth is finite should not be mistaken for an argument that standards of living should be low. Aquinas's view of the role of natural wealth in a virtuous life has room for our modern intuitions about the value of material goods. The crucial distinction is not whether one lives at a high standard of living or a low standard of living; it is rather whether one's desires for natural wealth are measured and bounded by the ends it is meant to serve. That is to say, the criterion for judging whether one's desires for natural wealth are rational is that those desires be satiable, that we be able to identify how much is enough.[7] To develop this point, it helps to begin with a more detailed exploration of Aquinas's account of the role of material goods in supporting virtue.

The Role of Material Goods in a Life Well Lived

In addition to distinguishing between the perfect happiness of the beatific vision and the imperfect happiness available to us in this life, Aquinas also identifies two forms of imperfect happiness. The more perfect form of imperfect happiness is that found in the contemplative life, which is ordinarily accompanied by the embrace of voluntary poverty.[8] As Christopher Franks suggests, Aquinas's affirmation of the traditional Christian view that voluntary poverty is a more perfect way of life should be borne in mind if we are to fully appreciate the theological dimension to Aquinas's economic thought.[9] Nonetheless, Aquinas regards an active life, one that is more engaged with the temporal world, as one in which we can meaningfully find a good measure of the happiness that is possible in this life. It is a form of life that we would recognize as flourishing, and it allows for an appreciation of the positive good of natural wealth, insofar as it is properly ordered to the higher end of achieving temporal perfection.

Natural wealth supports a virtuous life in various ways. First and foremost, it supports bodily life. Although our need or desire for material goods should be properly finite, that does not entail an argument that our need for natural wealth in support of bodily life should be limited to what is biologically necessary. Aquinas distinguishes between two forms of necessity. The first sort of necessity is that without which we cannot live. I might be able to make do without meat, but some food is absolutely necessary for me to live. But Aquinas also recognizes that we are social creatures and that our manner of feeding, clothing, and housing ourselves plays an important role. So he identifies a second form of necessity, namely, that we have sufficient material goods to lead lives appropriate to our social situation. I could get by with a tattered old T-shirt, but it would not be becoming for me to pay a call on my neighbors so attired.[10] The material goods that support our physical needs are thus also vehicles for cultural expression. Insofar as we are social animals, acquiring a decent wardrobe is a part of cultivating virtue in this life.

Second, natural wealth provides us with the implements we need to exercise virtue. On this account we can include things like transportation and instruments of communication that support our social lives. In addition, we properly desire implements that allow us to pursue excellence through various arts and crafts. The exercise of the technical arts is not, properly speaking, a virtue because one can exercise them well in pursuit of faulty ends.[11] Nonetheless, they can be perfective of human capacity, perfecting our ability to do good work, and in that sense can be considered virtues.[12] Since the arts and crafts depend on material goods, it is evident that material goods can be properly ordered to such endeavors, at least to the extent that the endeavors themselves are ordered to virtue in the absolute sense.

Finally, two of the proper virtues, liberality and magnificence, specifically require natural wealth for their exercise. Liberality refers primarily to giving gifts to others, with an emphasis on giving gifts suitably, that is, to those to whom it is fitting for us to give.[13] Liberality is thus distinct from almsgiving (considered in Chapter 6) in that it refers to gifts given in consideration of the relationship others have to us rather than in consideration of the needs of others. Because gifts are not simply transfers of wealth but rather markers of a relationship, they need not be directly related to the maintenance of physical well-being. Pictures or keepsakes have a proper function in a well-ordered human life. But Aquinas envisions an even grander role for natural wealth in his discussion of the virtue of magnificence.

Magnificence is the virtue of doing or making something great.[14] This is not primarily a matter of being lavish toward oneself, though it can have lavish expression. For example, it might fall within the purview of magnificence to throw a lavish wedding or live in a "suitable" dwelling.[15] What Aquinas has in mind here are great works or constructions that have lofty intent.[16] This would include projects done to "bring into effect what the whole state is striving for," that is, projects that embody the ideals of the community.[17] Projects to build museums or libraries would fall into this category. The highest exercise of magnificence would be projects that give honor to God.[18] In all of these examples, the aim is to use one's riches to embody some ideal worthy of human aspiration. Although Aquinas does not explicitly draw this point, all of these projects have a communal aspect—these magnificent projects manifest goods that can then be experienced by others, whether by being invited to the wedding, or seeing the stately home, or enjoying the public works that result.

So Aquinas's account of the role of material goods in a life of virtue allows for many of the elements we would associate with prosperity. As virtuous persons we can meet our bodily needs in the manner that is socially "becoming"; we can acquire the implements that allow us to travel and communicate with others; we can use natural wealth to pursue the technical arts; we can give material goods to others to mark our particular relationships with them; and we can use natural wealth to exercise magnificence in the pursuit of projects ordered to lofty ideals. Given all of that, we might well ask just what distinguishes Aquinas's account of the desire for natural wealth from our own. The answer is that Aquinas thinks that our desire for natural wealth is essentially finite, measured by the ends natural wealth is meant to serve. If we have sufficient wealth to meet those ends, further increases in income are superfluous. It thus would be irrational to seek ever-rising incomes. And it would also be irrational not to give away any excess income, should one be met with a windfall. Because our culture attaches a strong value to economic growth, it is helpful to consider Aquinas's thought on this more closely.

Why Our Desire for Natural Wealth Should be Bounded, or Finite

Aquinas's views about the importance of having a bounded desire for finite wealth can best be seen in his treatment of the virtue of liberality and the corresponding vices of covetousness and prodigality. As we have already discussed, liberality is the virtue of spending "becomingly," primarily by giving gifts to others but also through proper spending on oneself. It represents right relationship to material goods and is treated as an aspect of the virtue of justice. Broadly speaking, justice is the virtue of giving others what is their due, and liberality is a component of justice in that having one's interior affections for material goods rightly ordered is a component of the larger practice of handling material goods justly.[19]

The corresponding vices, covetousness and prodigality, work together to give us a picture of what is meant by the virtue of liberality. With respect to affections, covetous persons love riches more than they ought, while prodigal persons have deficient love for riches in that they are insufficiently careful of them. With respect to external actions, the covetous person is deficient in giving but excessive in retaining and acquiring material goods, while the prodigal person gives excessively and is insufficiently attentive to acquiring and retaining material goods.[20] In both cases, we should not confuse the vices in question with the vices associated with a failure to master one's passions or desires. The vices of covetousness and prodigality have to do directly with an inability to regard material goods with due measure, though as Aquinas observes, the prodigal who spends freely is apt to be prone to sins against temperance as well, sincc the habit of spending too freely can run in the direction of spending too freely on pleasures of the flesh.[21]

Our culture is still apt to view prodigality as a sort of failing. The prodigal is careless with his income and is therefore wasteful of material goods. From the perspective of the Thomistic framework, the defect is twofold. First, the prodigal does not dispose of his riches in a way that is ordered by reason. For example, he gives without regard to the fittingness of the gift.[22] Correlatively, the prodigal does not have a proper regard for the value of material goods. It is instructive to note Aquinas's sense that undervaluation of a good is as much a vice as is overvaluation. The overarching virtue is treating goods with due measure, valuing them neither more nor less than they deserve. The two defects come together to suggest that it is by virtue of not spending according to reason that the prodigal fails to fully appreciate the value of material goods. To arrive at a proper appreciation for material goods, one must see how they can be ordered to higher goods in a way that is commensurate with the end they serve.

While we continue to see prodigality as a failing, modern sensibilities are likely to be less offended by covetousness, or at least by the vice Aquinas designates by the term *covetousness*. Covetousness is not to be confused with envy, nor is it essentially related to a desire to have what others possess. It is, as already noted, an excessive regard for material goods, or an "immoderate love of possessing," whether or not that disposes one to covet what another possesses, using our sense of the term *covet*.[23] Although we might see that as a failing when it comes to things like Imelda Marcos's shoe closet or John McCain's seven or so residences, Aquinas's account of covetousness includes a set of attitudes we consider to be quite normal—namely, the notion that it is desirable to have indefinitely more material wealth. Indeed, covetousness underlies the widely accepted notion that the ideal economy would generate everrising standards of living.

Aquinas's affirmation of material goods as ordered to the maintenance of one's standard of living (the ability to live "becomingly"), to magnificent projects, or in support of the exercise of arts and crafts and so on thus comes with an important proviso. There is no vice in desiring material goods when they are ordered to an end, but it becomes the vice of covetousness when our desire for material goods is not "held in check by the rule taken from the nature of the end."[24] What does this mean?

As Aquinas goes on to argue, instrumental goods must be commensurate with the end they serve, and he uses medicine as an example, saying that it is "commensurate with health."[25] It is easy to see that a given substance can only serve as medicine up to the point that it restores health. Beyond that it is at best wasteful and at worst can become harmful. If it takes two pills a day to keep one's blood pressure in check, one wants two pills a day, not five or six. That logic extends to all material goods. If it takes a house of a given size to live becomingly, then one wants a house of that given size, not one twice as big. For Aquinas, our considered ideas about the end come first and serve as a measure of what material goods we actually need. All of this is consonant with the idea that our highest end in this life is a perfection of our nature. So long as we are finite, our need for natural wealth to support that end should also be finite.

The modern understanding of the relationship between wealth and the ends for which wealth is desired, as embodied in the rational choice model, inverts this relationship. In that model, we begin not with an end at which we are aiming but rather with a series of possible ends ranged according to desirability. Expansions in natural wealth allow us to attain more desirable bundles of goods. On that view, more wealth is always desirable. The reasoning we make in our decisions can sound deceptively similar to the sort of reasoning Aquinas commends. One person desires more income so she can meet her needs in a more becoming fashion. Another desires more income so he can construct a larger library for the public good. Yet another desires more income so she can get better equipment with which to pursue her avocation as a rock climber. The difference between Aquinas and the modern view thus does not lie in the fact that we can articulate why the material wealth is useful. Instead, it stems from the fact that the indefinite string of ends captured by the rational choice model can never serve as a measure of what is sufficient, because the string of ends is indefinite. Once the rock climber has attained the best equipment, she decides more money would be helpful because there is some further end that might be desirable to pursue.

As discussed in Chapter 3, Aquinas does not believe it is coherent to conceive of the final end as a string of increasingly desirable bundles of goods. When the end is constructed that way, it cannot serve as the measure of instrumental goods. Instead, the instrumental goods become the measure—determining how far up the ladder of desirable ends we can reach. In essence, the tail wags the dog. The instrumental good of wealth ends up being pursued as though it were the ultimate end, since it is the key to getting further up the ladder of successively better ends.

A parable might help illustrate the point. Consider two families, the Aardvarks and the Warthogs. The Aardvarks make a living as potters, but their lives are ordered around their avocation, which is musical. They decide that a grand piano would best help them to pursue their musical interests, and so they work hard at their craft, with the aim of earning enough to support themselves and buy the grand piano. Indeed, they decide that their needs would best be met by a particular grand piano, which happens to be rather expensive. So they work hard. When the Aardvarks finally have enough to buy the piano, they do so. They reduce their hours at the pottery shop to the point where they can generate enough income to meet their ongoing needs, and they spend the rest of their time playing their piano and hosting musical soirees. They become good musicians, and they enjoy a rich life sharing their musical gifts with their neighbors.

Their cousins, the Warthogs, also make their living as potters, and they are also musically inclined. Like the Aardvarks, the Warthogs decide to work hard so they can buy a grand piano. When they finally get their grand piano, they are pleased. But it occurs to them that it would be even better to supplement the piano with a cello and a violin. That way they could play those lovely trios by Schubert. So they go back to their pottery shop and keep working. When they finally get enough for the cello and the violin, they are again pleased. And then they think that it would be good to branch out into other forms of music, say jazz. So they earn enough money to get a saxophone, a trumpet, and a bass. Now their house is a bit crowded, and so they decide they need to get a larger house. And so they redouble their efforts at the pottery shop. And on it goes. At the end of the day, the Warthogs never do have much time for music; their hours are mostly spent making more pots. None of the ends pursued by the Warthogs are bad per se. But because their desires are open ended, the pursuit of more income ends up de facto being the real good that they pursue. Instrumental goods can only remain instrumental if they are in service of clearly specified ends.

The reasoning embedded in the rational choice model thus turns out to be a simulacrum of proper reasoning. It was in thinking of their pursuit of happiness as an exercise in maximizing their utility, reaching out to ever more desirable goods, that the Warthogs ended up never enjoying the good of music that they actually desired. Economists might argue that the essential difference between the Aardvarks and the Warthogs is that the Aardvarks have a better-specified utility function. The Warthogs' utility function depends on the number of instruments at their disposal, but this would be irrational if their ultimate end is to develop their musical talents. The Aardvarks do better simply because they see that their utility function depends on time spent making music on a quality instrument. But the Aardvarks are nonetheless still maximizing. Their decision to stop at the grand piano would simply reflect the fact that the marginal utility of additional instruments fell off rapidly for them, and so they rationally shifted time toward playing the instrument they had. On this account, the Aardvarks would benefit from economic progress. They would not want or need extra income, but if advances in productivity allowed them to earn more per hour, they could shift even more time to their desired activity of playing the piano, and they would thus be better off.

While it is possible that a family like the Aardvarks could think that maximizing time available for playing their piano is their ultimate end, such a family would simply end up with a variant of the problem that plagued the Warthogs. Their efforts would center on maximizing free time, rather than money for the purchase of more instruments, but the heart of their problem would still be on loosening the constraints that prevent them from moving higher up an open-ended ladder of successively better goods. While it is easy to see the mistake in thinking that more instruments translates into a better musical experience, thinking about a better musical experience in terms of time is not much better. To see this, simply notice that time spent on an enjoyable activity cannot be aggregated. If we pause to think of the good that is pursued when one takes up the avocation of music, the good is not a matter of extension, made better by more instruments to play or by more time in which to play. It is rather being present to the activity itself, in its proper perfection. If a three-hour session on the piano is the fitting time for a good musical soiree, one is not made better off by having five hours available. The deepening of the good of music is a matter of taste, talent, and application—but none of these are ultimately limited by external goods, whether in the form of natural wealth or of time.

This principle extends to one's life project as a whole. Once the Aardvarks have found a good balance of pottery making, music, and the ordinary business of life, they have no further need of extra income or extra time. To think that extra time could allow them to pursue a second avocation is again to conceive of the ultimate end as a matter of extension—increased command of finite goods of one sort or another. But such an extension of one's aim would simply dilute the good that one seeks. We are finite creatures, and the aim is to find the range of activities that allow us to pursue the aspects of the good we choose to manifest in our lives. Once that has been identified and achieved, again, one would not be made better off by a further increase in either natural wealth or time.

The point requires some elaboration because it is foreign to modern habits of thought, most especially as embodied in the rational choice model. The notion that purposive human action entails optimizing something subject to constraint is pervasive, especially among economists. Tibor Scitovsky takes up the question of whether such behavior is genuinely rational, in his essay "Are Men Rational or Economists Wrong?," which serves to both document and critique the way economists think about constrained optimization.[26]

Scitovsky begins with a type of irrationality that economists acknowledge: money illusion. Money illusion is the mistake of looking only at listed prices without thinking about their relationship to the general price level. For example, if over the course of a year inflation runs at 10 percent, it would be a mistake to look at one's 10 percent raise in salary as an increase in real income. Yet people do often fail to adjust listed (nominal) prices for inflation. Scitovsky argues that there are other sorts of illusions that economists should also worry about. He looks at three broad types of questions individuals face: how to maximize income, how to save time, and how to save effort. Beginning with the first, he notes that we seem to overwork, earning more income than we can spend. Economists use the life-cycle model of consumption to argue that we save over our working lives to finance a retirement. That model should leave people dying with some net wealth if individuals are risk averse and therefore have saved enough to cover the contingency that they will live long past retirement.

But empirically, people die with far more net wealth than could be accounted for simply as a matter of individuals wanting to ensure they do not survive their nest eggs. Moreover, the very wealthy make staggeringly large charitable donations. As Scitovsky argues, it is not irrational to give money away. What seems irrational is to work very hard in order to give away large sums of money. It seems easiest to explain large bequests and philanthropic donations as resulting from a divorce between decisions about earning and decisions about spending. As Scitovsky puts it, people seem to desire money for its own sake without reference to how it will be spent. He dubs this a form of money illusion.

Scitovsky then takes up the consideration that perhaps it was rational to earn as much money as possible so that one need not worry about economizing on money. It is nice to be wealthy enough to not have to pinch pennies. Among other things, pinching pennies takes time, and time is also scarce. So perhaps the behavior of the very rich is rational in that they are trying to earn a lot of money so they do not have to waste time trying to be frugal. Perhaps what is ultimately desired is time, because that can be spent at leisure—doing the things we wish to do.

The difficulty with that argument is that we see the same pattern when it comes to time. Unlike money, we cannot save up time, but we can end up with surplus remainders of time that have no clear purpose. Drawing on Gary Becker, Scitovsky observes that as income rises there should be two effects on the way we trade off money and time. First we should desire more leisure because leisure is a good. But second, as earnings go up, the opportunity cost of time goes up. Taken together, we would expect the demand for leisure to rise with incomes but not at the same rate as income. What we find looking at time-use studies is that the rise in income has shifted people away from spending time cooking and sharing meals, public entertainment, reading, club activity, and walking for pleasure toward watching television, shopping, and running errands.

As Scitovsky notes, there are some paradoxes here. For starters, part of the increase in shopping time is a result of a reduction in customer support. We spend more time in lines, more time bagging our own goods, more time assembling goods that are not fully assembled. All of this seems to be related to the desire to save money, but that is paradoxical since the behavior shifts occur in the context of rising incomes. We were supposed to be using our excess money precisely to avoid having to spend time pinching pennies.

The second paradox is the time spent watching television, which Scitovsky treats as parallel to the way surplus wealth issues in large bequests and charitable donations. It is not plausible that people work hard so that they can spend money in order to save time so that they can go home and watch television. To use Aquinas's language, the only way to make sense of this pattern of behavior would be to say that time spent watching television is our ultimate good, the thing toward which our other choices are ordered. Yet that seems to be an implausible account of what people are intending. When asked, most people say they watch a lot of television at the end of the day as a way of relaxing—presumably because all of that energy spent earning money so we could save time, and simultaneously spending time so we could save money, has left us rather exhausted. Scitovsky concludes that we suffer from a "time illusion" similar to our money illusion.

Finally, he considers that maybe our aim in all of saving money and time is to minimize effort. We like the idea of surplus money and surplus time because we could use that time and money in various ways to spare ourselves effort. But as Scitovsky notes, that explanation does not work either. One result of our affluent lifestyle is that we become prone to obesity and other diseases related to lack of exercise. And so we work hard to get a lot of money and time so that we can spare ourselves effort, and then promptly go to the gym to expend on treadmills all the effort that we have saved ourselves the rest of the day.

The patterns of behavior described by Scitovsky all involve "optimizing" behavior that reflects an underlying premise of the rational choice model, namely, that an expansion of resources (money, time, labor-saving innovations) allows us to move to higher-ranked bundles of goods. In other words, it is a picture of human behavior consistent with the thought that our ultimate end involves pursuing a sequence of ever higher levels of happiness. From the Thomistic perspective, such a project is ill conceived because our ultimate end involves perfection rather than endless progress. And as Scitovsky observes, a symptom of that irrationality is that we end up with a surplus of instrumental goods, surplus because at the end of the day the ladder of successively better goods is really an illusion.

The observation that our culture is excessively obsessed with material progress is hardly unique. Nor is the concern that such obsession is ultimately irrational. While it is true that the disorder Aquinas would identify as covetousness existed before the advent of modern capitalism, it is only in modern capitalism that it has become so widespread that rationality comes to be identified with the irrational effort to climb a ladder of successive goods that are not coherently ordered to a well-conceived end. Aquinas himself associates the disorder with the monetary economy. Although the rational choice model was not available for Aquinas to consider, his thought suggests that the root of the logic that underlies that model can be found in our tendency to confuse money with happiness. In his discussion of whether covetousness is a capital vice, by which is meant the sort of vice that begets other vices, Aquinas suggests that money is prone to being mistaken for happiness in ways that beget this ersatz form of reason.[27] As Aquinas argues, happiness is the most desirable end; it has the property of being self-sufficing, that is, of setting our appetites at rest. Money gives the promise of self-sufficiency, because all things seem to "obey money."[28] That is, money gives us command over that which can be purchased.

Although money does not occupy a principal position in a well-ordered life, it does occupy a principal position with respect to sensible goods, again because it gives us a general command over sensible goods.[29] That general command means that money can seem to contain all possible goods, which furthers its likeness to happiness.[30] The problem is that money, which seems to give us command over whatever it is we might desire, cannot truly be self-sufficing, because it can only give us command over goods that can be bought and sold, and human nature cannot be fulfilled only by having command of such goods.[31] The rational choice model mirrors this faulty logic by imaging an indefinite array of goods before us, with our final choice being determined by the constraint of our finite resources (that is, money and time). If only we had more, we would finally have enough. But that logic never comes to an end, and an effort to find happiness in that manner must always be in vain.

In his discussion of the confusion between money as a final end and genuine happiness, Thomas uses the term *money* to refer to that which economists would call income. It is a measure of our command over as-yet-unspecified material goods. But the fact that income is measured in terms of money leads to our tendency to confuse money with happiness in the way Aquinas suggests. The abstraction of money allows us to see it as something that can be turned toward an indefinite array of possibilities, which, in turn, leads us to falsely conclude that our desire for it is properly unbounded. To see this, we need to turn to Aquinas's discussion of the role artificial wealth plays in our lives.

Artificial Wealth as Ordered to Natural Wealth

Aquinas defines *artificial wealth* as that which is "not a direct help to nature . . . but is invented by the art of man, for the convenience of exchange and as a measure of things salable."[32] It is only desired for the sake of the natural wealth it commands. In other words, it is an instrumental good in service of an instrumental good. Aquinas's account of the role of money is similar to the one offered by modern economics. Money serves as a medium of exchange, a store of value, and a unit of account. Its primary function as a medium of exchange helps us to overcome the multiple difficulties involved in bartering. Because we typically do not spend at the same moment in which we earn, money needs to hold its value across time. These two functions reflect money's role in making exchange convenient. The third function, money's role as a unit of account, is what Aquinas refers to as serving as a "measure of things salable." It allows us to name the prices of goods and services in terms of one common measure, rather than having to name the prices in terms of all other goods and services. (It is easier to know that the price of a gallon of milk is two dollars, rather than having to know that the price of a gallon of milk is a dozen eggs, or a half a loaf of bread, or three quarters of a gallon of gas). Money's function as a unit of account is necessary, but it is also a primary source of the problems money causes.

Although Aquinas's understanding of money mirrors the one developed by modern-day economists, his further reflections on artificial wealth are not so easily reconciled. He seems to curtail the role of the market mechanism in arguing that prices should be just.[33] And he rules out lending at interest in his doctrines on usury.[34] Such doctrines have led the historian of economic thought, Mark Blaug, to argue that the medieval scholastics play no essential role in the development of economic thought.[35] A cursory glance at Aquinas's doctrine on, say, usury suggests that such dismissals are justified. His remarks about usury are rooted in a premodern setting and can sound naïve to those who appreciate the role that complex financial transactions play in promoting economic growth. Theological efforts to evaluate the soundness of Aquinas's strictures against usury are confronted with the daunting task of untangling both the scholastic teachings on usury and the vast economic literature on the unresolved questions about the nature of capital and interest and then to somehow correlate the results. Not surprisingly, no consensus on the question of how to apply Aquinas's specific doctrines on usury to modern financial institutions has been achieved.[36] However, we can take Aquinas's broader principles about the relationship between artificial wealth, natural wealth, and happiness to create a modern Thomistic framework for thinking through the role monetary and financial institutions should play in economic life.

Aquinas's framework offers two basic principles for thinking about the economy. The first, as we have seen, is the importance of ordering lower ends to higher ends. Markets and financial instruments are ordered to the provision of natural wealth, which, in turn, is ordered to human happiness understood as perfection. In other words, markets and financial instruments are of value only insofar as they facilitate the provision of natural wealth. And natural wealth, in turn, is of value because it supports happiness. Neither markets nor natural wealth have value independent of their role in serving the higher goods they support. On this view, the good of economic efficiency carries no weight in its own right. Rather, in confronting situations where there seems to be a tension between economic productivity and higher goods, the question is resolved not in terms of trade-offs but rather in terms of what solution best serves those higher goods. For example, lower taxes tend to spur productivity. That might be an important consideration in a country where individuals need more natural wealth to meet basic needs or to have the sort of autonomy necessary to cultivate a good life. But it would be a less important consideration in a country where there is enough natural wealth to support good lives.

The second basic principle is that our economic exchanges must be just. There should be some rough equivalence in exchange. Leaving aside the vexed question of what constitutes a just price, the key intuition is that it shifts the focus away from the monetary aspects of the transaction. For example, I buy a quart of milk. The fact that money is used for that exchange can tempt me to think of myself as a customer who has the means to "demand" the milk. In thinking that way, I can overlook the fact that real people have produced the milk, packaged it, and placed it in a location that is convenient for me to access. They have done me a real service, and I should appreciate it. By the same token, the grocer might think of me as a source of revenue that enhances his bottom line rather than as a person who benefits from the quart of milk. The monetary habit of thought blinds us to the real good we do for one another in and through our economic activities. I provide teaching and mentoring services to my students. The grocer provides me with the milk I will pour on my cereal in the morning. We are deeply involved in helping each other out, but the market system masks that. As Karl Marx has observed, we see things and their prices rather than the extensive network of human relationships that form the fabric of our economic lives.[37]

Worse, the tendency to see the monetary aspect of economic exchange as primary can lead to unjust economic practices. I "demand" the cheapest possible milk, heedless of whether the price I pay is enough to appropriately compensate the producers of that milk for their efforts on my behalf. The grocer thinks of me as revenue, heedless of whether he has provided me a good product at a fair price. The problem runs deeper than the obvious concerns about exploitation or fraud that might come to mind. Firms flood our culture with advertising and marketing campaigns aimed at persuading us to buy products regardless of whether such products are actually helpful to us. In 2016 news broke that Wells Fargo employees had created millions of unauthorized accounts for their clients. The news focused on the fraud involved. But behind the fraud lay a corporate culture that had put enormous pressure on employees to cross-sell, that is, to persuade existing clients to purchase more services.[38] Even if the employees had striven to meet their sales goals in a nonfraudulent manner, the corporate policy was unjust in the sense that the point was to get people to purchase products for the sake of Wells Fargo's revenue stream rather than out of any desire to meet existing genuine needs of their customers. That most of us would fail to see the injustice of a firm aggressively marketing its products regardless of whether its products meet genuine needs is a measure of how deeply the monetized view of the economy has penetrated our culture.

Both of Aquinas's principles (the ordering of ends and the character of justice) work to inculcate a habit of thought that refuses to mistake monetary measures for the underlying reality they represent. They insist that we think first about the real goods and services that are being produced and, even more importantly, about the human needs that are supported by those goods and services. But once those principles are accepted, there is room in the Thomistic framework to accommodate modern insights about the usefulness of markets in coordinating economic activity. To see this, it helps to begin with an account of what a virtuous firm would look like.

Aquinas himself does not have a full account of the role of economic production in a virtuous life. His emphasis is on the instrumental character of economic production. We labor to provision ourselves with necessary goods. But the very act of being responsible for oneself and one's family is part of the perfection of our beings. In performing this labor we exercise providence for ourselves. In addition, the act of provisioning is part of the perfection of our social nature. We are members of society, and our productive activities work to support others as well as ourselves. Part of this social function takes place when we offer material support to those in needs, as discussed further in Chapter 6.

But Aquinas also recognizes the social character of economic activity. In taking up the question of whether voluntary poverty is a legitimate practice, he addresses the objection that those who adopt voluntary poverty are failing to provide for themselves and are also thereby rendered incapable of providing material assistance to others.[39] Aquinas concedes the premise of the argument but defends voluntary poverty on the grounds that mendicants contribute to society through their prayers in exchange for the material support they receive from lay people.[40] Indeed, Aquinas explicitly appeals to the value of specialization in labor. Because many different things are required to support life, and because no one person could do all those jobs, we rely on the labor of others to support our own lives. The practice of voluntary poverty can be incorporated into that division of labor by simply noting that spiritual goods are among the goods that we all need. On this account, the essence of what a firm does is to produce goods and services of value to other members of society.[41]

The principle of thinking of business activity in terms of its function of provisioning extends to the financial industry as well. Although banking and insurance services trade in cash flows, the financial instruments they produce are ordered to genuine human goods. For example, financial instruments allow people to live in their own homes decades before they would be able to afford them; they allow workers to essentially trade present earnings to current retirees for a claim on future workers to support them in their retirement; and they allow a multitude of households to combine resources to finance great projects that are beyond the scope of any single individual. These are real services, and the individuals involved in developing and offering the instruments that make such transactions possible deserve recompense for their efforts. It takes skill to discern which households can handle a mortgage, which economic ventures are deserving of funding, and so on. Aquinas condemns the taking of interest on a loan of money (usury) on the grounds that in such transactions the lender receives payment without having rendered any good in return.[42] Insofar as most interest serves as compensation for expected inflation, risk, and the effort expended in originating and servicing a loan or an insurance contract, the Thomistic framework can accommodate such activities. The outstanding question, which I do not pursue further here, is whether the portion of interest that reflects the inflation-adjusted risk-free time premium is just. But most interest reflects just compensation for real services or real risks, or both, and is therefore moral.

Although Aquinas focuses on the function of provisioning, his framework is compatible with subsequent Catholic reflection on the role of work in a virtuous life. As John Paul II puts it, "Work is a good thing for man—a good thing for his humanity—because through work man not only transforms nature, adapting it to his own needs, but he also achieves fulfillment as a human being and indeed in a sense becomes 'more a human being'."[43] In our work we develop our abilities, and even exercise creativity, thereby perfecting the capacities latent in our nature. A virtuous firm, therefore, provides workers with an opportunity to cultivate their own human excellence. In addition, insofar as it brings workers together into a community, the firm is a place where human relationships can be cultivated, both among colleagues and with other firms and customers.[44] On this view, a firm should be evaluated in terms of the real goods and services it produces and the role it plays in fostering virtue and developing community.

The immediate question is what role do profits play. After all, firms are also in business to make money. Aquinas recognizes that in fulfilling their role of provisioning others with necessary goods and services, people also work to provide for themselves. That is, they expect to earn a living through their work. On this view, it is reasonable for firms to expect a fair return for their efforts in providing goods and services. Their revenues should be sufficient to allow them to justly compensate their employees. In addition, the revenues need to be sufficient to justly compensate the owners of the firm for their entrepreneurial and managerial work and for the risks they bear. Having produced goods and services of value to the community, the stakeholders in a firm can expect to receive a fair return as a matter of justice.

Modern insights into the workings of markets can be integrated into Aquinas's framework on this point. In particular, as Friedrich Hayek stresses, prices serve an invaluable role in conveying information to both producers and consumers.[45] In a complex economy, it would be difficult for the virtuous firm to gather enough information to know what goods and services are of genuine value to the community, especially relative to other potential uses for the resources devoted to production. But prices convey the relevant information efficiently. A shirt manufacturer does not need to conduct population surveys in an effort to determine how many shirts to produce. Instead, she can rely on the price of shirts to tell her what she needs to know. Higher prices mean that shirt production should be expanded. Lower prices mean that shirt production should be curtailed. The prices of inputs work the same way. The shirt manufacturer does not need to know about the drought that reduced the supply of cotton. All she needs to know is that the high price of cotton suggests that she shift production from cotton shirts to shirts made of other materials in more abundant supply. The price system works to coordinate the behavior of independent agents toward the end of producing the set of goods and services that best meet the needs of the community.

The virtuous firm thus attends to profits, but not with the aim of maximizing them. Rather, the aim would be to ensure that the goods and services it produces are of value to the community and that the resources used in the production of those goods and services are being used wisely. Profits that are insufficient for the firm to be adequately compensated for the labor it has expended and the risks it has borne are a signal that a different line of work should be considered. Profits that exceed the levels the firm would need to be justly compensated are a signal to expand production and will most likely encourage other firms to enter into the business. If the stakeholders in the firm have a virtuous relationship with natural wealth, higher-than-normal returns to their business would represent surplus income that would be available to give away to worthy causes or perhaps to be set aside to sustain the business during hard times.

Aquinas's framework thus gives us scope for imagining a humane economy, one that is in service of the higher goods that constitute genuine human happiness. The artificial economy—money, prices, profits, and markets—has a proper role in a humane economy. But for that to work, participants in the market need to act out of Aquinas's basic principles. Natural wealth is desirable only insofar as it meets genuine needs; instrumental goods are properly ordered to the ends they are meant to serve; and as social creatures we have an interest in making sure our exchanges are just. Participants in the modern economy, of course, typically do not act out of such principles. Most stakeholders are interested in maximizing their returns. Workers aim for higher salaries. Businesses aim at maximal profits. The interest in optimizing with respect to monetary measures extends even to consumers, who typically aim at paying the minimum possible price for the goods and services they receive. Incomes and profits, all measured in monetary terms, have come to be seen as more "real" than the actual exchange of goods and services they represent. And these two habits of thought—the desire to maximize income and the correlated tendency to view economic transactions primarily in terms of their impact on our bottom line—tempt us into economic transactions that are not just, even though we often blind ourselves to the injustice involved in such exchanges.

For Aquinas it is not happenstance that market participants in a commercial society would tend to act out of faulty principles about the proper ordering of artificial wealth to natural wealth and of natural wealth to happiness. Although money or artificial wealth can play a useful function in a humane economy, there is something about money that leads to a disordered understanding of the role of economics in human life.

The Trouble with Money

After rejecting natural wealth as a possible last end, Aquinas goes on to argue that artificial wealth is an even less likely candidate for final end than is natural wealth since it is (properly) sought only for the sake of natural wealth.[46] In other words, as we have seen, it is an instrumental good in service of an instrumental good. Aquinas then connects the desire for artificial wealth with what he calls "disordered concupiscence."[47] Disordered concupiscence is any lower desire that is not subordinate to our highest reason and is manifested in the vice of covetousness, the immoderate love of possessions.

Aquinas takes up an objection to his position that asserts that desire for the last end never fails and must therefore be infinite. Since the desire for wealth seems to be infinite, it must therefore be the last end.[48] In reply, Aquinas begins by arguing that this objection cannot establish natural wealth as a final end, since the desire for natural riches is not infinite. Our natural needs are finite, and there is therefore a natural limit to what we need. On the other hand, "the desire for artificial wealth is infinite, for it is the servant of disordered concupiscence, which is not curbed."[49] In a subsequent discussion of concupiscence, Aquinas elaborates as follows: Desire for an end is always infinite, since it is desired for its own sake. On the other hand, desire for the means to an end is limited by the end. Thus, for example, the desire for health is boundless, but the desire for a given medicine is finite, because it is measured by the end it serves (recall that ten aspirin are not better than two). Those who place their end in riches will have boundless desire for it.[50]

This serves as an argument for why the desire for goods and services will be unbounded for individuals who hold goods and services as their final end, but it does not explain how the disorder connects to money, which is merely the medium of exchange. What does it mean that the desire for artificial wealth is infinite, and that it is the servant of disordered concupiscence? In his discussions about both artificial wealth and disordered concupiscence, Aquinas refers to Aristotle's *Politics,* so it is useful to consider his commentary on that work for more insight into how Aquinas connects artificial wealth, understood as money (and presumably other financial instruments), with disordered concupiscence.

In that commentary, Aquinas distinguishes between "true" wealth, which corresponds to what he calls natural wealth in the *Summa,* and that "other" wealth, the acquisition of which is unlimited and which cannot properly be called wealth "since it does not *satisfy* the desire of human beings."[51] It is this other wealth that Aquinas is referring to in the reply to the objection we are considering, because he goes on in that reply to argue that the desire for such goods is infinite because they fail to satisfy and therefore leave us wanting more. As Aquinas proceeds in his commentary, he links the desire for such "other wealth" with the art of moneymaking, as distinguished from the proper use of markets, which is to assist households in procuring natural or true wealth.

The connection begins with a historical claim about the evolution of money. As human communities grew, and especially as foreign trade emerged, it was useful to conduct transactions with easily transported metals, which evolved into a medium of exchange, or money. As Aquinas has already said in the corpus of the question on wealth, this artificial wealth is properly meant to be in service of the procurement of natural wealth—that is, facilitating trades among households or across regions, which help people arrive at a sufficiency of what they need.[52] But as markets evolve, merchants enter into the picture. Whereas households enter into the market with one kind of good and exit the market with another kind of good, merchants begin with money, which they use for the purchase of goods, and end with money, which they obtain by reselling those goods. Merchants appear to be engaged in the art of moneymaking, which is "directed to making a great deal of money and wealth as its end."[53] It is this evolution that leads to the confusion between money as a medium of exchange and moneymaking as an art in service of the disordered concupiscence that places riches as an end rather than as a means.

The nub of the problem, then, is that the activities of households in markets (selling and buying goods to maintain the household) and the activities of merchants (buying and selling goods to make money) appear to be similar. Because household management and moneymaking seem to be similar, the logic of moneymaking can encroach on the logic of household management, inviting households to see their task as accumulating unlimited wealth. As Aristotle puts it, households that make this shift do so because they desire to live but not to live well, that is, to live without virtue. Such households live according to their own will, satisfying their desires. Alternatively, they can desire to live well "but add to living well what belongs to physical pleasures, since they say that human beings enjoy the good life only by living immersed in such pleasures." In either case, the result is that the household becomes preoccupied with maximizing what we would call income "because they do not have the right endeavor for the good life."[54] On this account, households give way to disordered concupiscence in the wake of the rise of commerce, which introduces the possibility of pursuing wealth as an end.

Once this corruption sets in, it can extend to all of the arts involved in sustaining human existence. First the art of household management itself becomes distorted when its end is accumulating wealth rather than ordering material goods to the end of supporting a virtuous life. Second, individuals who cannot accumulate wealth through commercial activities will turn to other modes of doing so. In particular, instead of pursuing their occupations for the ends inherent in that occupation, they will instead pursue their occupations as a vehicle for making money. The doctor, for example, shifts from aiming at healing to aiming at making money.[55] As Aquinas stresses, the two practices are deceptively similar. The doctor who aims at healing will charge patients for services rendered, but only in accordance with the needs of sustaining the doctor's family and not as the ultimate end of the practice. In other words, the virtuous doctor is going to heal someone whether or not they can pay and is not going to enter into practices, like plastic surgery, that have a dubious connection to the end of producing health but are commercially lucrative. The doctor whose end is to make money is going to gravitate to whatever specialties are commercially lucrative, prescribe medication with more attention to what is lucrative than to what is needed, and so on.

An economist might object here that Aristotle and Aquinas are laboring without benefit of the insights of Adam Smith and others into the way market pressures constrain producers to produce what is actually good and useful. A doctor whose patients suffer higher morbidity and mortality rates as a result of the doctor's subordination of the practice of medicine to the art of making money will soon lose patients and will end up making less money rather than more. The doctor truly interested in making money has an incentive to be a good doctor. But if we bear in mind that both Aristotle and Aquinas say that the two practices are deceptively similar, we can say in reply that they are both talking about the corruption that only becomes visible in the places where the market mechanism is not sufficient to constrain the corrupt to practice their arts the way a virtuous practitioner would. That there are doctor shortages in poor areas in desperate need of general practitioners but an abundance of cosmetic surgeons should be enough to secure this point.[56]

Although Aristotle seems to see merchants as necessarily involved in the art of moneymaking, Aquinas offers room for a merchant to practice his art in service of household management much the way the virtuous doctor would practice his art. In his discussion of whether merchants are necessarily engaged in vice, Aquinas observes that a virtuous man "may intend the moderate gain which he seeks to acquire by trading" for the upkeep of his household or for other virtuous activities. Moreover, such trading can be intended as providing a real service to the community, for which a merchant should be justly compensated.[57] For Aquinas, that real service is the importation of goods to a community that lacks them. A modern-day economist could add that, in addition, merchants provide real services by generating information about commodities and making them conveniently available to households. Notice that on this account, we could imagine an art of being a merchant that has as its end helping customers obtain the goods they need. And one can imagine that there are, in fact, merchants who practice that art.[58] Although Aquinas makes a move in this direction, he still sees the end of the art of trade as being gain, not "assistance in the allocation of goods," and as such he does think that unlike other arts, trade has a "certain debasement" attached to it because by nature "it does not imply a virtuous or necessary end."[59]

To return to the key point, the connection Aquinas (following Aristotle) makes between the rise of commerce and the temptation to pursue disordered concupiscence depends on the parallel between the pursuit of profit in commerce and the pursuit of accumulation in households. But insofar as it is possible that individuals were tempted to pursue disordered concupiscence in a barter economy, the connection between the desire for artificial wealth and disordered concupiscence seems a bit thin.[60]

However, in his discussion of concupiscence, Aquinas offers a second reason why "non-natural concupiscence is altogether infinite." In the previous article, Aquinas has established that in addition to the concupiscence we share with animals, wherein we desire what we require by nature, there is a second peculiarly human concupiscence rooted in our ability to apprehend something as good and suitable for our needs. That sort of concupiscence operates through our reason.[61] In this article he observes that because this secondary concupiscence operates through reason, it has a tendency to proceed to infinity.[62] However, it is a concupiscence that is disordered insofar as it perceives the relevant infinity as being a progression of numbers, indefinitely stretching out.[63] The only way it can motivate a person is if the individual takes delight in each of the succession of goods as they appear, but as we have seen in Chapter 3, to conceive of happiness as the realization of a succession of ends is simply a mistake.[64] The problem of disordered concupiscence that fixes on wealth as its highest good is not that it aspires to the infinite; it is that it does so by following a type of infinitude that can never truly satisfy.

The infinitude we are built for, of course, is God. In his discussion of wealth, Aquinas explains the difference: "Yet this desire for wealth is infinite otherwise than the desire for the sovereign good. For the more perfectly the sovereign good is possessed, the more it is loved, and other things despised." By contrast, when we try to fulfill our yearning for the infinite in finite temporal goods, we find that "when we already possess them, we despise them and seek others. . . . The reason of this is that we realize more their insufficiency when we possess them: and this very fact shows that they are imperfect, and the sovereign good does not consist therein."[65] And here is the nub of the problem. Money tempts us to a false conception of the infinite, at least as it relates to our desire. Disordered concupiscence is clearly possible in a barter economy, but there is greater temptation to it in a money economy. When we begin to exchange goods through the instrument of money, and especially to measure goods in monetary terms, we begin to think about goods in the language of arithmetic, with the attendant invitation to conceive of the good as an endless ascension. While our status as rational creatures means it is proper for us to yearn for the infinite, we can only achieve our true happiness if we pursue the true infinitude of the sovereign good, rather than the accidental infinitude of a succession of things. The problem with money, then, is ultimately theological.

Theological Analysis of the Dangers of Money

The confusion over the nature of infinitude is central to our experience of material discontent, because an economic system that is ordered to disordered concupiscence cannot be ordered to our true happiness. If we want to use our limited material resources wisely and well, we need to understand what it would mean to properly exercise our properly infinite desires. The account of Aquinas's economic framework thus far has largely drawn on principles Aquinas adopted from Aristotle. But to fully understand the dangers posed by money, we need to consider the issue in the context of the explicitly theological dimension of Aquinas's thought.

Recall that for Aquinas, the created world is an analogical reflection of God, and the happiness we can know in this life is analogically related to the happiness we will know in the next life. To establish the theological diagnosis of the dangers of money, it helps to begin with a theological discussion of the role of material wealth in promoting temporal human happiness in light of its analogical relationship to our ultimate beatitude. Aquinas's account of our eternal happiness delivers us a concept of happiness that at first blush is quite remote from anything we might construe as temporal happiness. Indeed, material goods do not play any role at all in perfect happiness. However, despite that vast gap, imperfect happiness does give an analogical reflection of perfect happiness, and that can be useful in thinking about the role material goods play in supporting the imperfect happiness possible to us in this life.

In brief, perfect happiness consists in the beatific vision, as we have seen. Happiness understood as perfection entails a fullness of act, a realization of our capacities. On this view, our ultimate happiness is one continuous act.[66] It is primarily an operation of our intellectual powers, though in the resurrection the happiness of the soul will overflow to the bodily senses.[67] The final act consists in a vision of the divine essence and is thus primarily an operation of speculative reason, though fulfillment of the will necessarily follows on that exercise.[68] It requires rectitude of the will both insofar as we are ordered to our last end and because in achieving our last end of loving God we necessarily love all else in subordination to God.[69] Although our perfect happiness centers on the perfection of our soul, the well-being of our souls requires our bodies, and indeed, our happiness in heaven will overflow on to the body, which will thereby obtain its own perfection.[70] These bodies are, however, spiritual bodies. As a result, material goods are "nowise necessary" for our ultimate happiness.[71] Finally, the fellowship of friends is not necessary in that perfect happiness, but that same fellowship "conduces to the well-being of happiness."[72]

So how can any of this be related back to the imperfect happiness possible in this life? As Aquinas puts it, imperfect happiness participates in perfect happiness, or alternatively it "partakes of some particular likeness of happiness."[73] By that he means that we order our lives to the ultimate good, which is God, insofar as is possible in this life. There are two principal sources of the imperfection of our happiness. First, we cannot know and love God in this life as we will be able to in the next. Second, we are enmeshed in a creation that involves multiplicity and materiality. The latter should not be understood as some Manichean principle wherein we are pulled down by that which is not God. As argued earlier, creation itself mirrors God, and thus our dealings with the imperfections of creation are themselves to be understood not so much as substituting not-God for God but rather as loving God in the only way possible to us in this life, namely, through that which reflects God.

Turning to the first source of imperfection, we can observe that the difficulty lies in the chasm between God and creation. Our proper happiness is found in knowing and loving God. But to truly know something, we must know its essence. Unfortunately it is not possible in this life to know God's essence.[74] Our capacity for knowledge is related to the sorts of creatures we are. As Aquinas puts it, the mode of knowledge follows the mode of the nature of the knower. Our way of knowing is tied up with our corporeal nature, that is, we know from our senses. But God, who is entirely spiritual, cannot be known in this way.[75] It is only through union with him in the next life that we can have a vision of God's essence.[76] In this life, using natural reason, we can only know God through his effects, that is, creation. That path of knowledge limits us to knowing that God is, but not what he is in himself.[77] God's grace in this life can elevate our knowledge of God by a strengthening of our "natural light" and the infusion of divine images in the imagination, but this just improves our ability to understand God from his effects and does nothing to bridge us to knowing God's essence in a more direct fashion.[78] In short, whether we know God in this life through reason or through grace, we only know God as he is reflected through creation, not as he is in himself.

In addition to not being able to know God's essence, we are part of the multiplicity and materiality of creation, and this also keeps us from the full perfection of happiness. The first difficulty stems from the changing nature of things in creation. For example, perfection entails exercising our powers in one final continuous operation. However, in this life we cannot engage in such a culminating act. We have multiple things to attend to, must eat and sleep, and so on.[79] More obviously, we are subject to the vicissitudes of changing fortune. A human life cannot exclude all evils, and such goods as we attain themselves pass away.[80] We thus cannot simply rest in the achievement of our ultimate desire in this life, something Aquinas takes to be an essential component of true happiness. However, we can more nearly approach a likeness of this happiness to the extent that we live a life that has something of the unity that is essential to that one act of happiness. On these grounds, a contemplative life, which is consciously centered on that one thing, more fully participates in our ultimate happiness than does an active life, in which we are busy with many things.[81]

The consideration of the nature of temporal happiness as a reflection of the ultimate happiness we are built for underscores the earlier account of the role of natural wealth in a life well lived. Our highest temporal ends are good because they reflect the ultimate good we desire, which is knowing God. Because God is known as He is reflected in creation, all humans, believers and nonbelievers alike, approach happiness by approaching a deeper understanding of creation. Insofar as humans are made in the *imago Dei,* the preeminent way of growing in this knowledge is through cultivating our own excellence and our relationships with others. Any economic practices, such as focusing on maximizing profits, that invite us to subordinate human goods to lower goods thus move us away from the happiness that is possible in this life. So too would any habits of thought that invite us to think of happiness as a matter of extension—whether of material goods or experiences. Such habits of thought undermine efforts to bring some sort of unity to life.

The purely instrumental character of material wealth is underscored in light of Aquinas's reflections on the relationship between temporal happiness and our ultimate beatitude. In particular, we rely on material goods to support our bodily needs. Although Aquinas's view of perfect happiness does not entail a denial of our bodily natures, he does think our bodies will be transformed. Accordingly, external goods are "nowise necessary" for our happiness in the next life. It might seem to be something of a concession to the limitations of a created world that we do need material goods to attain the happiness that is possible for us in this life. Because we have "animal" bodies, we need material goods to support ourselves and the exercise of virtue. That this is a concession would seem to be implied in Aquinas's observation that a life of contemplation approaches more nearly a likeness of perfect happiness than does a life of action, and "therefore it stands in less need of these goods of the body."[82] Part of the superiority of contemplative life to an active life is precisely that such a life minimizes our need for material goods.[83] It would thus seem that Aquinas rank-orders states of happiness in this life in terms of how strongly the life is focused on God and on how little the life depends on material goods.

If this were all there were to Aquinas's teachings, it would seem he has less to say to us about modern economic life than he does. Some might find asceticism attractive, but it seems to leave us with no vocabulary with which to articulate the genuine good of material flourishing. However, Aquinas does offer us some arguments that subtly move in that direction. In particular, he suggests that even though material goods are distinctly lesser goods, they are nonetheless goods because they reflect God's goodness. It might be better to focus directly on God, but a person who pursues goodness on more ordinary terms is implicitly also pursuing God.

To get a feel for how this move works, consider what Aquinas has to say about whether happiness could consist in consideration of the natural sciences. Perfect happiness cannot consist in such considerations because sciences consist in knowledge of sensible things, which are lower than scientists themselves. Our perfection lies in consideration of things above us. That said, insofar as sensible objects "partake of a certain likeness" to that which is above us, namely, the intelligible light or something of that kind, so an imperfect happiness can be found in considering them.[84] In other words, science can help us see the intelligibility of nature, and it is contemplation of that intelligibility that is ennobling. The objects, which of themselves are beneath us, can perfect us insofar as we find in them that which can only come from God, that is, intelligibility.

Just so, Aquinas opens the door to the possibility that material goods can likewise reflect something of God's goodness and thus possess a status as a good independent of their utility to us as embodied creatures. In his discussion of whether material goods are required for happiness, Aquinas takes up two objections that open up room for such possibilities. The first objection suggests that material goods must be part of perfect happiness, because scripture promises such goods to the saints in heaven.[85] His reply is that such promises are to be understood metaphorically. Scripture describes the joys of heaven in corporeal terms because those are terms we understand. "Thus food and drink signify the delight of happiness; wealth, the sufficiency of God for man; the kingdom, the lifting up of man to union of God."[86] But if allusion to such goods is scripture's way of communicating our ultimate good to us in a form we can understand now, it would seem to follow that we are invited to see those goods now as representing something of the ultimate good we hope for.

The second objection opens the door further to that possibility. In it, Aquinas takes up Boethius's statement that happiness is "a state made perfect by the aggregate of all good things." Even though external goods are of least account, they are nonetheless goods and therefore must be part of our perfect happiness.[87] Aquinas replies that goods that serve for animal life are incompatible with the spiritual life, which is perfect happiness. However, whatever good that can be found in those external goods *is* part of our perfect happiness, because God is the "fount of goodness."[88]

Aquinas's accent is on the negative because he is asking whether external goods are part of our perfect happiness. But if, instead, we ask what role external goods play in the imperfect happiness available to us now, it would be the case that part of what they can do is reflect to us that "fount of goodness." If the question is whether we will have grand banquets of marbled roast beef and fine wine in heaven, the answer has to be no. It is important to correct the error that stems from taking the goods we perceive in this world as the measure of any good we might hope for in the next life. But if we are clear of that error, it would seem reasonable to consider the possibility that we could look at the banquet table we encounter today and see in it a hint or reflection of the fullness of goodness that we hope for. Asceticism is necessary to help us see that we are built for a greater good than can be found in material goods. But that asceticism could open up to an aestheticism that would allow us to see the goodness of the world as reflective of God's goodness.

In essence, this is an argument that material goods should be viewed as sacramental signs, representing God's goodness to us in the only way possible in a finite creation. Recall that for a finite creation to reflect God, the qualitatively distinct goods we find in the world represent some aspect of God's goodness. The appleness of the apple tells us something of God, distinct from what the orangeness of the orange tells us. On this view, a full appreciation of the material goods in our lives would entail seeing them not only as they are ordered to higher ends but also as they are in themselves. To put it another way, the apple is not merely a device for delivering us nutrition, one that is interchangeable with a pill containing the same set of nutrients. It is a way of sustaining bodily life, along with the goodness communicated in the crunch, smell, and taste of biting into an apple.

And here we find one of the key dangers of money. Money is a quantitative abstraction that does not respect qualitative distinctions. It invites us to see goods as fungible, veiling the distinctiveness of the various goods. In doing so, it interferes with the twofold role material goods play in the imperfect happiness we can pursue in this life. First, when we think in monetary terms, it becomes difficult to think of how to order goods properly. If the essence of pursuing temporal happiness entails harmoniously arranging the goods in our lives, ordering lower goods to the higher goods they serve, we need to think primarily in terms of what the goods are and how they relate to one another. By reducing all goods to a single metric, money makes it difficult to think in terms of that ordering. All monetary measures can do is compare the price of one good to another. But while prices may contain a lot of information about how to coordinate economic activity, they do not contain enough information to help one decide what material goods one needs to support a becoming and virtuous life. The perfect couch for my living room is not the most expensive couch. It is the couch that has the right dimensions and brings harmony to the living room. The practice of thinking about how material goods are ordered to their ultimate purposes and how they can be harmonized to form a sort of unity leads more naturally to the thought that one has finite need of them than does the practice of thinking in terms of incomes and budgets.

Second, when we think in monetary terms we are invited to see the underlying goods as essentially fungible. Apples and oranges become alternative vehicles for delivering nutrition. In his book, *What Money Can't Buy*, Michael Sandel argues that the language of money makes it difficult for us to make moral distinctions between various goods. In a world that has been shaped by the language of money, it can be difficult to see, for example, the difference between writing a note of apology and hiring someone to do it for you.[89] The argument here builds on that concern by observing that when we become tempted to see material goods primarily as commodities we are more apt to overlook the intrinsic good contained in the goods themselves. The appleness of the apple is overlooked in our rush to move on to the next thing.[90] As a result, the apple is not as fully satisfying as it might be if we were more fully present to the way it represents goodness to us, through its texture, smell, taste, and form. The modern sense that our desires are fundamentally insatiable or unlimited stems from our inability to think in terms of ordering goods, and possibly also from our inability to be fully present to the goods before us. The abstraction of money thus encourages a habit of mind that makes it harder to give material wealth its proper due, and no more than its proper due.

On this view, we would be able to draw more genuine fulfillment out of the prosperity we enjoy if we could learn to see material wealth as a reflection of God's goodness and as properly ordered to the higher intangible goods that even more fully reflect that goodness. The abstraction of money deflects that understanding, and as a result, we continue to think of ourselves as economically pressed despite the fact that by historical standards our material prosperity is unprecedented. Money does not merely set out a faulty conception of the infinitude we properly desire; it also mimics God in other ways. As Aquinas argues, happiness is the most desirable end, which has the property of being self-sufficing, that is, of setting our appetites at rest. Money gives the promise of self-sufficiency, because all things seem to obey money.[91] That general command means that money can seem to contain all possible goods, which furthers its likeness to true happiness.[92] It is like the unopened package under the Christmas tree, which almost always seems more full of promise and excitement than the actual gift once it is opened. The rational choice model mirrors this faulty logic by imaging an indefinite array of goods before us, with our final choice being determined by the constraint of our finite resources (that is, money). If only we had more, we would finally have enough. But this logic never comes to an end, and an effort to find happiness in this manner must always be in vain.

In her lengthy critique of financial capitalism, Katherine Tanner argues that the logic of relentless profit maximization distorts our sense of time, with respect to both the past and the future.[93] From a Thomistic perspective, the specific problem is that the language of money deflects our attention away from the goods that are present to us now. By presenting a false hope for indefinite goods to come in the future, it makes it more difficult for us to properly receive the good before us now. We access the past through memory and the future through imagination. It is in the present that we have contact with reality and thus with God (to the extent possible in this life). It is the combination of not fully absorbing the present good and comparing that vague sense of dissatisfaction with the goods we imagine enjoying in the future that leads to the belief that what we need is more income. As individuals come to think increasingly in terms of maximizing income, it becomes even more difficult to recall that the proper end of firms is to provision society with useful goods and services. Instead, it comes to be seen as self-evident that the aim of business is to maximize profits. The consequence of the widespread adoption of the language of money and the correlated language of profit maximization is that the genuinely good role of markets in coordinating economic activity and provisioning society well is undermined.

The Consequences of Adopting the Logic of Profit Maximization

Although Pope Francis's encyclical, *Laudato si,* was justly criticized for undervaluing the good that markets can do, his fundamental critique of what he calls the technocratic paradigm is consonant with the analysis offered here. As he writes,

> The basic problem goes even deeper: it is the way that humanity has taken up technology and its development *according to an undifferentiated and one-dimensional paradigm.* This paradigm exalts the concept of a subject who, using logical and rational procedures, progressively approaches and gains control over an external object. This subject makes every effort to establish the

scientific and experimental method, which in itself is already a technique of possession, mastery and transformation. It is as if the subject were to find itself in the presence of something formless, completely open to manipulation. Men and women have constantly intervened in nature, but for a long time this meant being in tune with and respecting the possibilities offered by the things themselves. It was a matter of receiving what nature itself allowed, as if from its own hand. Now, by contrast, we are the ones to lay our hands on things, attempting to extract everything possible from them while frequently ignoring or forgetting the reality in front of us. Human beings and material objects no longer extend a friendly hand to one another; the relationship has become confrontational. This has made it easy to accept the idea of infinite or unlimited growth, which proves so attractive to economists, financiers and experts in technology.[94]

The language of profit maximization invites us to collapse the diverse goods around us into what Francis calls an "undifferentiated and one-dimensional paradigm." In doing so, it obscures the complex reality that we inhabit. The underlying problem is the problem of abstraction, which is essential to the role money plays in facilitating trade. The resulting habit of thought issues in three problems. First, the economy's proper role in provisioning society with useful goods and services is undermined. Second, the economy becomes subject to instability. And finally, the pressure for relentless economic growth puts pressure on the environment and makes it more difficult to achieve economic justice.

The first concern has already been touched on. As a matter of principle, setting profit maximization as the goal, or *telos,* of business activity inverts the proper relationship between wealth and the goods natural wealth is meant to support. Goods and services are produced to make money rather than to provision our neighbors with useful products. Employees become a cost line in financial statements rather than human beings seeking to develop their human potential through their efforts to produce valuable goods and services. The financial accounting comes to seem more real than the actual goods and services produced and the human beings who are both served by firms and work in firms. The ubiquity of the practice can make it harder for us to see how dehumanizing the modern economy can be.

In some cases the consequences of prioritizing money over human concerns is obvious. The major tobacco firms, for example, have been stigmatized for profiting by selling products that are harmful to their clients, and especially for their decades-long efforts to prevent their customers from knowing the dangers of smoking.

But tobacco is not the only industry subject to these sorts of critiques. In her book *Addiction by Design,* Natasha Dow Schüll offers an anthropological study of the machine gambling industry.[95] The focus of the industry is to maximize profits, which can only be done by extracting as much money from their customers as possible. To that end, they design gambling halls with no sense of time, with machines laid out in a disorienting maze, so that gamblers will remain at the machines as long as possible. Everything from the payout rates to the sounds emitted by the machines has been engineered to hook gamblers into the machines. Frequent-customer cards are used to monitor gamblers, so that interventions can be made when a customer is likely to leave owing to a losing streak, by having someone offer a drink or some free chips. Although not every person who plays at the machines in Las Vegas becomes addicted to gambling, the industry has discovered that its real profits come from those who can become trapped by their obsession with machine gambling. As a result the industry gears its practices not toward providing innocuous entertainment to large numbers of people but rather toward converting some of those customers into the habitual gamblers who can be relied on to bleed their life earnings into the gambling machines.

In the conventional view in which firms are expected to seek to maximize profits, an external ethical standard is necessary to draw boundaries between acceptable and unacceptable modes of exploiting one's customers. But from the Thomistic framework, the problem is straightforward. Such firms are failing their primary role, which is to provision members of the community with goods and services that support flourishing lives.

The same objection can be brought to a wide-ranging set of business practices in industries that do not produce goods or services that are actively detrimental to their customers. The case of Wells Fargo noted above is an example of these sorts of distortions. Marketing strategies are aimed at boosting sales, irrespective of whether the resulting sales serve any real human need. Increased sales effected by advertising campaigns that appeal to emotions or by strategic positioning of products for impulse buys are aimed not at meeting existing needs but rather at profiting by selling to an artificially induced desire. Such critiques are hardly novel. In their book *Phishing for Phools,* George Akerlof and Robert Shiller document many of these practices and suggest that we need to recognize that the market forces that induce firms to produce goods and services that provide real benefits will often likewise induce those firms to produce goods and services that do not.[96] In her Gifford Lecture series, Kathryn Tanner offers an extensive analysis of the way the profit motive distorts the relationship between firms and their employees as well.[97] Once one begins to look for examples where human goods are subordinated to the demands of profit seeking, it becomes clear that a substantial proportion of economic activity fails to secure real human goods. As a result, measures such as GDP are not good measures of the true well-being of a nation.

Although the problems are widely acknowledged, what is generally lacking is a vocabulary for distinguishing between good and bad economic practice. Akerlof and Shiller can only say that market mechanisms can produce both good and bad outcomes. Tanner can only say that the profit motive should be rejected. The Thomistic framework allows us to pinpoint the problem. All things related to money are meant to be in service of genuine economic activity. Prices and profits serve the real economy by acting as signals that facilitate economic coordination and by working to justly compensate producers for the efforts they have expended on behalf of their customers. Profits cannot play their proper role if they come to be seen as ends in themselves. It is the reification of profits that is the problem. Instead of thinking primarily in terms of the real goods and services that are produced, the real human activities involved in production, and the extensive network of human relationships that the economy comprises, we begin to think in terms of the monetary measures of economic activities as having an independent reality. Thus, although Aquinas argues that artificial wealth has a proper role to play, he also flags it as the likely source of our inability to come into right relationship with natural wealth.

Not only does the practice of maximizing profits divert a substantial proportion of economic activity away from the end of serving genuine human needs, it also introduces instability into the economic system. This happens primarily through the financial industry. As we have already seen, the financial industry provides real service to the economy. The problem is that all these transactions take the form of exchanges of money for money, and as Aquinas highlights in his discussion of merchants, this opens up directly to the danger of shifting focus from the real task of provisioning to the ephemeral goal of pursuing artificial wealth.[98] Stocks and bonds and other financial instruments are exchanges of money now for streams of money later. The more one focuses on the instruments themselves, abstracted from the real economic activities that give rise to them, the more money looks like the thing that matters. One starts to look for investments that promise high rates of return or are likely to appreciate in value over time. And the minute these become the focus, we have entered into the world of profit maximization. As Tanner suggests, the rise of finance has played a major role in exacerbating the ills associated with modern economic practice.[99]

The faulty approach to pursuing happiness issues in two problems. First, as Aquinas observes, fraud and deceit are daughter vices of covetousness.[100] Although it is certainly possible for fraud to arise in sectors of the economy dealing directly in real goods (think of the proverbial snake-oil salesman), the problem is particularly pronounced in finance. Enron and Bernie Madoff are only the modern exemplars of the pyramid schemes and the like that have haunted finance from its inception. Even Robert Shiller, in his defense of the essential value of finance, concedes that the sector offers practitioners "more than the usual temptation to be manipulative or less than honest" in their business practices.[101] The abstraction of money is a strong temptation to manipulate financial instruments for one's own gain, and the complexity of financial instruments creates great scope for fraudulent schemes.

More insidious is the second problem with the financial sector stemming from perfectly legal transactions, namely, the problem of speculative bubbles. These bubbles emerge when an asset begins to rise in price, and individuals scramble to buy it not because of its intrinsic value but rather because they hope to profit from further price increases. The increased demand for the asset, in turn, does boost the asset prices, inviting a further round of increased speculative demand. Although economists have been sometimes unwilling to admit that such bubbles can occur, the economic historian Charles Kindleberger offers a compelling history of their ubiquity in his classic work, *Manias, Panics, and Crashes: A History of Financial Crises*.[102] Although some bubbles involve real goods, most notably the tulip mania in Holland in the early seventeenth century, they overwhelmingly involve financial assets. The reason for this is rather simple. Because financial instruments are measured in terms of the abstraction of money, it is easier to imagine that their true value is significantly greater than the underlying fundamentals would justify. It is difficult to imagine a bubble forming around milk, because the true value of milk is more immediately apparent.

The 2008 financial crisis is a clear example of the problem. Its most visible symptom was the asset bubble around housing. Now this might seem to be a counterexample to the claim that financial assets are most prone to speculative bubbles. But the reasons the bubble was able to emerge rest almost entirely with the financial side of housing transactions. The underlying asset, the mortgage, is a good thing in itself. It allows a family to live in their own home without waiting to amass the savings needed to buy it outright. Because the transaction involves the concrete entity of the house and requires the real service on the part of the loan officer of discerning the buyer's ability to handle the mortgage, it is unlikely to be part of the dynamic that fuels speculative bubbles.

But in recent decades, the practice has emerged of banks selling off their mortgages to third parties. The issuing lender stands to profit from the fees charged in generating the mortgage, with an increased incentive to issue risky loans because they will not suffer any losses on default. A second layer of abstraction was introduced when mortgages began to be bundled together and sold as securities to the investment market. Now individuals could buy bonds that were backed by these bundles of mortgages. The assets were deemed to be even safer because the income flowing from a bundle of mortgages would not be severely affected if a few of the mortgages defaulted. A further level of abstraction was introduced when these mortgage-backed securities were divided into tranches, which divided the investors in these securities into classes, with higher returns going to those investors willing to "own" the part of the income stream that would first be affected by defaults, and lower returns going to those investors "owning" the safer part of the income stream. Taken together, these financial innovations gave issuing lenders a large incentive to generate ever more mortgages, with a notorious decline in standards. The easy availability of mortgages, in turn, bid up housing prices, and the resulting bubble embellished the sense that mortgage-backed securities were a safe investment, because even if there were defaults, the underlying housing assets would be valuable.

The speculative bubble still would not have been as catastrophic if there were not yet still another level of abstraction added, in the form of a further financial innovation that allowed investors to bet on whether these mortgage-backed securities would rise or fall in value. These financial instruments, known as derivatives because they are financial instruments drawn around the behavior of other financial instruments, created the staggering tower of paper that threatened to destroy the global financial system in September and October 2008. Each step of increasing abstraction increased the likelihood of destabilization because the assets involved were so far removed from the very real human activity of buying a house. The people investing in the various tranches of the mortgage-backed securities were looking only at risks and returns, not at the question of whether a particular family could afford a $400,000 house on an income of $30,000. Even those who were aware that something was awry in the housing market were complacent because they thought a collapse in the housing bubble would have limited effects, much like the Internet stock bubble of the early 1990s. They were unaware of the tower of derivatives that would implode with the collapse of the housing bubble.

As Carmen Reinhardt and Kenneth Rogoff argue in *This Time Is Different: Eight Centuries of Financial Folly,* economic contractions that are precipitated by a financial crisis are longer and more harmful to the economy than are economic contractions originating in other sectors of the economy.[103] The 2008 crisis illustrates why. The illusions involved in pursuing ever-greater profits by trading in financial assets allow larger distortions in the economy to occur, because the movements of asset prices are not as firmly tethered to the real economy.

How might the Thomistic perspective have helped? First, financial transactions should always be referred back to the real economic values they are meant to represent. The first stages of increasing abstraction (the selling of mortgages to third parties) required nothing more than attention to the incentives of the originating loan officers. But the subsequent stages (starting with the bundling of the mortgages into mortgage-backed securities) were predicated on the abstract considerations of the diversification of investment portfolios and risk management. The successive stages all involved complex financial calculations that could be done without reference to the actual housing market. That abstractness is what made it possible for the financial industry as a whole to fail to recognize how precarious were the underlying mortgages and how vulnerable they were to a bursting bubble in the housing market.

From a Thomistic perspective, the increasing abstraction promotes a second danger, owing to the tendency of the abstraction of monetary values to bleed into a quest for indefinite gain. The sophisticated financial instruments that are scarcely understood, even by those who created them, positively invite a focus on nothing but income streams, with the attendant thought that more is always better. In addition to creating a climate ripe for more fraud and other forms of abuse, the mania for more that emerges during speculative bubbles serves to blind people to the fact that a real economy does not, in fact, magically produce soaring rates of return out of nothing, as seems to be the case when the market is caught up in a mania. It was only after the bubble burst that people collectively looked around and wondered how any sane person could have thought that housing prices could or should rise by double-digit rates for years on end.

A financial environment in which people were vigilant to remember that finance serves the real economy and is only of value to the extent that it promotes real transactions that produce real economic value, and in which they were also vigilant to remember that the abstraction of money can fuel a quest for more that frequently blinds even very smart people to obvious realities, would be less subject to the instability of bubbles and manias. Nor is this merely an arcane problem. As the extensive damage that ensued in the wake of the financial collapse of 2008 attests, the consequences of financial instability for the real economy can be quite severe.

Finally, as Pope Francis suggests, the language of profit maximization supports the idea that indefinite economic growth is desirable. It is beyond the scope of this book to take up the question of whether a paradigm committed to unlimited economic growth is compatible with environmental sustainability. The Thomistic approach could assist such debates by asking us to reevaluate the trade-offs. In such discussions, economic growth in poor countries should count as a more obvious good than further economic growth in affluent countries. It further invites us to reflect on what genuine human good is achieved through the energy-intensive lifestyles that are associated with affluence in the modern world. But as Pope Francis also suggests, the emphasis on profit maximization also makes it more difficult to work for economic justice. To see the contributions that the Thomistic framework can make to the topic of economic justice, we need to take up Aquinas's account of private property. Aquinas's qualified approval of private property is worth examining in its own right because it provides a platform that allows us to embrace some of the best insights modern-day economists have while retaining a critical distance. But in addition, Aquinas's discussion of private property hinges on a concept of economic justice that, in turn, hinges on an understanding of how to be in right relationship with material goods. To that subject we now turn.

6

From Liberality to Justice

Aquinas's Teachings on Private Property

———————————

The argument thus far has been that it is crucial that any theological economics begin with an account of the role economic goods play in human life. Because Aquinas's thought lends itself to that sort of analysis, I have found it useful to engage economic thought from a Thomistic framework. But to get a deeper grasp of how useful Aquinas's economic thought can be for engaging modern economic life from a Christian perspective, it is necessary to move on to consider his thought about the institutional arrangements that undergird economic life. The obvious starting point for that inquiry is to consider Aquinas's understanding of property rights, especially in view of the fact that private property is an essential component of our market-based economy. As Chapter 1 notes, many theologians view the institution of private property with suspicion. In doing so, they simply pick up an ancient Christian tradition that likewise views private property with suspicion, though that tradition at least grants private property some standing as a concession to sin.[1] Economists, by contrast, hold private property to be a positive good, properly reflecting the reality of human nature and serving to channel human self-interest to the benefit of society as a whole.

Aquinas is a useful interlocutor for modern-day economists because he does argue that private property is legitimate, and not solely as a concession to fallen human nature. At the same time, his argument is rooted in his view of the role of economic goods in human life that has been set out in Chapter 5. It is thus a Christian account of private property, and as such, it offers the possibility of affirming what is good in modern economic thought, while maintaining a critical stance. To put it another way, Aquinas's account of private property can help us see what a truly humane economic system might look like.

Another reason to offer a close reading of Aquinas's teachings on private property is that it gives us an opportunity to better understand how the principles set out in Chapters 4 and 5 would cash out in an explicitly Thomistic economics. Aquinas's account of private property can be used to better understand our creation in the *imago Dei,* the role of proper self-interest, and what it means for economic life to be ordered to virtue. To see this, the chapter begins with an exegesis of Aquinas's teachings on private property.

That same exegesis reveals that there is a deep connection between Aquinas's account of our proper relationship to material goods and his account of economic justice. Accordingly, the second section takes up the question of proper consumption, showing the relationship between the theory developed thus far and Aquinas's account of private property. In addition, Aquinas's teachings on private property introduce a social element to our consumption practices that needs to be developed if Aquinas is to have application to modern life. The third section takes up the implications for economic justice that are contained in Aquinas's account of private property. Aquinas's discussion goes no further than addressing the question of how much we can properly consume and how much is due to others in need, but the same principles turn out to be at work in Aquinas's argument that prices and wages should be just. We cannot know what justice requires if we do not have a sense of what standards of living are appropriate, but that, in turn, requires the theory of consumption that this book has been developing.

Aquinas on Private Property

Aquinas takes up the subject of private property in the section of the *Summa theologica* devoted to the virtue of justice.[2] The specific questions on private property are set out in his treatment of theft and robbery.[3] To determine what constitutes theft, it is necessary to first inquire about possession, and so the first two responses to that question deal with private property explicitly. Aquinas's first move is to place the issue within a theological setting, beginning with the question of whether humans can be said to possess external goods at all, given that God created all things and exercises dominion over all things.[4] Aquinas answers that with respect to their nature, external things are subject to God's power, but with respect to their use, humans have a natural dominion.

Aquinas offers two reasons for human dominion over external things. First, he argues that God created those things so that humans could use them. As noted in Chapter 3, humans are more perfect than are all non-rational beings because they more fully image God. Insofar as the imperfect is ordered to the perfect, humans can and should have dominion over external goods. Although this argument takes an instrumental view of nature, it is not an invitation to despoil the planet to serve our own ends. For starters, Aquinas explicitly rules out the human right to manipulate the nature of things, because that is part of God's exclusive dominion.[5] Second, as stressed below, the invitation to have dominion over things is intended only insofar as they are ordered to our proper use, in the sense of right relation with material goods discussed in Chapter 5. The key here is that we encounter the theme of order. Humans may use the goods of the world for their use, provided that those goods are ordered to genuine human good.

The second reason humans have dominion with respect to the use of external goods relates directly to our creation in the *imago Dei*. Our dominion over other creatures derives from our possession of reason, which, in turn, is the key respect in which we are made in God's image. Aquinas cites Genesis 1:26, which connects our creation in the image and likeness of God and our dominion over other creatures. This observation should further alleviate our concerns about whether human dominion over creation is a license to despoil it. If we are to exercise our reason as an image of God, our exercise of dominion over other creatures takes on an aspect of stewardship, since exercising our reason should be done as a reflection of God's providence for creation.

The first article on property thus serves to ground our consideration of private property against a backdrop that reminds us that the world itself is a gift to us. The first attitude toward property and wealth, then, is properly one of gratitude. The second note that is introduced is that with property comes a sense of responsibility. We have dominion because we are trusted to make right use of external goods and to use our reason in an exercise of stewardship. In other words, the material world is the field over which we should exercise our powers virtuously, that is, under the auspices of right reason. Having established that humans can properly possess external things, Aquinas then takes up the vexed questions of whether individuals may possess external goods privately.

As the objections make clear, Aquinas inherited a tradition that holds that material goods that have been given to humans in common are ordained for common use.[6] Aquinas accommodates that intuition by arguing that we should distinguish between the "power to procure and dispense" external goods and their use. The "power to procure and dispense" is the power to use property for productive purposes and to be in charge of allocating the resulting income. "Use" refers to what we would call consumption. With respect to the power to procure and dispense, private property is not only lawful, it is also "necessary to human life." Aquinas offers three reasons for this:

> First because every man is more careful to procure what is for himself alone than that which is common to many or to all: since each one would shirk the labor and leave to another that which concerns the community, as happens where there is a great number of servants. Secondly, because human affairs are conducted in more orderly fashion if each man is charged with taking care of some particular thing himself, whereas there would be confusion if everyone had to look after any one thing indeterminately. Thirdly, because a more peaceful state is ensured to man if each one is contented with his own. Hence it is to be observed that quarrels arise more frequently where there is no division of the things possessed.[7]

With respect to use, however, individuals ought to possess external things not as their own but as in common, namely, by being ready to share them with others in their need. A casual reading of the text would seem to affirm the tradition's take on the matter—worldly goods are ordered to the common good, but in a concession to fallen human nature we must conclude that it is lawful to own private property.

Yet consideration of the three reasons Aquinas gives for being allowed to hold private property with respect to the power to "procure and dispense" undercuts that reading. While the third reason is surely related to fallen human nature, in that one assumes that saints are not prone to quarreling, the second reason, referring to the need for order, obtains whether humans had fallen or not. That second reason seems instead to relate directly to human finitude. Even if all humans had good will, it would be difficult to know what we should do each morning if we walked out our doors and had to decide which of the wide array of tasks that would need to be done for the common good ought to be done by us. By assigning property, we properly match a finite person with a finite piece of the collective work that is to be done. We could contemplate such assignments being made by a central committee in a command economy, but Aquinas himself does not seem to contemplate that possibility, nor should he.

The reason for this is that a person who owns a given plot of land or a given business is able to develop expertise about his property. While we can and should learn from experts, the person who is most likely to be able to judge well which techniques should be employed in a given set of circumstances is the person whose business it is to tend to that piece of property. Moreover, as previously discussed, command-and-control economies fail because the amount of information required to coordinate the myriad tasks that go into making even a common object like a shirt is too vast. One might say that the mistake of centralized economic planning is to think that a small committee can have godlike knowledge of the whole economic order. The combination of a proprietor's particular knowledge of his own business or property and the market's ability to coordinate economic activity has historically proved to be vastly more productive. Aquinas's instincts here about the way private property matches finite individuals with finite spheres of economic activity both reflects his understanding of the proper relationship between the finite and the infinite and accords well with modern economic insights.

If the third reason for owning private property with respect to the power to "procure and dispense" stems from fallen human nature, while the second would hold even had we not fallen, what are we to make of the first reason Aquinas supplies? There is an apparent tension between his argument that we are "more careful to procure what is for [ourselves] alone" and the further claim that we should nonetheless use the goods we procure as if they were common goods. If we are too selfish to work for others, why would not the command to use the goods we earn by our labor to meet the needs of others undercut our motivation to work? Given that Aquinas holds that material wealth is a good only insofar as it is in service of happiness, that is, the exercise of virtue, he cannot be arguing that we should permit private property as a way of channeling the vice of greed toward productivity, thereby avoiding the vice of shirking.

We can resolve part of the problem by appealing to the material developed in Chapter 5. Aquinas does not believe that procuring the goods that we genuinely need is an instance of greed. Greed entails desiring goods that are not ordered to a good life, that is, that are more than we properly need. So we can read him here as saying that one reason for private property is that it channels our proper self-interest. We are more careful to procure for ourselves what we need to live an orderly virtuous life. Yet there still seems to be a remaining tension, because Aquinas seems to be saying that we are more concerned with our own material needs rather than those of our neighbors. Love of self seems to take priority over love of neighbor, and that does not sound very Christian.

As it turns out, this is precisely what Aquinas is saying. Indeed, he thinks it is a virtue to prioritize proper self-concern over concern for one's neighbors.[8] We can begin by noticing that Aquinas believes that it is part of natural law that we should provide ourselves with the necessities of life.[9] At the same time, natural law also dictates that we should be concerned with helping others.[10] However, as Aquinas makes clear in his treatise on charity, our love of ourselves rightly takes precedence over our love of our neighbors.[11] This claim only makes sense if we begin with the observation that our first love is the love of God, who is the cause of all happiness.[12] Were we to bypass ourselves to love other creatures more than ourselves, we would be bypassing our direct point of contact with the supreme good, which is God. In doing so, we would undercut the proper basis of our love for our neighbor, which is that they are our fellows in that good.[13] To put it another way, to attempt to love our neighbors more than ourselves would be essentially to love our neighbors more than God. Aquinas applies this principle when he takes up the question of almsgiving, when he asks whether we should give alms out of that which we need for ourselves. His answer is emphatic: "It is altogether wrong to give alms out of what is necessary to us [to sustain our own lives]."[14]

We are now in a position to give a full account of Aquinas's first reason for defending private property. The problem with common property would be that it is not commensurate with the proper ordering of our concerns. Although shirking in such circumstances would be a failing, a regime of common property would not give us scope to exercise our natural and proper concern for ourselves. This, along with the second reason, sets private property apart as something that human reason can discern as an instrument in service of natural law.[15] Private property channels proper self-interest and orders human affairs. On both counts it is fitting to finite human nature. Although Aquinas is writing without benefit of economists' subsequent insight into the workings of markets, that these arrangements also tend to increase the material prosperity of society as a whole fits in nicely to round out a picture of private property as an institution that is in accordance with natural law, and not simply as a remedy for fallen human nature.

Although Aquinas's basic teaching affirms private property for reasons that resonate with economists' intuitions about the benefits of private property, he qualifies his support of private property in important ways. We have already seen one crucial difference in that for Aquinas, self-interest refers to the desire to provision ourselves with what we need. Whereas economists refuse to distinguish between natural and disordered concupiscent desires, Aquinas would deny that the pursuit of disordered concupiscent desire is an act of self-love.[16] Thus for Aquinas, a person who overconsumes in a world where many suffer the deprivations of deep poverty is not exercising self-interest at the expense of altruism; she is acting against her own interests and harming her neighbor at the same time. This difference is explored further below.

But there is another important difference between Aquinas and modern economists with respect to property rights. To begin with a subtle but important difference, Aquinas does not follow Locke in grounding the right to a particular piece of private property in any act of the individual.[17] C. B. MacPherson has linked Locke's theory of property rights to a phenomenon he calls "possessive individualism."[18] Although MacPherson can be challenged on the question of whether he has read Locke rightly,[19] I think he does have something to say about how Locke has been received. MacPherson essentially argues that although Locke does start with the thought that the world was given to humans in common, he goes on to derive a right to private property from the fact of our possessive ownership of ourselves. In particular, the claim is that when we mix our labor with external goods, those goods become ours by extension of our right to ourselves. The sentiment boils down to the idea that private property is justifiable because people have worked for what they own. I built it, therefore it is mine.[20]

By contrast, Aquinas does not ground the right to private property in anything we do. The reasons for permitting private property explored above all explain why the institution of private property is useful and suitable to human nature but say nothing about how those property rights are to be distributed. Indeed, Aquinas argues that "considered absolutely" there is no reason why a given piece of land "should belong to one man more than another."[21] Human reason discovers that it is useful to match one person with a particular piece of property, but it is a matter of human convention to determine how to allocate that property. For Aquinas, at least, that allocation does not derive from any inherent rights the person has with respect to his own body or his own labor.[22]

The more obvious difference is that for Aquinas the right to private property extends only to the power to procure and dispense goods. With respect to their use, external goods are to be held "as common."[23] What does that mean? If we read a bit further on, we learn that whatever we have "in superabundance is *due,* by natural law, to the purpose of succoring the poor."[24] Private property exists as a means of provisioning ourselves, but our claim to a given piece of property does not confer on us the right to use the fruits of that property in any way we like. According to the natural order, material goods are ordered to the maintenance of human life, and the institution of private property does not override that basic purpose. Nor is this a matter of giving lip service to the idea of the common destiny of material goods. If a person is in dire and urgent need, to take the property of another is not "properly speaking theft or robbery."[25] Indeed, it is the person who consumes too much who might be liable to that charge.[26] The entire point is a reflection of Aquinas's insistence on order. Material goods are ordered to the human good. If I am misusing my material goods in pursuit of the satisfaction of disordered desires while another person is starving, I am not ordering material goods to the human good.

The import of this difference between Aquinas and modern-day economists is that Aquinas sees the value of private property as a way of helping us to order our behavior in a way that is fitting with human nature. But he never forgets that production of goods is not the end of the task. An economic system is healthy and of use to the extent that it helps us order material goods to a life well lived. To the extent that private property serves that goal, it is moral. Indeed, it is *because* it can serve that goal that it is moral. What we ought not to do is exalt the property right to the point where it becomes an absolute whether it does or does not serve the human good.[27] Just as the language of money and profits ought not to be reified to the point of distorting the purpose they are meant to serve, so ought not an absolute conception of property rights to be taken as license to overlook the true role of economic goods in human life.[28]

Aquinas's teachings on private property, taken as a whole, seem to serve as a valuable bridge, affirming what is true in economic thought but pushing back against economic thought to the extent that it fails to order economic goods to the higher good of authentic human happiness. However, to use this material to think about modern economic life, we need to attend to the ways it needs to be adapted to our setting. In particular, to live out what Aquinas says about private property, we would need to have some idea of how to distinguish between what we need and what is abundant to us. In addition to building on the material on right consumption developed in Chapter 5, we need to take into account the social setting in which we make our choices. A virtuous consumer who has resisted the modern temptation to covetousness will nonetheless experience social pressure that makes it difficult to identify how much is enough.

How Much Is Enough: The Role of Standard of Living in Aquinas's Thought

If we acknowledge that private property comes with an obligation to use the resulting fruits for our own proper good, with the surplus reserved for supplying the needs of others, we need to have some further guidelines on how to exercise that duty. One set of questions would be about how to allocate the surplus among the many people who are in need. I defer this question to the next section, where I take up the question of how Aquinas's teaching on private property relates to questions of economic justice. The other set of questions would center on how we distinguish what is surplus to us. It is, in fact, the question that gets raised every time I speak on the subject of Aquinas and economics.

As we have already observed, Aquinas holds that we are not to give to others when doing so would deprive us of the means of sustaining our own lives. That would seem to leave open the possibility that we are to subsist on a minimum of bread while donating everything else to needy others.[29] But as Aquinas goes on to observe, economic necessity is not merely a matter of biological survival. There is a sense in which things are economically necessary to us to keep with our social station. It would be wrong to give out of what is economically necessary to us in the first sense but permissible to give out of what is necessary to us in the second sense, albeit in due measure.[30] It would, as Aquinas says, be "inordinate to deprive oneself of one's own, in order to give to others to such an extent that the residue would be insufficient for one to live in keeping with one's station and the ordinary occurrences of life: for no man ought to live unbecomingly."[31]

We could cut into this necessity if doing so were to require but a temporary dip in our standard of living or if we were confronted with a case of extreme need on the part of the other. But ordinarily abundance would be defined as whatever we earn that is beyond what is necessary to our station in life. The force of the teaching, though, is that while we might in some circumstances give of what is socially necessary to us, we absolutely should want to part with whatever is surplus to us. If we cling to goods beyond the measure of what is socially necessary, we would be guilty of covetousness, which is a mortal sin, if in doing so we sin against our neighbor.[32] And we would be sinning against our neighbor if people were left in dire want as a result of our own overconsumption.[33]

If there is something of a bright line about the duty to give away what is surplus to us, it would seem we need some account of what is necessary for us to live "becomingly." Aquinas himself points to what he calls our "station in life." The difficulty for us is that Aquinas was appealing to socially determined norms about the distribution of the goods of society for which we have no counterpart. In particular, although there was a trend toward commercialization and urbanization, the medieval economy was relatively static compared with ours.[34] It was an economy still subject to Malthusian rhythms, with prosperity fueling population growth rather than raising standards of living.[35] Market forces were beginning to change the world in which Aquinas lived, but there was still a strong social sense of what constitutes an appropriate standard of living. As Stephen Marglin describes, it was a world in which one's occupation defined one's standard of living rather than a world like ours, in which our standard of living is determined by the income we have at our command.[36]

We might wonder why Aquinas accepted social norms that allowed some persons to live at higher standards of living than others. Why would the high standards of living of the lords not constitute robbery with respect to the many peasants who lived on the margin of survival? Aquinas himself does not say. Presumably it was a world order that seemed natural to him. However, while one would not want to go back to Aquinas's day, it is worth observing that there was some wisdom to those static, if unequal, social norms. In particular, they provided for a social expectation that consumption be capped. If it is not seemly for a baker to wear a purple cloak, the baker in a prosperous year is not going to buy the purple cloak and will instead have surplus funds available to care for the poor.

A consideration of Aquinas's discussion of merchants suggests that such concerns were on his mind. In Aquinas's day, merchants were an emerging social class, and there would have been no well-established norms as to what constituted an appropriate standard of living for them. Insofar as merchants were the driving force for economic and social change, there was reason to be concerned that if no norms could be established for them, that lacuna would tend to erode the sense that anyone was subject to a social expectation that their consumption levels remain capped.[37] When Aquinas takes up the question of whether trading for gain is lawful, he begins by citing a tradition that was hostile to the practice on the grounds that trading for profit is unseemly.[38] Such unqualified critiques sound economically naïve because, in fact, merchants perform a real service to society—namely, bringing goods from places where they are plentiful and delivering them to places where they are scarce. Transportation of the goods, information gathering, and risk taking all produce real economic value, and it would seem just for merchants to expect compensation for their labors.

As it turns out, Aquinas himself is not naïve. In the last paragraph of his response, he makes precisely this point. On such a view, there is no reason to distinguish the occupation of merchant from other occupations. They provide a service. They have a right to earn a living by doing so. Yet before that concession, Thomas cites the line of argument from Aristotle associating merchants with the perversion of the meaning of money discussed in Chapter 5. As Aquinas puts it here, merchants are susceptible to "the greed for gain, which knows no limit and tends to infinity."[39] Merchants in their pursuit of unbounded profits risked diverting the market from its proper end of facilitating the trade of economic goods that the specialization of labor requires. That transition also risked eroding socially prescribed standards of living.

Our difficulty is that while one can see the value of having socially determined norms about what standard of living is sufficient, a social order with such norms lacks social mobility. The merchants may have been trading for profit so they could afford more luxurious clothes, but in retrospect it also seems clear that they were simply trying to climb a social ladder. Indeed, that is probably the main reason to desire more luxurious clothes in the first place. As Adam Smith asks in his *Theory of Moral Sentiments*, "To what purpose is all the toil and bustle of this world? What is the end of avarice and ambition, of the pursuit of wealth, of power, of preeminence? Is it to supply the necessities of nature? The wages of the meanest labourer can supply them." He then goes on to answer his question: "To be observed, to be attended to, to be taken notice of with sympathy, complacency, and approbation, are all the advantages which we can propose to derive from [all the toil and bustle]. It is the vanity, not the ease, or the pleasure which interests us."[40] While it might be a matter of vanity for those pursuing the highest rungs of society, Smith is even more eloquent on the subject of the disregard that attaches to being at the bottom of the socioeconomic ladder. To be in the lowest ranks of income is painful, not so much because one lacks necessary goods but more because of the disrespect that attaches to being at the bottom of society.

In a world with such attitudes, it seems only fair to be in favor of widespread social mobility. The trouble is that insofar as we measure status by income, our mode of pursuing status obliterates Aquinas's bright line about how to understand the proper balance between attending to our needs and to those of our neighbors. In a society where social position is largely determined by income, there is no gap between the income one might happen to generate in the market and the consumption level appropriate to one's station because there is no station. But Aquinas relies on that gap to distinguish between genuine economic need and the abundance that is owed to the poor. We thus have an account of why we, who are so very rich by all global or historical standards, can feel that we have little to spare for others. As our incomes rise, we move into higher classes, and with that comes a higher standard of living that is socially necessary to us to live "becomingly." And even for those of us who are uninterested in climbing the social ladder, the steady rise in standard of living across all classes means that our increases in income are largely absorbed by increases in the "necessary" standard of living.

Thus even if we avoid falling into the faulty relationship with material goods that is so common in the modern world, there will be strong social pressure on us to move our standards of living up along with our incomes, and we will not feel that we have the surplus income that is the likely situation of virtuous consumers. The plight of the genuinely indigent in faraway places will rouse our sense of concern, but we give far less than we might, and I would argue this is largely bound up in the way we translate rising income into rising norms for what is necessary in order to live becomingly, which, in turn, has a good deal to do with the otherwise desirable thought that social mobility is a good thing. Rich as we are, we simply do not feel like we can afford to do right by others.

In modern economic thought, the concept of a standard of living only surfaces in discussions about poverty. Amartya Sen and others have argued that to measure the needs of the poor, we cannot be worried simply about whether their basic physical needs are met; we must also be concerned about their ability to meet the requirements of social decency.[41] But there is no modern vocabulary for invoking standard of living when it comes to defining an upward bound on social norms of consumption.

In the first half of the twentieth century, there was a cluster of women largely employed by home economics departments who developed an economics of consumption. The founding figure of that movement, Hazel Kyrk, set forward a theory of consumption that centered on standards of living.[42] According to Kyrk, humans organize their various economic values into one coherent set of practices, which she calls a "standard of living." These standards, which are socially determined, designate goods that are essential or desirable. From an individual's point of view, the standard of living is as binding a constraint as are price and income because there are social costs to not conforming to it. A drop in the standard of living necessitated by a drop in income is regarded as painful not just because there are fewer goods but because it involves a loss of social status.[43] By contrast, an increase in income is experienced primarily as a decrease in concern about maintaining the essential elements of one's standard of living. Surplus income is regarded as discretionary. A sustained rise in income would allow an individual to adopt a higher standard of living and would afford the increase in social status that comes with it.

On this point, Kyrk provides us with an important point of contact with Aquinas's thought. Her "discretionary income" functions much as Aquinas's "abundance" does in dividing between what is necessary to a person and what is not. Kyrk goes beyond Aquinas, however, by raising the question of how standards of living are formed. She argues that they evolve as individuals with discretionary income experiment with new goods and services. Successful experiments are added into a culture's standard of living. For example, streaming music services like Spotify are a successful experiment, whereas eight-track tapes were not. The rate of change in standards of living depends on whether a society places an irrational premium on custom or novelty; the degree of interaction with other societies; the presence or absence of a scientific spirit; the amount of economic surplus with which experiments can be performed; and the relative absence of rigid social classes, because social fluidity gives more impetus to experimentation.

Kyrk's analysis helps us diagnose the difficulty we have in practicing economic virtue in developed countries. Individuals who seek to restrain their spending might be disposed to allocate their discretionary income to the needs of others, as Aquinas prescribes. In a culture such as ours, however, that values a rising standard of living, gains in economic productivity tend to be translated into rising standards of living. As those standards of living rise, even practitioners of economic virtue will feel socially compelled to raise their own standard of living. This reaction need not be taken as a matter of envy. In the past decade, for example, we have moved to a world in which the social norm is to have a smart phone, and accordingly we all have one more bill to add to our monthly pile, on pain of being regarded as eccentric.

Aquinas, who lived in a society that places a premium on custom and did not have such social mobility, did not contemplate the situation that Christians in the developed world currently face. We may be giving out of our abundance, but our substance entails a standard of living that is very high and cannot be just in a world in which dire poverty is an ongoing problem. Nor is the difficulty likely to abate. As our incomes grow, so too will our sense of what is socially necessary. The absence of an upper cap on our social norms leads us to a situation in which we can have an inconceivably high material standard of living by historical standards yet still find we are unable to exercise proper stewardship of that abundance. Moreover, if global poverty somehow disappears, our ever-rising standards of living put pressure on the environment. And even if we were somehow to find a way to overcome that problem, we would still be trapped in a world in which material concerns consume a great deal more time and energy than would be rational on Aquinas's account.

Although Kyrk herself was not concerned with such difficulties, her theory of consumption offers us one final element that might be of use. In particular, she points out that the fact that standards of living are socially determined does not mean that we cannot bring the spirit of inquiry to bear on the question of what constitutes a desirable standard of living that is commensurate with genuine human flourishing. She argues that it is a mistake to blithely assume that an expensive standard of living is necessarily the most desirable. Although standards of living are not completely irrational, they develop in a haphazard and unexamined fashion. Once we have adopted certain goods and services as necessary, we are no longer free to do without them. Kyrk argues that just because these norms are formed through amorphous social forces, we need not simply take them as given. On the contrary, we can investigate the values that are reflected in the standards of living we adopt, discerning between what genuinely serves a good human life and what does not. Insofar as Aquinas's thought contains the seeds of a compelling theology of consumption, he has something to contribute should we ever launch such conversations.

The rational choice model, which is silent about the ends we pursue, cannot help us with a consideration of how to construct good standards of living.[44] To address that question, we need to exercise practical reason in light of Aquinas's metaphysical framework. There are two ways his framework can point us to a theology of consumption. First, Aquinas's analogical framework and his conception of all goods as ordered to one another and to God can help us to take a holistic approach to decision making. As shown in Chapter 2, the primary focus of modern economic thought is on asking how we can maximize our income, that is, our means, while little attention is paid to the ends economic goods serve. A theology of consumption would refocus our attention on the question of the ends to which economic goods are ordered. From Aquinas, we learn that we are created in the *imago Dei,* and so the question would be how our consumption choices serve that end. The issue would become not whether we should acquire the latest new thing but rather, given our aims, what goods and services would be helpful to achieving those aims.

I once gave a talk on this subject and was confronted with the observation that while dishwashers may not have been strictly necessary it is now inconceivable that we would want to do without them. What is missing from that concern is an argument about what end is served by having a dishwasher, save perhaps the implicit argument that dishwashers are labor-saving devices, and saving labor is intrinsically good. That would be the sort of irrationality to which Tibor Scitovsky alerted us. It sounds like a good argument, but it really is just an argument about efficiency with respect to means. In other words, the dishwasher helps us economize on time. But that invites the question of what we want to use that freed up time for.

The Thomistic approach would be to first ask what the dishwasher is ordered to. If we ask that question, we might encounter the following sorts of considerations. In a family, the labor of preparing a meal and cleaning up after it is a service for our loved ones. We could imagine a mother and one of her children working together to prepare dinner, and a father and another of his children working together to clean up afterward. Doing the dishes would be labor but not labor understood merely as cost. Instead, the activity of dishwashing would be inflected by the fact that it is a shared activity directed toward the well-being of the family. Understood that way, it would be an exercise of virtue, exercising our capacities in an ordered way to achieve an identifiable human good. The ill-considered introduction of a dishwasher into such a situation might serve to shift attitudes toward that time, such that the labor involved becomes viewed as something unpleasant that is to be done as quickly as possible so that the individual members of the family could turn to some unspecified set of activities.

It is entirely possible that the dishwasher could be part of a set of choices that decrease both the sense of community in the family and the sense that labor done for the good of others is valuable of itself.[45] By contrast, we could imagine another family that has chosen to entertain frequently, serving the needs of the larger community by providing gatherings where friends and more distant family can come together and share a meal. In such a family a dishwasher might well promote that end by making it easier to host larger gatherings and might well then be a genuine addition to the good of the family (and the larger community). The question of whether the dishwasher promotes or hinders the flourishing of the household thus depends on what the dishwasher is really ordered to.

The key here is that proper decision making involves looking at goods and services in a larger context, asking what role they play in constructing the shape of our lives. What values are embedded in those goods and services? How are the goods and services ordered to one another in service of genuine human flourishing? Notice how this mode of thinking is suitable to a world that is an analogical reflection of the infinite good. We are to look at the qualities of the various goods for what they are and to order them together into a pattern of life that is coherent. Along with the exercise in prudential reasoning involved in discovering a coherent order of life, there is an aesthetic dimension as well. A well-ordered life is beautiful, because the parts are fittingly arranged so that the deeper meaning of things is preserved. If our decisions are made such that the pieces of our lives fit together to form a harmonious whole, we are exercising prudence.

Rational choice, by contrast, invites us to make our choices in a piecemeal fashion without thinking carefully about how various goods and services fit into the overall pattern of our lives. We can easily end up in a sequence of choices that are irrational taken as a whole. Various kitchen appliances are appealing as conveniences. But then our kitchen is too small to hold all those appliances. So we need to remodel the kitchen or buy a larger house. Perhaps that requires that one of the spouses works overtime. And so on, and so on. If, instead, we consciously order our lives in a harmonious way, we are exercising our particular providence in God's creation, which itself orders things to one another. In general, it would increase the sense of purposeful behavior in an arena of our lives that is too often overtaken by whim or by desires that are not thought through.[46]

A second Thomistic notion relevant to a theology of consumption follows directly upon this. Our modern notion of practical reason understands it as instrumental reason, deliberating about means to reach a given end. Moreover, the means are considered to be interchangeable, or fungible. What matters is the effectiveness with which the means promote the end. If our aim is to maximize utility, the particular means used to achieve that end are a matter of indifference. On this view, life is a series of trade-offs. Would I maximize my utility by buying a dishwasher or by taking a weekend trip to Chicago? In economic jargon, my opportunity cost of buying a dishwasher would be forgoing that weekend trip. Such language creates a sense of scarcity, which, in turn, fuels the notion that more is better.

Aquinas's virtue of prudence likewise centers on reasoning about the means used to achieve ends, but it differs from the rational choice model in important ways. First, it takes the end as given to us (namely, the realization of our creation in the *imago Dei*) rather than as being defined by our unreflective desires. Although the end is given to us, the function of prudence is to discern what that end looks like in the specific circumstances of a given human life. Part of living out our creation in the *imago Dei* is to become virtuous human beings, but that leaves open the question of what a virtuous response to various situations entails. This leads to the second point, which is that the means cannot be understood apart from the end. The path toward virtue is simply the practice of virtue. Because of the particularities involved in each individual life, virtuous practices cannot be set down as some sort of code to be followed. Virtuous practice involves discernment of the order of things, discernment of oneself, and a judgment of how to fit one to the other. Under the economic model of practical reason, the means are fungible because all that matters is whether they most efficiently move us toward the end. By contrast, under Aquinas's understanding of prudence, the means themselves are part of the end.[47]

Thus we have some key contrasts. Economic logic is a matter of calculation, whereas prudence is a matter of discernment. Economic logic lends itself to choices made in piecemeal fashion, whereas prudence judges how the particulars fit into the overall pattern of a virtuous life. Economic logic sees goods as fungible and measures them by the single metric of utility, whereas prudence respects the qualitative differences of goods, fitting those diverse goods into an orderly and harmonious pattern. Economic logic sees choice as a matter of trade-offs, whereas prudence sees choice as being more like the artist's discernment that painting a central figure with a blue robe rather than a red robe better fits the overall meaning and mood of the painting. One could choose to think of the choice to marry one's spouse as a trade-off against the possibility of having married someone else. But a marriage is more likely to work if one recognizes that one's spouse is a fitting partner in life. Prudence thus invites us to appreciate our finitude and sink into the life choices that we make.

Not surprisingly, Aquinas's understanding of the virtue of prudence harmonizes with his understanding of the nature of God's creation.

Recall that God represents himself in a finite world by using the qualitative differences in individual goods as a way of representing his superabundant goodness and by ordering those heterogeneous goods harmoniously as a way of representing his oneness. In exercising prudence, we enter into a pattern of thinking that respects the diversity of goods and the unity expressed by their proper ordering. In seeing that order and acting on it, we move to conform ourselves to the *imago Dei.*

In doing so we not only become more virtuous, exercising human reason to its fullest, we also end up with a bounded set of desires. As presented in Chapter 5, to see material goods as ordered to particular ends is to let those ends serve as a measure of the material goods that we need. But that boundedness of desire is exactly what can serve to help us to distinguish between what is necessary to us and what is superfluous. Indeed, it can help us better discern cases where the pressing needs of others might require that we give up some genuine goods. Concern for others is part of the good that we seek in the pattern of our lives, and it is the development of wisdom that can help us judge when our own excellence is best pursued by genuine sacrifice.

Finally, because we are inherently social creatures, the effort to discern and achieve a rational standard of living cannot be undertaken in isolation. If my neighbor's children have limousines to take them to the prom, it will be hard to resist paying for limousines for my children. The virtuous consumer who does not find a community to support his desire to resist ever-rising standards of living will face trade-offs between making his surplus available to those in need and the requirement that he spend more and more to meet the socially accepted standard of living.[48]

Thus far I have been focusing on the question of almsgiving. How do we know how much of our income is due to others? Yet most theologians writing about economics are worried less about whether the rich are sufficiently charitable than about whether the economic system as a whole is just. As it turns out, the principle of having a bounded sense of economic need, and a standard of living that is correspondingly capped, is essential to the subject of just prices and wages that Aquinas also takes up. To that topic I now turn.

Standard of Living and Economic Justice

In *Deus caritas est,* Pope Benedict XVI responds to those who argue that the poor are better served by calls for social justice than by the exercise of charity, arguing that *caritas* (charity) would be necessary even in the most just society.[49] Benedict makes this observation in response to those who object to the Church's focus on charitable work, fearing that it is "in effect a way for the rich to shirk their obligation to work for justice and a means of soothing their consciences, while preserving their own status and robbing the poor of their rights."[50] Indeed, this concern was voiced by Pope Paul VI in his encyclical *Quaregesimo anno.*[51] Daniel C. Maguire, a contemporary moral theologian, gives voice to the concern that Catholics are "distracted by charity to the neglect of justice."[52] According to Maguire, Catholic thought treats justice as an inferior virtue that is concerned only with the "materialities of relationships."[53] Moreover, Maguire associates the American Catholic conception of justice with what he dubs "American justice," which he finds inadequate to the biblical concept of justice. Among other things, Maguire's American justice makes no special provision for the poor and the marginalized; is blind to systemic injustice; overemphasizes the individual at the expense of a more communitarian view; is premised on an overvaluation of material and economic success; and is, therefore, too conservative and too dispassionate.[54]

Maguire views charitable giving as an inadequate response to the plight of the materially impoverished.[55] Because he frames this question in terms of the American understanding of justice, his concerns are well taken. In particular, what Maguire might have in mind is the role charitable giving would play in a world described by the values that undergird modern economic analysis. As discussed in Chapter 2, economists can easily accommodate charitable giving in their models of consumer behavior.

In principle, an individual's utility can be a function of anything: one's own consumption, the consumption of others, abstract goods like a sense of justice, and so on. Nonetheless, charity, or almsgiving, is marginalized in this model. The central focus of the model is on the individual's efforts to secure her own happiness. Almsgiving will be chosen only to the extent that the individual's subjective happiness depends on the well-being of others. And even then, it will only be chosen if the utility function is configured such that giving to others generates more subjective happiness for the individual than spending the money on herself. Thus while individuals can certainly choose to give to charity, it is a choice that is made at the discretion of the giver. And while it is universally assumed that a person's subjective happiness is necessarily enhanced by greater personal consumption, it is only granted as a possibility that for some individuals subjective happiness is enhanced by giving to others.

If we incorporate the points developed in this chapter, charitable giving would seem to be an even less adequate response to the poor. To the extent that individuals in our culture take it for granted that higher consumption levels are always desirable, there would be a systematic tendency for them to overweight their own consumption in their utility functions. Even for those who actively want to strike a better balance between their own consumption and almsgiving, the ever-rising standard of living would act as a constraint on how much they could give without experiencing some sense of sacrifice. Moreover, in a culture with a Lockean sense of property rights (in the possessive sense described by C. B. MacPherson), forcing the poor to rely on almsgiving would seem to undercut their human dignity in important ways.

Were Thomas's framework on private property and right relationship to material goods to be widely adopted, many of Maguire's concerns would be lessened. Thomas's teachings on private property straddle the subjects of charity and justice. His discussion of almsgiving does, indeed, appear in the treatise on charity, but his discussion of private property, with its stricture that we must stand ready to give our surplus income to those in need, appears in the treatise on justice.[56] In addition, almsgiving being anything but a purely optional matter, Aquinas's teachings, properly followed, would free up income for charitable donations. Individuals with a right relationship to material goods would not experience a sense of sacrifice in giving to others, especially if they were part of communities that had consciously engaged the question of what constitutes a genuinely good standard of living, such that the socially required forms of spending were more restrained.

More deeply, a culture formed around a Thomistic understanding of the proper role of material goods would find it easier to pursue the sort of justice Maguire calls for. Maguire is concerned that we cannot rely on charitable giving to meaningfully improve the lives of others because our culture is too individualistic. Yet if that is so, why are we not also too individualistic to resist the call to energetically work to restore social justice? If we can prophetically persuade people to work for social justice, could we not also prophetically persuade them to be more generous with their surplus wealth? If there were no prior restraint in our conception of what we need, such justice would demand the same sort of sacrifice that almsgiving currently demands. That sacrifice would take the form of our expenditure of effort to bring about social justice; the likely necessity of reducing our own claims on material goods (if we are rich) in the new social order; and any material losses to society as a whole that would result, to the extent that efficiency is undermined by the effort to achieve greater equity.[57] To call for the primacy of justice in a world of people who are only capable of exercising the weakest form of almsgiving is likely to be an exercise in futility. You might well get one political party arguing for higher taxes on the rich and a corresponding expansion of programs for the poor. What you will not get is a political party arguing for the taxes on the broad middle class that would be necessary to actually sustain such policies.

To understand why it is difficult for us to move toward a genuine economic justice, we must first understand what the obstacles are. The obstacles largely reside in the fact that we do not have a proper account of the role material goods can and should play in a life well lived. On the one hand, we are tempted by the logic of the maximization that leads us into thinking that more goods will somehow facilitate our realization of our highest ends. On the other hand, our society links status with economic wealth and thus makes it difficult for us to discern the gap between the income we possess and the material goods we genuinely need to live well. In both cases, the argument would imply that part of our discourse about economic justice should be a prior discourse about the role economic goods genuinely play in a life well lived. In other words, we need to act through the cultural space in which these social norms are set, at least as much as we need to work through the political space (if not more.) We can and should have conversations about what it really takes to live becomingly. We can and should have conversations about whether there are ways to delink social status from income. In other words, we should pursue economic justice through both political and cultural conversion. But as we move onto those sorts of questions, it is helpful to step back and ask a further question, namely, to what extent is our conception of economic justice itself distorted by our distorted understanding of the proper role of material goods in a life well lived?

When we bring up concerns about economic justice, there are a variety of concerns we might have in mind. We might be worried about the plight of the poor. We might be worried that workers are paid unjustly for their labors. We might be worried that the distribution of income or wealth is too concentrated. Obviously the theme is too vast for me to tackle here. But I do want to raise the concern that we are too apt to think about these issues in terms of material goods and too little apt to think about the goods that are really important. Furthermore, our tendency to talk about the problems of economic justice in material terms might make it even more difficult for us to put material goods back into their proper place as instrumental goods, the need for which is properly bounded. My basic principle for beginning to think about these questions is simply that when we think about economic justice in its various facets, we need to think more in terms of the ends material goods are meant to serve and less in terms of the material goods themselves.

Since economic inequality has become the hot topic, and because it is in many ways the most problematic of the concerns about economic justice, I use that subject to illustrate the point. Over the past several decades there has been a noticeable increase in the concentration of both wealth and income.[58] This is true not just of America but of most of the developed world as well. The Organization for Economic Cooperation and Development has recently informed us that the eighty-five wealthiest individuals together own as much wealth as the poorest 50 percent of the world population—a staggering figure.[59] For the most part, conversation in America revolves around our own income distribution, with increasing worry about the 1 percent or the rise of the plutocrats.[60] To be clear, I think rising income inequality represents a real danger to our society. But by definition, the entire conversation about income distribution is conducted in terms of material goods, and as I have been arguing, material goods are only instrumental. So we need to ask what real goods are under threat by the rise in income inequality.

The analogy between wealth and medicine should give us pause as we think about income inequality. If we are already very wealthy, is there not a danger that we resent the wealthiest of the very wealthy for having ten blood pressure pills a day, vastly more than the four we have to make do with, all ignoring the fact that nobody needs more than two?[61] Around the web it is hard to avoid click-bait articles about the multimillion-dollar homes of the rich and famous, homes that boast every luxurious feature one could imagine and then some. But are we really to envy Bill Gates or resent him for rattling around in his 66,000-square-foot house? What about the rich man whose downstairs bar has an underwater view of his pool? Properly understood, these are manifestations of a disordered relationship with material goods, and as such such people are to be pitied rather more than envied or resented. That said, there are real reasons to be worried about increasing income inequality.

First, quite simply, our concern about the excessive wealth of the few simply reinforces our idea that money is what matters most. Second, there is a real reason to be worried that the high concentration of wealth threatens our democracy. In addition to concerns about whether campaign finance delivers disproportional political influence to the very wealthy, there are problems with the symbiotic relationship between Wall Street and Washington and the deployment of regulations and tax codes to the benefit of the well connected. As Luigi Zingales observes, the returns to lobbying are quite high, and so we can expect a further deployment of business resources to the business of manipulating Washington, which not incidentally is the one big boomtown in our country these days.[62] The corrosive effect of this on our polity should concern us all. Third, there is some reason to worry that an excessively unequal distribution of income is destabilizing to the economy as a whole.[63] The last time income distribution in the United States was this skewed was in the late 1920s, right before the Great Depression.

Finally, increasing income inequality both reflects and contributes to the increasing economic segregation that we are seeing in our country, and this creates a multitude of disturbing social dynamics. As the rich retreat to their own enclaves, the problems discussed above with respect to standard of living simply become more pronounced. The rich who live in such enclaves give a smaller portion of their wealth to charity than do the rich who live in more economically mixed neighborhoods.[64] Why? The analysis about the social formation of standards of living suggests an answer: if everyone around you is quite wealthy, there will be a tendency to think it is socially necessary to live at a higher standard of living. The rich in mixed communities feel a sufficiency of wealth because their standard of living is probably already elevated relative to the people around them. Worse, by segregating themselves this way, the rich cease to play the more constructive communal roles they may have once played. Robert Putnam illustrates this with a poignant account of the loss of communal support for disadvantaged youths in a small town as a result in the changing economic structures. In decades past, if there was a promising boy from a poor family, money would materialize from wealthier members of the community to help get him to college, for example. As we segregate economically, those opportunities for financial assistance or simple mentoring begin to evaporate, and it can be harder for the poor who are left behind to find opportunities.[65]

Social networks matter, and we are letting money create barriers between the economic classes, barriers that break down those networks. Would policies that redistribute income help here? They would not hurt. But the real ailment may be more pernicious—this breakdown of community and the use of material goods to build a new barrier between the classes—and it is that cultural shift that is problematic. As long as we frame the issue as a question of whether everyone has an equal shot at getting to the place where they can fly first class, we will fail to ask the harder question about whether we want to be the sort of society where a few get to board an airplane from a red carpet with much personal attention while the masses wait their turn to be herded into the cattle cars in the rear.

The danger, then, of our talk about income inequality is that it will just reinforce our idea that money is what matters and that the real problem with poverty is that it might diminish the opportunity of some to reach for the brass ring themselves. There is nothing wrong with the idea that all people, no matter what their families' economic status, should have the opportunity to enter into the niche of the economy that will allow them to best exercise their talents on behalf of the community. The poor girl with the right set of skills should be able to become a neurosurgeon. But with that mindset we will continue to think of success as a matter of getting into the right occupations with the right level of income. What does that do for the boy whose dream is to be a really good first-grade teacher? What does that do for the dignity of the person who contributes to the community by taking on the highly unpleasant and even dangerous occupation of being a sewer worker?[66]

Shortly after my conversion to Catholicism, I came to know Hector, who was one of the prominent members of my parish. As it turns out, he was also a gardener at the college where I worked. Until then, I had thoughtlessly paid no mind to the gardeners and janitors who worked hard to maintain a beautiful campus. I simply failed to value work that has little status in our society. Programs to enhance labor mobility for Hector's children will not address the situation of the gardeners and janitors of the future—who will continue to provide invaluable services to us all. But as I came to know Hector, I came to realize that economic and social status is a very poor measure of a person's worth. Hector was a wise leader of our parish community. Surely the Christian call to deal with poverty extends to the demand that we recognize the value of what people do apart from the incomes they happen to earn by doing it. Yes, we can pay gardeners more. But a big part of what matters is the respect we accord them and the cultivation of our ability to see the wealth—which is the true sort of wealth—that the poor have to offer us.

These are just a few examples of what it means to think about economic justice by first thinking about the role of economic goods in a life well lived. We do not have to distribute status and respect according to the market's distribution of income. We do not have to value people by what they have or what they do not have. The call to think about the role of economic goods in a life well lived is a call to think about what really matters. In doing so we could perhaps begin to free ourselves from the materialism of our culture, and in becoming so liberated we might well find that we indeed enjoy an abundance of material wealth such that we can address the burdens of poverty that are directly related to material lack. Meanwhile we could begin to open up the prospect of being enriched by drawing into community those who are wealthy in other ways but marginalized because of our overemphasis on money. We could notice that the lives of the money-obsessed are often quite impoverished in the goods that really matter. The call for economic justice is deeply rooted in the Christian tradition. But to fully answer that call we have to come into right relationship with material goods themselves. If we cannot do that, we will remain spiritually impoverished and correspondingly unable to answer the call of the materially poor.

In addition to providing a framework that urges us to think through broad questions about economic justice in light of the higher goods material wealth is meant to serve, Aquinas explicitly calls for justice in our individual transactions, notably, arguing that prices should be just. Aquinas thus does lay out some principles that belong to the question of economic justice in the sense Maguire seems to mean. In the case of that argument, however, we can see that the principle that prices should be just still turns on the question of an appropriate standard of living. In his discussion of just prices, Aquinas does not explicitly discuss just wages, but the two are directly connected. As Joan Robinson argues, the medieval concept of a just price is closely related to the economic concept of a long-run price, which, in turn, should reflect the costs of the factors of production, including wages.[67] To pay a just price for a shirt, say, requires that one pay enough so that the weavers can earn a just wage. But what is a just wage? Surely, the just wage is what is sufficient to maintain the weaver at an appropriate standard of living. To the extent that our own income is the result of paying prices that are insufficient to maintain producers at an appropriate standard of living, and to the extent that we hire workers directly at less than a just wage, we violate the principles of economic justice.

But to come to an assessment of how justice plays out in these transactions we must have a sense of what would constitute an appropriate standard of living for the people we interact with, since that is the crucial determinant in what constitutes a just price or wage. Furthermore, our willingness and ability to pay a just price or wage would have a good deal to do with what sort of standard of living is justly appropriate to us. If I have a surplus of income as compared with the economic requirements of my station in life, I can have no excuse for paying workers the market wage rate if that wage is unjust in the sense that the workers could not maintain a just standard of living at that wage rate. On the other hand, if I have no such surplus, my response to a situation in which market wages seem to deliver a standard of living that is unjustly low to the people I hire (either directly or indirectly) would require a rethinking of what the relative standards of living should be, given that the market is signaling that we cannot afford to let everyone achieve the standard of living that is deemed socially just.

This raises the question of how we should think about relative standards of living. Aquinas simply accepted the socially determined standards of living as his benchmark for how individuals should practice economic justice; accordingly, he offers us no tools for thinking about whether those socially determined standards of living are themselves just. I find Hazel Kyrk's argument that we should not let the socially determined nature of standards of living prevent us from bringing a spirit of inquiry into what constitutes a compelling standard. There is not any obvious reason to think that such standards should be resolutely egalitarian. As Aquinas does observe, the question of how the goods of a community should be distributed will reflect the values of that community.[68] There is reason to think, for example, that a doctor who has spent years in school accumulating the knowledge and experience required to practice medicine well deserves a higher standard of living as a way of marking practitioners' special contributions to the community. Our conversations about appropriate standards of living would have to include a conversation about such distinctions and the extent to which they reflect communal judgments about the relative contributions of individual members of society. The point is that we cannot really begin a discussion of economic justice without thinking through the question of appropriate standards of living, which, in turn, requires clear thinking about the role material goods play in a human life well lived. Without appeal to that question, it is not clear what would ground our conception of what constitutes economic justice in the first place.

To give a complete account of economic justice would be a complex task. For Aquinas, economic justice hinges on a prior account of how material goods should be properly ordered to a life well lived. That is to say, if we are to understand what an ideal of economic justice would look like, it would be based on and would reflect a pattern of virtuous consumption. Of course, we do not live in a world in which such virtuous consumption is common. In our world, economists' models seem to be more accurate in predicting the response of individuals to various economic policies and the consequent social impact of such policies. This raises a series of difficult questions of how to integrate a science built around the analysis of humans "as they are" and a framework ordered around what humans are meant to be. The concluding chapter takes up this subject.

7

Toward a Humane Economy

A Pragmatic Approach

Aquinas's framework offers us a vision of what a humane economy would look like. Virtuous individuals would have a proper relationship with material wealth, ordering them to higher, more fully human goods, and would have a clear sense of how much was enough. Because their demand for natural wealth would be satiable, they would be able to identify income above the level they need as surplus and would be able to generously make that surplus available to others. Indeed, they would not experience such altruism as coming at their own expense. Because their own desire for wealth would be satiable, it would be easier for them to vote for taxes to support public programs aimed at promoting the common good. Because they understand their fulfillment as coming from leading lives that reflect God's ultimate goodness, they would be in a position to draw more genuine satisfaction out of the natural wealth with which they are blessed. Being free from the relentless pressure to raise their incomes, they would have more time to attend to their families, cultivate their relationships with friends and neighbors, and pursue higher goods.

Virtuous firms would see their main goal as provisioning goods and services that are of real value to their community and as opportunities to exercise their own creativity and skill. Such firms would use prices and profits as signals about how to best direct their efforts. Because their aim would not be to maximize profits, they would more often be in a position to offer fair wages to their employees. They would view customers as fellow humans to be served, not as wallets to be emptied, and would accordingly be less likely to produce shoddy goods or to pressure or persuade customers into buying goods and services they do not genuinely want or need. In short, the economy would be in service of human life.

In such a world, private property would be a useful institution. It would assign to owners the finite slice of creation that is their special responsibility, allowing them the chance to become expert about how best to cultivate the resources at their command. Aquinas's framework thus affirms economists' intuition about the value of specialization. In such a world, markets would play a valuable role in coordinating economic activity. Money would be a useful instrument for facilitating trade, but it would never be pursued as an end in itself. Financial services allowing people to make trades across time and to allocate risk would play a suitable role but would be immune to the temptation to trade for profit at the expense of destabilizing the system. The health of the economy would be measured in terms of genuine human flourishing and its ability to serve the community.

That all sounds wonderful. It is also, frankly, a utopian vision of what economic life could be. In the world we inhabit, the disordered relationship with wealth is ubiquitous and almost impossible to escape. Even virtuous consumers face social pressure to steadily raise their sense of how much would be enough, a phenomenon so pervasive that many if not most people in our astonishingly affluent society feel economically strapped.[1] Virtuous firms are pressured by the demands of stockholders to maximize profits, forcing them to face difficult choices about how to balance the demand for more profits with the impetus to provide good products to customers who actually need them and to offer just wages to their employees.[2] And, of course, there are many individuals and firms that do not have a virtuous relationship with natural wealth and who accordingly pursue happiness as though it were an exercise in constrained maximization, such that the overriding imperative is to loosen those constraints by raising income. The resulting pressure for sustained economic growth and rising living standards pressures the environment and makes genuine economic justice difficult to achieve.

If Aquinas is right about human nature, it is also wasteful. Economists have long warned laypeople against the mistake of assuming that a country rich in resources must necessarily be rich. What matters, they will say, is whether the country can efficiently convert those resources into income. But a similar warning should be made against the mistake of assuming that a country rich in income must necessarily be flourishing. That income needs to be well spent in order to support genuine flourishing, and too much of our consumer culture is devoted to spending aimed at pursuing illusory goods that leave us feeling vaguely dissatisfied.[3]

Nonetheless, this is the world we inhabit, and it might be difficult to see how the Thomistic framework is actually useful. We seem to have foundered on the problem that animated the first chapter. Theological economics can deliver a compelling vision of what our economy should look like, but its vision depends on an account of human nature as it should be. For theological economics to be relevant, it would need to grapple with a more realistic appraisal of human nature as it is, such as the one provided by economists. As it turns out, the Thomistic approach to economics contains resources for integrating the best insights of modern-day economics into a more comprehensive account. Indeed, I argue that the pragmatic value of modern economic analysis would be enhanced if it were understood in light of the more comprehensive account of human life such as the one offered by Aquinas. So what would an economics informed by Thomistic principles look like?

The Value of Economic Analysis

As discussed in Chapter 1, a good theological approach to economics needs to incorporate useful features of modern economic analysis while maintaining a critical stance. The approach developed in this book does this by embedding modern economic analysis within Aquinas's more comprehensive framework. As it turns out, the economic analysis of the impact of incentives on human behavior is valuable, provided we are clear about the ends that are thereby served and the limitations such analysis has. Indeed, the tools provided by economists are indispensable for anyone interested in pursuing economic justice or working to alleviate poverty.

As discussed below, Aquinas's own framework does not neatly follow the distinction economists would make between positive and normative economics. However, he is certainly interested in realistic descriptions of humans as they are. Indeed, as discussed in Chapters 3 and 4, Aquinas's own account of human behavior anticipates the findings of modern-day economists. People often act out of the lower form of reason that we share with animals and thus can be reasonably well described as responding to incentives in generally predictable ways. So a Thomistic economics would make use of positive economic analysis, which can help us think through the implications of the fact that humans often act to maximize subject to constraint.

But we need to ask what ends are served by developing predictive models of human behavior. Much modern economic analysis is tacitly written for policy makers, who can use economic analysis to determine how best to achieve desirable social goals. The key contribution of economics is an understanding of unintended consequences. Well-intentioned legislation can often be counterproductive if it creates incentives that induce behavior that undermines the efficacy of the policy. Thus, for example, one might think that one way of ensuring affordable housing for the poor is to impose rent controls. But economic analysis suggests that if rents are legally set below the market-clearing level, there will be a shortage of housing, and in the long run the housing stock might deteriorate because landlords would no longer have an incentive to maintain or improve properties when they cannot be compensated through higher rents. As a result, such policies might well make affordable housing even less available to the poor. Such conclusions are not meant to argue against the intentions of such policies. Rather, they are an invitation to find other approaches that will achieve the desired goal more effectively. In addition, economic analysis provides the best tools available for thinking about the stability of the monetary system and the maintenance of full employment.[4]

Aquinas's framework can accommodate economists' instincts about the value of positive economic analysis at least to a first approximation. His conception of the aim of lawmaking differs from ours. Not surprisingly, he believes that law is properly ordered to the happiness of the community, with happiness understood primarily as the cultivation of virtue.[5] That said, Aquinas also argues that the law must be useful. Insofar as many if not most citizens are not virtuous or even engaged in the project of cultivating virtue, the legislator should craft laws with the end of establishing peace and promoting general well-being.[6] The result is a vision of law as having a complex twofold character. Its ultimate aim is to promote genuine happiness in the form of the cultivation of virtue, but it must balance that concern with a pragmatic insistence that necessary lower goods be secured. Thus, for example, Aquinas suggests that a wise lawgiver would not legally mandate all acts of virtue, since law must meet people where they are. Instead, the lawgiver should prudently outlaw such vices as would undermine peace and the common good.[7]

Although Aquinas wrote before the concept of unintended consequences was well developed, his pragmatic conception of the law can be extended to benefit from modern economic analysis. Insofar as much human behavior is, in fact, shaped by incentives, economic analysis of the consequences of incentives should inform policy. It is not enough for a lawgiver to have good intentions. For example, one could conclude that economic justice requires that everyone receive a minimum wage of fifteen dollars an hour for their labor. But if we live in a world where such a law would cause many employers to reduce the number of workers hired, such a policy might end up harming more of the working poor than would be helped by such a law. This particular question is the subject of lively debate among economists. The point here is simply that good objective economic analysis has an important role to play in helping the virtuous lawgiver to craft good law.[8]

Modern economic analysis is particularly valuable in debates about government regulation of markets. As discussed in Chapter 1, economists have a well-developed apparatus for thinking through both market and governmental failures. Economic analysis in principle can handle both firms that narrowly seek profits without regard for the negative impact their actions might have on others and those that also aim to serve the common good through just practices. Likewise, it has the tools for describing governmental decisions that aim at the common good as well as those that are undertaken out of the narrow self-interest of legislators. It thus resists ideological attempts to characterize markets as bad (or good) and government as good (or bad). Although individual economists often have pronounced political leanings, the analytical tools economists use can be employed for a clear-eyed assessment of both the strengths and weaknesses of human behavior in both the private and the public sectors. It thus serves as a steady reminder that public policy debates should be about effective means of achieving good goals rather than about shoring up ideological attachment to one set of means over another regardless of their suitability to a given place and time.

The Thomistic framework thus has room to accommodate many of the best insights on offer from economics. That said, the Thomistic framework also identifies the limitations of economic analysis. In particular, Aquinas's account of human nature suggests that although we often make decisions based on the lower form of rationality we share with animals, we also can and sometimes do base decisions on the higher form of rationality that is proper to human beings. This distinction has implications both for positive economics and for public policy analysis.

With respect to positive economics, insofar as the goal of economists is to generate models that predict human behavior, they would do well to add some insights from Aquinas's teachings about the nature of reason to their tool kit. In particular, human choices depend on the discernment individuals make about what sort of goods they perceive, which means that economists need to find a way to capture the qualitative distinctiveness of goods. We have already seen one example where this matters. When policy makers following economists' advice offer incentives to induce certain types of behavior, they sometimes inadvertently change the way individuals perceive the good in question and can end up with perverse results. To see something as a social obligation, for example, is different from seeing something as a commodity, as in the case of the Israeli day care centers. The protracted debate about how to explain the "wasteful" practice of gift giving is another. Economists' insistence on using mathematical models carries with it a strong preference for denying that there are qualitatively important differences between goods and blinds them to important features of human life and human decision making.

At least one economist, the Nobel laureate Gary Becker, actively argues that we should ignore those qualitative differences. In a piece setting out his agenda, Becker describes the economic approach as a way of thinking that uses the "combined assumption of maximizing behavior, market equilibrium and stable preferences" "relentlessly and unflinchingly" and argues that it "provides a valuable unified framework for understanding *all* human behavior."[9] Among the examples of this approach Becker gives are suicide and marriage. On suicide, Becker argues that we should see that nearly all deaths as suicides, because most deaths could be postponed if we made different choices (buckling up, eating better, spending more on medicine). Indeed, he says that we should question the common distinction between natural deaths and suicides.[10] On marriage, Becker argues that it is a matter of calculation of utility such that a marriage is contracted when the two parties believe they can raise their respective utilities by marrying and is dissolved when one of the two parties believes she can raise her utility more by divorcing than by accepting whatever bribe her spouse might offer her to induce her to stay in the marriage.[11]

While the Thomistic framework certainly has room for a consideration of the effects incentives have on human choices, including choices such as the ones Becker describes, it also strongly suggests that the economic approach can only be partial and incomplete. A suicide prevention center that could not distinguish between an active desire to die and a willingness to make choices that are not ordered to prolonging life indefinitely would not be very helpful to people; and an account of marriage as a transaction seems incapable of getting at more traditional understandings of marriage with a corresponding loss in ability to explain human behavior.[12]

Fortunately, the growing field of behavioral economics is making more room for accounting for the importance social norms can have on behavior, and that work is being taken into account by policy makers. For example, in trying to predict the impact of the Affordable Care Act on the budget and on the number of uninsured in the country, the Congressional Budget Office was aware of the difficulty of predicting the impact of the mandate on individual behavior. The mandate that all individuals purchase health care is necessary if the law is to require insurers to insure individuals with preexisting conditions.[13] In its models, the office is taking into account the difference it might make if people view the mandate as a tax or a fine. If it is viewed as a fine that in some sense is punitive, people might be more likely to get insurance for a given fine level than they might be if they perceive the mandate instead as an optional tax. What matters is whether or not the mandate is perceived as a social obligation. If it ends up being perceived as an optional tax, it is less likely to be effective, since the mandate is much cheaper than getting the actual insurance, and as the law is written a rational agent would not buy the insurance but rather would just pay the tax, with potentially disastrous consequences for the efficacy of the law.[14]

From a Thomistic point of view, good policy requires attention to the fact that while humans often act out of the lower form of reason that can be manipulated through incentives, they also sometimes, and perhaps even often, act out of the higher form of reason that discerns which goods are genuinely worthy of pursuit. That the deployment of incentives can lead individuals to reframe a choice in terms of the lower form of reason needs to be taken into account as we consider our policy options. As it happens, economists are increasingly aware that good policy needs to think about the dual effect of incentives.[15] In his recent book, *The Moral Economy: Why Good Incentives Are No Substitute for Good Citizens*, Samuel Bowles takes up the challenge posed by research that suggests that policies that "incentivize" desired behavior might end up having counterintuitive results to the extent that the introduction of incentives might undermine social norms that promote that behavior.[16] He argues that a truly wise policy maker needs to consider the impact incentives have on norms to determine the best policy for achieving desired ends. This sort of research corresponds to Aquinas's two-tiered account of human nature and thus represents an encouraging convergence. That said, Bowles constructs the problem entirely in terms of thinking about how policy makers can achieve good outcomes by balancing the effects of incentives on behavior with the effects of changing norms on behavior.

This leads to a more hidden, but also more pernicious, limitation of economic analysis. It tends to think of human agents as objects to be manipulated rather than as human beings who can be addressed. Economists' default mode of speech is to address policy makers about the various options they face, while the policy makers themselves are thought of as manipulating incentives to induce behavior and outcomes they deem as desirable. Human beings themselves thus become objects rather than subjects. To address this problem, we need to think harder about the purpose of economic study and especially about the distinction between positive and normative economics.

The Limitations and Liabilities of Economics from a Thomistic Perspective

Granting that economic analysis is valuable insofar as it describes humans as they are at least reasonably well, there are reasons to be wary of economists' deployment of their central model. As we have already seen, the rational choice model is limited to a consideration of the form of reason that we share with animals and thus is not equipped to model the distinctively human form of practical reason. In addition, the rational choice model contains a dangerous temptation to think of the human end as an indefinite progression up a ladder of successively better goods, which for Aquinas would entail renouncing the possibility of ordering our diverse activities in a coherent way. And finally, the rational choice model emphasizes the satisfaction of preferences rather than objective progress toward happiness.

How we think about the relationship between economists' models of human behavior and that of Aquinas depends on which overarching framework we adopt. Because Aquinas places such emphasis on purposive behavior and the importance of thinking about how goods are ordered to one another, we need to ask, What is the purpose of engaging in an inquiry into human nature in the first place? Not surprisingly, Aquinas is pursuing a different sort of project than are economists, and this has bearing on how we should ask the question of the value of the rational choice model from a Thomistic perspective. So we need to ask two further questions: How is the rational choice model counterproductive with respect to the goals Aquinas is pursuing? Does the Thomistic framework offer any suggestions about the value of the rational choice model with respect to the ends economists are pursuing?

What Is the Purpose of Studying Human Nature?

In Aquinas's framework, all human action is done for a purpose, and we need to first ask what purpose is served by developing a model of human action. For economists, the putative purpose of the rational choice model is to describe or predict human behavior, as an exercise of a value-free inquiry into the nature of human beings. Aquinas's account of human behavior is likewise meant to be a description of humans as they are, but it is not intended to be predictive of human behavior. The reason for that difference lies in the ultimate end of the two practices.

Although economists see themselves as generating knowledge for its own sake, the prestige of the discipline is tied up with their ability to offer advice to policy makers on how to regulate markets to pursue various goals.[17] As Daniel Hausman has argued, the goal of controlling the economy is often used as a justification for the instrumental approach to economics exemplified by Milton Friedman's methodology described earlier in this book.[18] Indeed, that a given line of inquiry cannot issue in palatable policy prescriptions is frequently offered as a reason to abandon that line of inquiry.[19] The emphasis on policy prescription results in what I have elsewhere called the "control stance" economists take with respect to their subject matter. By that I mean that economists see themselves as analytically separate from the world they describe and think largely in terms of how agents within their models can be manipulated by shifting around incentives.[20] Note that the control stance is consonant with the rational choice model, which stresses that aspect of reason that we share with animals and is subject to manipulation through incentives. The emphasis on policy making explains why the ability of a given model to predict behavior is held to be a premium in economic research (beyond the function of simple empiricism).

Aquinas, of course, is not addressing an audience of potential policy makers. In the prologue to the *Summa theologica,* he says his intent in writing is to offer a better introduction to theological science than was then available. It is meant for the "instruction of beginners."[21] Aquinas's target audience was young Dominicans studying for the priesthood, and the immediate need for a coherent theological treatment was for priests to offer parishioners practical guidance. Aquinas's intent was to place moral theology within a comprehensive theological framework.[22] Thus his treatment of human nature has an inescapable practical component, and it was treated as such by his audience.

Aquinas was writing before we had adopted the idea that science proceeds through the accumulation of empirical data. But it should be noted that an empirically minded Thomist today would not approach data the way economists might, for the simple reason that on Aquinas's view human nature is understood as a potential to be actualized. Not all humans have exercised their capacities, and so, empirically speaking, we would expect to find humans at varying stages in the development of virtue. Evidence that most people lack a given virtue would not count as evidence that the virtue in question was not a potential of our human nature and desirable. This is not to say that there is no room for deliberation about people as they are. Although for Aquinas revelation assists us in discerning the truth about human nature, much of his virtue theory draws on the philosopher Aristotle, who offers knowledge drawn on observation of the world and reflection on its ways. A modern Thomist's reflections could surely be informed by what we learn from social sciences. But there would be no impetus for research projects aimed at using Thomistic models to predict human behavior because that is not the purpose of Thomistic thought. The aim is not to arm policy makers with data about how best to manipulate populations to achieve desired results.

From a Thomistic point of view, the knowledge offered by his inquiry is first and foremost intended to draw us into a better understanding of God. But secondarily it is to illuminate our path toward becoming what we are meant to become. It is knowledge that is meant to motivate us because that is the kind of knowledge it is. All humans are endowed with a desire to be happy, and a discussion about human happiness presents us with the practical question of what we will do in relationship to that knowledge.[23] But from a Thomistic point of view, *any* discussion of the project of pursuing human happiness would have a practical component in a similar way. If economists propose a model describing humans as pursuing their ends by maximizing utility, then economists are inviting us to pursue our ends by maximizing utility. And this is where the substance of Thomistic objections against economics would lie. From a

Thomistic point of view, the rational choice model is not a good model for how to pursue one's ends for reasons discussed immediately below.

Economists might object that they do not intend their model to be prescriptive and it is therefore unfair to hold them to that account. To this objection, I make two replies. First, regardless of the intent of economists, exposure to their models does seem to influence people's behavior.[24] Second, and more importantly, economists themselves clearly do intend to shape behavior, their protestations to the contrary notwithstanding. The aim in teaching economics is to teach students to "think like an economist," and that includes equating reason with the instrumental reason embodied in the rational choice model.[25] Yet the first thing any introductory economics text does is explain that people intuitively do *not* think like economists. In particular, students are told that their intuitions about how to calculate opportunity costs are simply wrong. Here is Greg Mankiw, author of the bestselling introductory text on the subject:

> Because people face trade-offs, making decisions requires comparing the costs and benefits of alternative courses of actions. In many cases, however, the cost of an action is not as obvious as it might first appear.
>
> Consider the decision to go to college. The main benefits are intellectual enrichment and a lifetime of better job opportunities. But what are the costs? To answer this question, you might be tempted to add up the money you spend on tuition, books, room, and board. Yet this total does not truly represent what you give up to spend a year in college.
>
> There are two problems with this calculation. First, it includes some things that are not really costs of going to college. Even if you quit school, you need a place to sleep and food to eat. Room and board are costs of going to college only to the extent that they are more expensive at college than elsewhere. Second, this calculation ignores the largest cost of going to college—your time. When you spend a year listening to lectures, reading textbooks, and writing papers, you cannot spend that time working at a job. For most students, the earnings given up to attend school are the largest single cost of their education.[26]

The first written assignment of any introductory course in economics will cover opportunity-cost problems that students typically find difficult because they do not naturally think this way. The same opening chapter that teaches students how to correctly calculate opportunity costs typically also tells students that economists confine themselves to a positive study of humans as they are.[27] That those descriptive models assume that economic agents calculate opportunity costs correctly is not usually pointed out to students, and students rarely notice the contradiction.[28]

The exhortation for students to think about these matters the way economists do is performed through an appeal to rationality. It is *rational* to make decisions the way economists model decision making. Here is Mankiw again:

> Economists normally assume that people are rational. **Rational people** systematically and purposefully do the best they can to achieve their objectives, given the available opportunities. . . . Rational people know that decisions in life are rarely black and white but usually involve shades of gray. At dinnertime, the decision you face is not between fasting or eating like a pig but whether to take that extra spoonful of mashed potatoes. . . . Economists use **marginal change** to describe a small incremental adjustment to an existing plan of action. . . . Rational people often make decisions by comparing *marginal benefits* and *marginal costs.*[29]

Insofar as nobody would wish to be less than rational, this constitutes encouragement for students to think like economists do, comparing "marginal costs and marginal benefits"—that is, to think at the margin. As we have seen, this sort of exhortation surfaces in economists' interactions with the public as well. Recall Joel Waldfogel's campaign against gift giving as a source of economic loss as an example.

Since economists in fact *do* want people to behave as they describe, they are vulnerable to the Thomistic criticism that people adopting the economists' model of reason as the quintessential model of reason would systematically fail to achieve genuine happiness. To that criticism I now turn.

That the Rational Choice Model Is a Poor Guide to
Achieving Happiness

From the perspective of the Thomistic framework, an agent exercising practical reason along the lines set forth by the rational choice model would be unable to achieve genuine happiness. By definition, happiness requires an exercise of the fully human form of reason involved in discerning goods and ordering goods into a coherent whole. Insofar as the rational choice model identifies rationality with the lower form of rationality we share with animals, individuals whose actions were entirely guided by the rational choice model by definition would not be exercising their human powers to the fullest and therefore would fall short of genuine happiness. But on its best account, the rational choice model allows for agents to make their decisions about what goods to pursue according to whatever lights they like. So the real question is whether individuals pursuing the happiness identified by Thomas could split their reason the way the rational choice model would prescribe: identifying goods worthy of pursuit as part of their exercise of virtue and then using the rational choice model to determine how to effectively realize those ends. My argument is that the rational choice model could only be used in limited circumstances, and that individuals using it as a general model would be ill equipped to cultivate virtue.

The first difficulty is that the rational choice model assumes that one has, in fact, identified the goods one is pursuing. One has an array of bundles of goods from which one could choose and an established preference ordering that is complete. But if Aquinas's account of practical reason as ordered toward cultivating virtue is correct, agents who are not yet perfected in virtue do not have one preference ordering, they have two. For example, who among us does not periodically think, "I know I should do X for my own good, but I am going to do Y anyway." People have one preference ordering according to their untutored desires and another preference ordering according to their higher desires. While it is true that some economists have written about how individuals with higher-order desires can rationally work to bind their lower desire, the situation of divergent desires within one agent is treated as an anomaly, whereas for Thomas it would be seen as a far more general condition.[30] Because the rational choice model has a default assumption that we have a single set of desires, one could argue that the rational choice model in fact encourages us to see our untutored desires as our ultimate desires, insofar as it is far more common for individuals to pursue their untutored desires than it is for them to have so perfected themselves in virtue that their desires are in alignment with their higher-order judgments.

Even if we assume that agents are pursuing the ends determined by their higher-order judgments, the rational choice model is still problematic insofar as it assumes that agents have a complete preference ordering. In Aquinas's model of practical reason, the whole project of developing virtue is learning what one should desire. Moreover, each choice conditions the choices an individual will make further on, the ramifications of which cannot possibly be known ex ante. For someone who desires to grow in virtue, choices are an exploration, learning what works and what does not work in the context of a particular life. For example, if I want to grow in the virtue of temperance, I can begin with some standard ideas about not eating too much and having a balanced diet. But it is only over time that I will learn what foods I am likely to start craving too much, or which foods work with my physical constitution, or how to take the proper pleasure in healthy foods that do not immediately agree with my palate. Many of our choices, in other words, are explorations. The basic rational choice model, with its fixed set of preferences, can offer no guidance here, and therefore cannot be accepted as a universal model of choice that is applicable regardless of the sorts of preferences agents are seeking to satisfy. Again, there are some models that seek to address consumer choice as an exercise in learning, but there are few such articles, and they are subject to more technical objections from a Thomistic perspective.[31]

That most individuals do not have comprehensive known preferences does not render the rational choice model entirely irrelevant, however. In cases where there are choices to be made with respect to a set of preferences that are known and stable, the rational choice model could be helpful in describing decision making. For example, a student with three hours available to study for an exam would do well to allocate time between rereading class notes and reworking problem sets using the logic described by the rational choice model. The primary critique of economic theory is not that it is wrong but rather that it overstates its range. In this case, we can accept that individuals are very far from having comprehensive preferences, while still thinking that there are situations where preferences are clear enough that the rational choice model could apply.

A second limitation of the economic way of thinking about choice is the emphasis on decision making along the margins. On that view, the proper way to frame a decision is to ask about incremental moves in one direction or another. Thus my question right now is whether the marginal cost *(MC)* of working for another hour outweighs the marginal benefit of working for another hour *(MB)*. If *MB* > *MC*, then I should work the extra hour. If not, I should go home. Decision making in this fashion is incompatible with a practical reason oriented toward virtue both with respect to intertemporal decision making and decision making at a given moment in time.

The project of cultivating virtue depends on the cumulative effect of decision making. Each act works toward building up habits for better or for worse, which means that decision making has an important intertemporal component. Although economists certainly have intertemporal models to focus on decision making across time, the emphasis on decision making at the margin tends to frame decisions as a sequence of isolated choices, which militates against thinking about the implications of decisions made across time.[32] This leads to conundrums that economists themselves have to deal with. In particular, any activity that requires persistence will not be well handled by decision making on the margin. If one is spending six months training for a marathon, it will be the case most days that the marginal cost of not training that day is low. One can take a day off without interfering with one's overall chances of success. The problem is that the marginal cost of taking a day off will be low every day, and one would rationally choose to miss too many days of training. This leads to a problem known as dynamic inconsistency, wherein the rational choice on a given day is incompatible with what would be rational in the long run.[33]

Consider patent policy. Patents are issued so that inventors can enjoy the higher prices (and profits) associated with having a monopoly for a fixed period of time. Monopolies are themselves socially inefficient, but the lure of monopoly profits encourages innovation. Once an invention has taken place, it would be socially optimal to void the patent in order to get rid of the inefficiency caused by the monopoly. The invention has already occurred and therefore is no longer relevant to decision making on the margin. The difficulty is that if you void an important patent today, innovators will realize that they are unlikely to enjoy monopoly rents during the life of the patents they aspire to obtain on innovations they make in the future and will therefore slow down innovation. The best social policy in the short run has detrimental implications for social welfare in the long run. The problem of dynamic inconsistency results in a situation in which it is better for policy makers to commit to following rules than to exercise discretion, and it has been used to argue against Keynesian-style intervention in macroeconomics.

These sorts of policy dilemmas are pronounced because of the election cycle. Policy makers who need to be reelected (or to have the officials who appointed them reelected) will always have an incentive to implement policies that are beneficial in the short run even if they are poor policies when judged from a long-run perspective. But similar issues surface for individuals insofar as untutored desires and aversions tend to weight the present more heavily than the future. It is immediately enjoyable to cheat on one's diet, and it is rational to observe that cheating on a diet on one day is not going to make much of a difference one way or another. The problem is that every time you cheat on the diet, you weaken any habit of temperance you might have been working on, making it that much more likely that on subsequent days the decision to cheat on the diet would seem rational.

The problem here is not that economists are blind to intertemporal decision making. As I said, such models are quite common. The problem is that from the point of view of virtue, these sorts of intertemporal problems are the rule, not the exception. If that is so, the presentation of decision making at the margin as a hallmark of rational thinking is misleading. Consider the early exhortation to introductory economics students to *not* factor sunk costs into their decision making. Sunk costs are costs that have already been incurred and therefore should not factor into decision making on the margin, since that cost exists whatever choice is made and therefore nets out. For example, suppose I have purchased a season pass to the opera. On the day of the fourth opera, I am just exhausted from work and really do not feel like going to the opera. I have paid for the ticket whether I go to the opera or stay home, and the cost of the ticket therefore is not relevant. To an economist, all that matters is whether the marginal cost of going to the opera (getting dressed up, driving downtown, and so on) is greater than or less than the marginal benefit (hearing the opera). If I am exhausted, the marginal cost of going is high and the marginal benefit is low, so I should rationally decide to stay home.

Introductory texts note that many people confronted with this situation would feel obliged to go to the opera anyway because they have already paid for it, and students are told that such feelings are simply irrational. But from the perspective of the cultivation of virtue they may not be irrational at all. For starters, ignoring sunk costs is a way of disassociating oneself from past decisions. If part of cultivating virtue is developing a coherent self over time, the habit of disavowing past choices would be counterproductive.[34] In addition to honoring decisions one has taken in the past, taking sunk costs into account could also work as a way of following rules rather than discretion, which, as noted, might be the rational thing for policy makers to do. To take a slightly different example, individuals may buy memberships in health clubs as a way of trying to foster the virtue of exercising regularly. If one has cultivated the mindset that sunk costs are to be disregarded, it becomes easier to flout the resolution one's past self was intending when the membership was purchased. If, by contrast, one has a mindset that says that one should use what one has paid for, the purchase of the membership at the health club will most likely help one get to the gym more regularly. To routinely disregard sunk costs is to give past decisions no weight in one's present calculations, and that can be counterproductive if the aim of practical reason is to help cultivate virtue.[35]

The stress on decision making at the margin is also counterproductive if we look at decisions taken within a given time frame. Here the point is quite simple. As we have seen, for Aquinas the higher exercise of human reason involves discerning the various goods before one and ordering them properly. It is a holistic exercise. To identify reason with decision making at the margin is to invite individuals to think of decision making as a series of discrete, unconnected choices, which is the antithesis of reason as Aquinas understands it. Interestingly, the noted economist Tibor Scitovsky has identified this precise problem in his article "Are Men Rational or Economists Wrong?," discussed in Chapter 4.[36]

A person trained to see the rational choice model as the best way for thinking about choice is thus impeded in multiple ways from pursuing happiness as Aquinas understands it. Insofar as descriptions of practical reason serve as guides to how we live, the rational choice model cannot be seen as neutral. Economists may deny that their models serve as guides, but their introductory textbooks show otherwise. To the extent that economists train their students to think like economists, they are training their students in a mode of thought that will thwart them in their pursuit of happiness. Moreover, the rational choice model used for the purposes economists do acknowledge is also not neutral. Economists who take Aquinas's framework seriously would have to make some adjustments in their practice.

The Implications of Thomas's Framework for Economic Practice

Economists identify their discipline with the tools they use—their models and their repertoire of statistical techniques. By contrast, a Thomist economist would define economics around the ends it is meant to serve. The overarching question is how economic life should serve genuine human happiness. This teleological orientation would distinguish a Thomistic economics from mainstream economics in two ways. First and most simply, this would entail evaluating economic questions in light of broader measures of human well-being than economic indicators alone. Second, Thomistic economics would be conducted in a way that is mindful of the fact that we can never merely describe human behavior. Economic analysis is always addressed to humans and therefore plays a role in shaping cultural conversations that can either promote or hinder our ability to translate economic wealth into authentic happiness.

Embedding Economic Analysis in a Holistic Account of Happiness

The disciplinary fragmentation of modern academia has made it seem natural for economists to focus primarily on economic outcomes. As discussed in Chapter 1, this coheres with the faulty modern notion that the pursuit of the good life properly belongs to the private sphere. Economists thus are experts on how to promote economic growth, which is taken to be a properly public concern, since increased prosperity provides individuals with the material means to pursue happiness however they conceive it. On such a conception, a primary concern would be how to balance policies that promote growth with policies that ensure that the resulting wealth is equitably distributed. But the essential insight of a Thomistic approach is that material wealth does not necessarily promote happiness, and indeed, can even interfere with it. An economics that is oriented toward promoting happiness would view GDP or wealth not as ends in themselves but rather as instrumental goods. The ultimate analysis would focus instead on the ends that are meant to be served by economic goods.

As discussed in Chapter 2, even secular economists have been taking up questions about these higher ends, in light of research calling into question any neat relationship between economic growth and happiness, especially in prosperous nations. The new field of happiness economics is one such example. However, its use of subjective measures of happiness does not suit the Thomistic framework, which operates out of a more Aristotelian conception of the possibility of objective study of human happiness.[37] On the other hand, the line of research developed by Amartya Sen and Martha Nussbaum known as the capabilities approach is more consonant with a Thomistic economics.[38] In that approach, philosophical discussion is used to think about the fundamental goods that serve human happiness.

For Sen and Nussbaum, that ultimate good is to be found in freedom, and they identify a set of basic goods such as food, housing, and education that are necessary in order to secure that ultimate good. These basic goods are not limited to material or economic goods but also include political and cultural structures that facilitate human freedom. It is thus an approach that specifically embeds economic analysis within a larger philosophical account of the human good and promotes empirical research that can help us better understand how economic and political institutions serve authentic human happiness. The capabilities approach's conception of the ultimate end is distinctly liberal. A Thomistic economics would have a different, somewhat thicker conception of the ultimate good, but before turning to that it is worth noting that philo-sophical differences, even if profound, do not lead to much disagreement about what sorts of goods should properly be measured in lieu of reli-ance on economic indicators such as per capita GDP. The simple fact of recognizing that economic goods are in service of higher ends produces a recognition that the primary good of material wealth is to secure ad-equate nutrition, housing, education, health care, and so on.

That said, a Thomistic version of the capabilities approach would also be more explicitly concerned with the good understood as the pursuit of virtue, which insofar as we are inherently social animals entails a con-cern for relationship and community standing. These goods can perhaps best be understood in terms of the Catholic notion of the common good. The Vatican II document, *Gaudium et spes,* defines the common good as "the sum of those conditions of social life which allow social groups and their individual members thorough and ready access to their own fulfillment."[39] Insofar as human fulfillment requires adequate provision of material goods, the production and equitable distribution of those goods is an important element in fostering the common good. But in-sofar as human fulfillment also requires relationship and social standing, we must also be concerned with goods that might more properly be studied by sociologists, psychologists, and anthropologists. As a result, a Thomistic economics would be explicitly oriented toward interdisci-plinary study.

To give an example of the difference the Thomistic approach would make, consider the subject of poverty. In addition to studying poverty in terms of income or consumption levels, the Thomistic economist would investigate the meaning of poverty within a given community. Individuals with low incomes would have different experiences of pov-erty depending on whether they were in a genuine community or in a more fragmented community of atomistic individuals. The material lack alone would not be enough to assess the human ills involved. The na-ture of the community, in turn, would most likely have an impact on the efficacy of various measures that might be considered to redress pov-erty. The Thomistic economist would thus want to work with other so-cial scientists to determine what mix of structural or cultural elements produce poverty in a given community. The social meaning of poverty and the wide array of possible causes of poverty vary from place to place. As a result, the best study of poverty would be granular—paying attention to local circumstances.

The abstract models of economists could be helpful in providing analytical tools for thinking about poverty in a given place and time but would not be a substitute for working in the community to understand the complexity of the human situation on the ground. Above all, the Thomistic economist would insist that in thinking about the human condition we need to think about both the impact of incentives and the impact of higher reason (mediated through cultural norms). Economic models thus have a role to play, albeit a circumscribed one. The same general principles would apply to all economic analysis oriented toward public policy questions. Questions should be framed in terms of the impact of economic variables on higher goods; there should be an openness to integrating economic analysis with insights from the other social scientists; and there should be an awareness that because of the complex mix of social, psychological, anthropological, and economic concerns, the best policy analysis should be granular, expecting different results from studies of different communities.

Economics as a Participant in Cultural Conversation

The second principal difference a Thomistic approach would make for the practice of economics is that it would require a self-awareness of the fact that economists are participants in cultural conversations that shape norms and understandings, which, in turn, either promote or hinder our pursuit of happiness. The Thomistic economist, thus, would recognize her task as complex because the objects of her studies are also the persons to whom the results of those studies are addressed. We can better see the complexity by considering the three audiences for economic analysis: policy makers, individuals making their own economic choices, and individuals participating in civic conversations. Beginning with policy makers, economists need to make clearer the provisional quality of their analysis. In particular, their predictions are sound insofar as people respond to incentives. As Samuel Bowles has suggested, economists can work to expand their tool kit to include analysis of how people are likely to respond to various policies given the effects of incentives on behavior but also the effect policies might have on people's choices insofar as policies might shift norms or other higher motivations.[40] The Thomistic economist would embrace Bowles's call for this sort of two-tiered analysis of human behavior. But, in addition, the Thomistic economist would be mindful of her own participation in and impact on cultural conversations about the ends economic analysis is meant to serve.

This mindfulness would make a difference in two ways. First, the Thomistic economist would work to remind herself and policy makers that the fact that humans can be the objects of study and the objects of manipulation through policy should not obscure the fact that these models are about human beings who are our fellow citizens and who can also be addressed directly. The habit of the social sciences of treating humans as objects of study has permeated our culture, making it easier to think of other people as objects subject to manipulation. This is the mindset that allows firms to go from thinking of customers as people to whom they are offering goods and services to thinking of them as consumers who can be manipulated in ways that are advantageous to the firms' bottom line, as discussed in Chapter 4.

For an example of the way the habit of thinking in terms of predictable (and manipulable) human behavior impacts our economy, consider the revolution in politics associated with the rise of "big data." In the wake of the 2012 election there were a spate of stories about how both campaigns placed cookies on the computers of anyone who went to their respective websites, allowing them to track the interests and concerns of those people. This, in turn, would allow them to target voters with appeals based on their preexisting concerns. In addition, they developed sophisticated models about which voters the campaign should work to make sure they would get to the polls.[41] The new conception of politics as an exercise in manipulating voters in this way undermines the more fully human approach to politics, which would involve conversations aimed at mutual persuasion on subjects related to the common good. Predictive models are useful tools, but they become pernicious if they become a template for how we view other human beings. The Thomistic economist would thus deploy her analysis with proper circumspection.

The second difference is that because economists are themselves human beings, they need to be careful about how their own conception of the good shapes their analysis. In particular, they need to be more cautious about their deployment of the concept of efficiency, which figures prominently in welfare analysis, as discussed in Chapter 2. Recall that economists treat efficiency as a desirable property and that much policy analysis depends on a social belief that policies should promote efficiency. The term is employed in a normative fashion, however much economists might like to deny that claim. Behind that normative usage is the thought that economic prosperity is an end in itself. But as discussed in the preceding section, economic activity needs to be evaluated in terms of the higher goods served by economic life. More deeply, the habit of thinking in terms of efficiency underwrites the cultural habit of thinking of the pursuit of happiness as an exercise in constrained optimization. If only we had more time or more income we could get more of the goods that make us happy. In other words, it is rooted in a world in which scarcity is the overriding problem.

Given that fact, efficiency is important because it allows us to get as much as we can from the limited goods we have. While it is true that in some situations scarcity is the paramount problem, the habit of thinking that it is always the problem distracts us from thinking about the more pervasive obstacle to temporal human happiness, namely, the lack of wisdom about how to order well the finite goods that are present in our lives. Efficiency is certainly better than inefficiency. But it should not trump the higher concerns about how to balance goods in a way that serves genuine human flourishing.

The second audience for economic analysis is individuals seeking advice about how to make their own decisions. As discussed above, although economists deny this is a feature of their practice as economists, they do, in fact, offer advice to their students and to the lay public on how to make "rational" decisions. The Thomistic economist would explicitly acknowledge the pedagogical role they play as economists. As discussed in Chapter 4 and above in this chapter, the Thomistic economist would guard against having students take the rational choice model as a general prescription for how to make good decisions. Because of its use in descriptive models of human behavior, the rational choice model would still be taught. But it would need to be taught in the context of a more complete anthropology that explicitly points out the two tiers of rationality. Placing the rational choice model within a larger account of human nature would serve two functions. First, it would prevent students from identifying rationality with the lower form of rationality. Second, it would set up a discussion of the complexity of policy making wherein the deployment of incentives needs to be balanced against the possibility of undermining social norms rooted in the higher form of human reason.

The recognition that an important role of economics is to serve individuals by giving them tools for thinking about the choices they confront would also open up lines of economic research that are often neglected because they do not naturally conform to the mainstream emphasis on model building. For example, in the early twentieth century there emerged a line of research on consumption and household production generated by women economists who were largely confined to teaching in home economics departments. They developed large bodies of data on time usage and household consumption patterns, which they deployed in textbooks to give their students more tools for managing their households well.[42] The material exposed students to a range of options they might consider, evaluated in light of the various goods the household manager might pursue. Although they produced much valuable information, the school of thought ultimately died. As Joseph Dorfman suggests in his extensive survey of American economic thought, the reason for the school's demise is that the subject matter did not lend itself to the sort of mathematical analysis that came into vogue later in the century.[43] An economist who confines himself to the control stance would not readily recognize the value of such research, though its value would be evident to any economist who recognized that economics is also part of a conversation.

Finally, the understanding of economics as part of a cultural conversation is particularly important when we turn to the third potential audience—individuals participating in civic discussions. Economists are eager to share their insights about the unintended consequences of policy and the counterintuitive fact that self-interested behavior channeled through markets can produce the substantial social good of widespread prosperity. But they tend to bristle when confronted by critics who accuse them of fostering greed and excessive materialism, which, in turn, produces economic injustice. The mutual misunderstanding arises because economists fail to account for the aspect of human nature that is not manipulable by incentives. Economists see themselves as simply describing human nature as it is. But the higher form of reason that identifies what goods are worthy of pursuit and seeks to order those goods into a coherent pattern is also part of human nature, most commonly mediated through culture in the form of social norms and cultural assumptions about the nature of the good life. Economists thus tout their insights based on their descriptive or predictive models, while critics are alarmed by the way economic discourse shapes culture and produces a faulty conception of the good life.

A recognition that economists inevitably contribute to the culture's understanding of human nature and the corresponding conceptions of the good life would do much to clear up the confusion. Economists could do this by emphasizing the fact that their insights are based on a partial view of human nature and that there is nothing normative about their descriptions. Recent research in the fields of behavioral economics, the economics of happiness, and identity economics suggests that economists are becoming more aware of the range of human nature, a fact that should receive more attention in civic discourse. The Thomistic economist would navigate these issues by embracing humility about the limits of economic knowledge. This would involve being clear about the following matters.

First, the Thomistic economist would emphasize that her research typically only speaks to economic outcomes, whereas civic conversations about the good life and the role of policies and institutions in securing it must necessarily be about the higher goods to which material goods are ordered. It is a cultural mistake to treat GDP and economic growth rates as ultimate goods. The prestige economists enjoy relative to other social scientists is a by-product of that cultural mistake. The Thomistic economist would present her findings in a way that emphasizes the instrumental nature of economic goods and refocuses attention on the higher goods that should be the ends of public policy.

Second, and correlatively, the Thomistic economist would be actively engaged in interdisciplinary work, learning from the other social scientists about other facets of human behavior, and taking those findings into account in her thinking about economic issues. The question of how to think about the two-tiered nature of human reason would be central, as would concern about the impact the culture has on the balance between the two tiers and our ability to think about how the culture shapes our ability to pursue genuine human flourishing. And finally, the Thomistic economist would insist that while empirical research is valuable, it is not a substitute for philosophical and theological discussion about the human good and human happiness. That we cannot quantify such knowledge or test it in labs does not mean that it is not knowledge. Indeed, it is the highest sort of knowledge.

Aquinas seems well suited as a starting point for how to think about a genuinely humane economy. His framework accommodates the valuable intuitions that undergird the best of economic science but orders them toward a much richer account of human happiness than the one deployed by economists. It is a framework that allows us to overcome the false dichotomy between economic considerations and ethical considerations. It is a framework that can help us see economic life in a theological light, with a corresponding diagnosis of many modern-day ills. It is, above all, a framework in which economists of good will and theologians could, at least in principle, have a meaningful and productive conversation. My hope is that such a conversation would open the door for serious thought about the ends served both by the economy and by economics. Rethinking of both is necessary if we are to move toward an economy that serves genuine human flourishing.

Notes

Preface

1. Steven D. Levitt and Stephen J. Dubner, *Freakonomics: A Rogue Economist Explores the Hidden Side of Everything* (New York: Harper Perennial, 2009); Tyler Cowen, *Discover Your Inner Economist: Use Incentives to Fall in Love, Survive Your Next Meeting, and Motivate Your Dentist* (New York: Plume, 2008). The cover of my copy of *Freakonomics* is graced with a blurb from the *Wall Street Journal:* "Genius . . . has you gasping in amazement." National Public Radio runs a podcast called *Planet Money* that embodies this spirit of evangelization—you might think one way, but you will think differently after you have heard from the economists.

2. Arjo Klamer and David Colander, *The Making of an Economist* (Boulder, CO: Westview Press, 1990), offer a portrait of elite graduate programs in economics in the mid-1980s based on surveys with students in those programs. The chief complaints about the excessive abstraction and emphasis on mathematic technique were a common refrain throughout. In response to the work of Klamer and Colander, the American Economics Association commissioned a study of the problem. Commission on Graduate Education in Economics, "Report of the Commission on Graduate Education in Economics," *Journal of Economic Literature* 29, no. 3 (September 1991): 1035–1053, finds that graduate programs in that era did, indeed, overemphasize technique over knowledge with real-world institutions. Since then, economics has significantly shifted away from pure mathematical abstraction.

3. The critiques date back to the emergence of political economy as an independent field in the nineteenth century. John Ruskin, *Unto This Last and Other*

Essays, edited by Clive Wilmer (London: Penguin Books, 1997), offers an early version of these critiques in 1860, arguing that the science of homo economicus was about as relevant as a science of gymnastics predicated on the assumption that humans have no bones would be. There are many branches of economics that resist the practice of making the rational choice model central to their thought, most notably that of institutional economics. Hazel Kyrk, an institutional economist, offers a typical assessment: "Men do not act . . . in the way the marginal theorists describe them as acting. We cannot recognize ourselves or our fellows in the hedonistic, individualistic calculators whom they described, nor find in their account any trace of the complexity of motives, impulses, and interests which lie behind market activities." Kyrk, *A Theory of Consumption* (Boston: Houghton Mifflin, 1923), 17. Irene van Staveren, *The Values of Economics: An Aristotelian Perspective* (London: Routledge, 2001), offers a representative example of modern variants of those critiques, along with an ample bibliography.

4. Milton Friedman, "The Methodology of Positive Economics," in *Essays in Positive Economics* (Chicago: University of Chicago Press, 1966), 3–43.

5. The seminal article that launched the study of cognitive bias in economic decision making is Daniel Kahneman and Amos Tversky, "Prospect Theory: An Analysis of Decision under Risk," *Econometrica* 47, no. 2 (March 1979): 263–291. Edward Cartwright, *Behavioral Economics* (London: Routledge, 2011), offers a good overview of the field of behavioral economics.

6. Luigi Zingales, *A Capitalism for the People: Recapturing the Lost Genius of American Prosperity* (New York: Basic Books, 2012), 175; Gary Becker, *The Economic Approach to Human Behavior* (Chicago: University of Chicago Press, 1976).

7. Becker, *The Economic Approach to Human Behavior,* 10.

8. Daniel Klein, "Does Economics Need an Infusion of Religious or Quasi-Religious Formulations? A Symposium Prologue," *Econ Journal Watch* 11, no. 2 (May 2014): 97–105, raises the question of whether economics is suffering from an "undue flatness" (97). As discussed at length in Chapter 2, Amartya Sen, "Rational Fools: A Critique of the Behavioral Foundations of Economic Theory," *Philosophy and Public Affairs* 6, no. 4 (Summer 1977): 317–344, offers a classic argument that we should distinguish between pursuing preferences and honoring commitments, but it is an argument that does not decisively show that the rational choice model cannot accommodate that distinction.

9. Richard A. Easterlin, "Does Economic Growth Improve the Human Lot?," in *Nations and Households in Economic Growth: Essays in Honor of Moses Abramovitz,* ed. Paul A. David and Melvin W. Reder (New York: Academic Press, 1974), 89–125. At a given point in time, those in the higher-income brackets are typically happier than those in lower-income brackets. But across time, it is difficult to find a strong correlation between income and happiness.

Surveys across nations show a strong improvement in happiness as income lifts countries out of poverty, but the correlation flattens such that it is difficult to say that very rich nations are any happier on average than moderately rich nations. Bruno S. Frey, *Happiness: A Revolution in Economics* (Cambridge, MA: MIT Press, 2008), offers a good overview of the literature. While there is some debate about whether there is a correlation between wealth and happiness once countries reach a certain level of prosperity, even studies finding a positive correlation do not show a strong positive correlation.

10. For a good account of why it is plausible to hold orthodox views about God in the modern world, see David Bentley Hart, *The Experience of God: Being, Consciousness, Bliss* (New Haven, CT: Yale University Press, 2013).

11. Mary L. Hirschfeld, "Standard of Living and Economic Virtue: Forging a Link between St. Thomas Aquinas and the Twenty-First Century," *Journal of the Society of Christian Ethics* 26, no. 1 (Spring–Summer 2006): 61–77. Aquinas's views on private property are discussed at length in Chapter 6.

12. Thomas Aquinas, *Summa theologica*, trans. Fathers of the English Dominican Province (Allen, TX: Christian Classics, 1948).

13. Charles Taylor, *A Secular Age* (Cambridge, MA: Belknap Press of Harvard University, 2007).

1. To Serve God or Mammon?

1. Albino Barrera, *Biblical Economic Ethics: Sacred Scripture's Teachings on Economic Life* (Lanham, MD: Lexington Books, 2013), offers an excellent account of the extensive biblical teachings on economics, along with an exhaustive bibliography of modern scholarship on the subject.

2. Dierdre N. McCloskey, *The Bourgeois Virtues: Ethics for an Age of Commerce* (Chicago: University of Chicago Press, 2006), 1–53, provides a classic panegyric of capitalism along these lines.

3. Examples of secular criticism of the excessive materialism of capitalism include Herbert Marcuse, *One Dimensional Man: Studies in the Ideology of Advanced Industrial Society* (Boston: Beacon Press, 1964), and John Kenneth Galbraith, *The Affluent Society* (Boston: Houghton Mifflin, 1958). Karl Marx's atheism is well known, as is his entrenched critique of the exploitation he believed to be an essential feature of capitalism. Although he disclaims any Marxist influence, Thomas Piketty, in *Capital in the Twenty-First Century* (Cambridge, MA: Harvard University Press, 2013), offers a variant on the argument that capitalism necessarily creates economic injustice (for Piketty, in the form of excessive income inequality).

4. David J. O'Brien and Thomas A. Shannon, *Catholic Social Thought: The Documentary Heritage* (Maryknoll, NY: Orbis Books, 1992), collects the key

documents from Pope Leo XIII's *Rerum novarum* (1891) through John Paul II's *Centesimus annus* (1991). Since then, the tradition has been extended by Pope Benedict XVI in his encyclicals *Deus caritas est* (2005) and *Caritas in veritate* (2009) and by Pope Francis in his exhortation *Evangelii gaudium* (2013) and his encyclical *Laudato si* (2015).

5. D. Stephen Long, *Divine Economy: Theology and the Market* (London: Routledge, 2000), delivers a magisterial survey of the range of theological responses to the modern economy.

6. Christina McRorie, "Heterodox Economics, Social Ethics, and Inequality: New Tools for Thinking Carefully about Markets and Economic Injustices" (unpublished manuscript), offers a valuable critique of the naturalistic metaphors employed by mainstream economists.

7. Charles Taylor, *A Secular Age* (Cambridge, MA: Belknap Press of Harvard University, 2007), 2.

8. In this book, I use the umbrella term *economics* to refer to the mainstream discipline of economics. Other schools of economic thought (for example, Marxist or feminist) are identified using more specific terminology. I use the word *economy* to refer to the workings of the market, an important component of the subject matter studied by economists of all stripes.

9. A. M. C. Waterman, *Political Economy and Christian Theology since the Enlightenment: Essays in Intellectual History* (New York: Palgrave MacMillan, 2004).

10. John Rawls, *A Theory of Justice,* rev. ed. (Cambridge, MA: Belknap Press of Harvard University Press, 1999).

11. The idea that goods should be ordered is simply the idea that some goods are valuable because they help us procure the higher goods that we really value. When I buy eggs at the store, the good of those eggs is ordered to the higher good of the omelet I intend to cook. The omelet, in turn, is ordered to the still higher good of nourishing my family and perhaps also to the aesthetic goods involved in fine cuisine. As the twin goals of achieving some aesthetic purpose and nourishing one's family suggest, ordering goods also entails identifying which higher goods to value and thinking about how to arrange those higher goods into some harmonious pattern. The idea of ordering goods is developed more fully in Chapters 3 and 4.

12. Lawrence Iannaccone, "Introduction to the Economics of Religion," *Journal of Economic Literature* 36, no. 3 (September 1998): 1466.

13. Economists have long been more open to dialogue with philosophers; Amartya Sen, an economist-philosopher, has even been awarded a Nobel Prize in economics. And there are at least a few economists interested in engaging theology. A relatively small group of Christians have formed the Association of Christian Economists, which publishes a journal called *Faith and Economics* that tackles questions that arise along the boundaries of the two dis-

ciplines. More recently, *Econ Journal Watch* devoted an entire issue (11, no. 2 [May 2014]) to the question of whether economics could not profit from some engagement with theology, indicating that even some secular economists are open to dialogue with theology.

14. Niccolò Machiavelli, *The Prince,* 2nd ed., trans. Harvey C. Mansfield (Chicago: University of Chicago Press, 1998), 61.

15. The tension between thinking of humans in light of what they could or should be and thinking of them as they are echoes the tension Charles Taylor identifies between a life lived in pursuit of self-transcendence and a life lived in pursuit of ordinary human flourishing, understood as health, prosperity, family, and so forth. Taylor, *A Secular Age,* 44.

16. Samuel Bowles, *The Moral Economy: Why Good Incentives Are No Substitute for Good Citizens* (New Haven, CT: Yale University Press, 2016), provides a discussion of the trajectory from Machiavelli to modern economics. See also Albert O. Hirshman, *The Passions and the Interests: Political Arguments for Capitalism before Its Triumph* (Princeton, NJ: Princeton University Press, 1977). Machiavelli himself does not argue that we should disregard the cultivation of virtue altogether. My employment of Machiavelli here is heuristic.

17. This complaint goes back to the earliest days of political economy. See, for example, John Ruskin, "Unto This Last," in *Unto This Last and Other Essays,* ed. Clive Wilmer (London: Penguin Books, 1997): 167–179. Irene van Staveren, *The Values of Economics: An Aristotelian Perspective* (London: Routledge, 2001), offers a roundup of more contemporary criticism along these lines.

18. Milton Friedman, "The Methodology of Positive Economics," in *Essays in Positive Economics* (Chicago: University of Chicago Press, 1966), 3–43. Andrew Yuengert, *Approximating Prudence: Aristotelian Practical Wisdom and Economic Models of Choice* (New York: Palgrave Macmillan, 2012), 9–30, offers a good discussion of the aims of economic modeling and its limitations.

19. Dani Rodrik, *Economic Rules: The Rights and Wrongs of the Dismal Science* (New York: W. W. Norton, 2015), offers an overview of the strengths and weaknesses of current economic practice from the perspective of an economist.

20. Chapter 2 presents a full discussion of the economic approach to human behavior and a survey of its strengths and weaknesses.

21. Michael Sandel, *What Money Can't Buy: The Moral Limits of Markets* (New York: Farrar, Straus and Giroux, 2012), 83.

22. Adam Smith, *The Wealth of Nations* (New York: Bantam Books, 2003), 23–24.

23. Friedrich Hayek, "The Use of Knowledge in Society," *American Economic Review* 35, no. 4 (September 1945): 519–530.

24. Kenneth J. Arrow, "An Extension of the Basic Theorems of Classical Welfare Economics," in *Proceedings of the Second Berkeley Symposium on Mathematical Statistics and Probability,* ed. Jerzy Neyman (Berkeley: University of

California Press, 1951), 507–532; Gerard Debreu, "The Coefficient of Resource Utilization," *Econometrica* 19, no. 3 (July 1951): 273–292.

25. Piketty, *Capital in the Twenty-First Century.*

26. Joseph E. Stiglitz, *The Price of Inequality: How Today's Divided Society Endangers Our Future* (New York: W. W. Norton, 2012).

27. Luigi Zingales, *A Capitalism for the People: Recapturing the Lost Genius of American Prosperity* (New York: Basic Books, 2012).

28. George A. Akerlof and Robert J. Shiller, *Phishing for Phools: The Economics of Manipulation and Deception* (Princeton, NJ: Princeton University Press, 2015).

29. Robert J. Shiller, *Finance and the Good Society* (Princeton, NJ: Princeton University Press, 2012).

30. Jeffrey D. Sachs, *The Price of Civilization: Reawakening American Virtue and Prosperity* (New York: Random House, 2012), 3.

31. Long, *Divine Economy,* 6, observes that both disciplines are fragmented, though he acknowledges that while there is little agreement among theologians as to what distinguishes good theology from bad theology, economists appear to have agreement about fundamental principles. The fragmentation he identifies in economics derives from the fact that economists differ about how to apply those principles. Even if we accept Long's basic observation, fragmentation about what the principles of a discipline should be is a much more fundamental fragmentation than is one that is about the application of those principles. Long's basic observation greatly understates the difference between the two disciplines. Economists' shared notion of what it means to think like an economist is so standardized that any economist could teach the core economics courses in any department in the country without having to write a single new lecture. The same is clearly not true of theology, where introductory courses, even within the same department, vary greatly by instructor, with an even larger variance if we compared introductory courses across departments.

32. Long, *Divine Economy,* 5–6.

33. Long, *Divine Economy,* 10. The theologians Long identifies as exemplars of this approach include Michael Novak, Max Stackhouse, Dennis McCann, Ronald Preston, and Philip Wogaman.

34. Long, *Divine Economy,* 72.

35. Long, *Divine Economy,* 35–38; 32–33. As Long puts it, the theologians in the dominant tradition "use a similar theology to arrive at different economic prescriptions" (71).

36. The first edition of Paul Samuelson's *Economics* was published in 1948, and the book has gone through nineteen editions since then. It is no longer the best-selling introductory text, but it was for decades. The most recent edition appeared in 2010.

37. Paul Krugman has claimed otherwise. In a column entitled "Knaves, Fools, and Me (Meta)," *New York Times,* April 28, 2013, he writes that "the anti-Keynesian position is, in essence, political. It's driven by hostility to active government policy and, in many cases, hostility to any intellectual approach that might make room for government policy," arriving at that conclusion as the only possible explanation for the fact that not all economists share his views on austerity. His declaration that there is no room for "respectable" disagreement with his position prompted Miles Kimball, a professor of economics and survey research at the University of Michigan, to post a lengthy excerpt from John Stuart Mills, *On Liberty,* on the value of those who disagree with you on his blog, *Confessions of a Supply-Side Liberal,* http://blog .supplysideliberal.com/post/49083238303/let-the-wrong-come-to-me-for -they-will-make-me-more. A week later, Tyler Cowen, a professor of economics at George Mason University, offered an oblique reply to Krugman on his blog, *Marginal Revolution,* using Jamaica to point out the difficulties in making the sort of macroeconomic inferences Krugman would like to make, http://marginalrevolution.com/marginalrevolution/2013/05/why-is-no-one -talking-about-jamaican-fiscal-policy.html. The point is simply that Krugman ruffled feathers in asserting that there can be no principled disagreement on these points, and I take the entire incident as reflective of the fact that however heated the controversies can become, economists are, in fact, operating out of a shared sense of what counts as a reasonable argument, even if the contestants do not come to an agreement about the best diagnosis of the economy or the appropriate policy recommendations.

38. Long, *Divine Economy,* 83, includes James Cone, Gustavo Gutiérrez, Rosemary Radford Ruether, and Jon Sobrino in this tradition.

39. Long, *Divine Economy,* 86.

40. Mary Jo Bane, "Public Policy and the Common Good," in *Empirical Foundations of the Common Good: What Theology Can Learn from Social Science,* ed. Daniel Finn (Oxford, UK: Oxford University Press, forthcoming), offers an extended reflection on the way public policy analysis that draws on economics and allied social sciences can provide technical assistance to the bishops or other theologians reflecting on public policy issues.

41. U.S. Catholic Bishops, *Economic Justice for All,* in *Catholic Social Thought: The Documentary Heritage,* eds. David J. O'Brien and Thomas A. Shannon (Maryknoll, N.Y.: Orbis Books, 1992), 572–680.

42. U.S. Catholic Bishops, *Economic Justice for All,* introduction, 4, 572.

43. U.S. Catholic Bishops, *Economic Justice for All,* introduction, 7, 573.

44. U.S. Catholic Bishops, *Economic Justice for All,* introduction, 12, 574.

45. U.S. Catholic Bishops, *Economic Justice for All,* introduction, 3, 572. In point of fact, a perusal of their references suggests that the bishops did not widely consult. They exclusively cite liberal economists, a point to be taken up below.

46. U.S. Catholic Bishops, *Economic Justice for All,* introduction, 13–18, 574–575.

47. U.S. Catholic Bishops, *Economic Justice for All,* introduction, 20, 576.

48. Peter L. Berger, "Can the Bishops Help the Poor?," *Commentary* 79, no. 2 (February 1985): 31, reports that the bishops publically announced that they would withhold publication of the letter until after the 1984 elections, because their proposals closely mirrored the Democratic Party platform of 1984 and they didn't want to be seen as making a political endorsement. Conservative Catholics responded to an early draft of *Economic Justice for All* with their own letter: Lay Commission on Catholic Social Teaching and the U.S. Economy, *Toward the Future: Catholic Social Thought and the U.S. Economy—a Lay Letter* (New York: Lay Commission on Catholic Social Teaching and the U.S. Economy, 1984).

49. The enthusiasm for Keynesian-style government intervention had waned in the wake of the stagflation of the 1970s. And by the mid-1980s rational expectations models of the macro economy were widely deployed to argue against the efficacy of discretionary fiscal or monetary policy. It was only later in the decade, after *Economic Justice for All* was promulgated, that there was a resurgence of left-leaning macroeconomic analysis in the form of the New Keynesianism.

50. Partha Dasgupta, "What Do Economists Analyze and Why: Values or Facts?," *Economics and Philosophy* 21, no. 2 (October 2005): 222–223.

51. Anthony Randazzo and Jonathan Haidt, "The Moral Narratives of Economists," *Econ Journal Watch* 12, no. 1 (January 2015): 49–57.

52. Long, *Divine Economy,* 177.

53. Long, *Divine Economy,* 4.

54. Kathryn Tanner, *God and Creation in Christian Theology: Tyranny or Empowerment?* (Oxford, UK: Blackwell, 1988). See Robert Sokolowski, *The God of Faith and Reason: Foundations of Christian Theology* (Washington, DC: Catholic University of America Press, 1995), for a similar set of arguments.

55. Kathryn Tanner, *Economy of Grace* (Minneapolis, MN: Fortress Press, 2005), x.

56. Tanner, *Economy of Grace,* 32.

57. It is unclear whether the irony of using the language of contestation to assert that we should be noncompetitive is intentional on Tanner's part.

58. Tanner, *Economy of Grace,* 10–29.

59. Tanner, *Economy of Grace,* 29.

60. Tanner, *Economy of Grace,* 29.

61. Julie A. Nelson, "Review of *Economy of Grace* by Kathryn Tanner," *Journal of the American Academy of Religion* 74, no. 3 (September 2006): 783–784; Rowena Pecchenino, "On Tanner's 'Economy of Grace': An Economist Responds," *Irish Theological Quarterly* 72, no. 1 (2007): 96–104, offers an extended criticism along the same lines.

62. Tanner delivered her series of six lectures in Edinburgh in May 2016. Kathryn Tanner, "Christianity and the New Spirit of Capitalism," Gifford Lectures,

http://www.ed.ac.uk/humanities-soc-sci/news-events/lectures/gifford
-lectures/gifford-lectures-2015-2016/professor-tanner-christianity-and
-capitalism. A monograph of the lecture series is forthcoming from Yale.

63. Bernard Dempsey, *Interest and Usury* (Washington, DC: American Council
on Public Affairs, 1943). Brian M. McCall, *The Church and the Usurers: Unprofitable Lending for the Modern Economy* (Ave Maria, FL: Sapientia Press
of Ave Maria University, 2013), offers a more recent argument in the same
vein.

64. Bernard Dempsey, *The Functional Economy: The Bases of Economic Organization* (Englewood Cliffs, NJ: Prentice Hall, 1958).

65. A fear of social disapprobation might be one explanation for why stores run
out of batteries in the days leading up to a big storm, rather than raising the
prices quite high in order to allocate the batteries on hand to those in most
need of them.

66. Thomas Aquinas, *Summa theologica,* trans. Fathers of the English Dominican Province (Allen, TX: Christian Classics, 1948).

67. Aquinas, *Summa theologica,* I.2. pr.

68. Note that the finite goods need not be simply material goods. Whether we
want more electronic gadgets or more time to read more books, the key idea
is that we want more of an array of finite goods.

69. John Paul II, *Centesimus annus* (1991), 36.

70. Aquinas, *Summa theologica,* II–II.66.2.

71. Aquinas, *Summa theologica,* II–II.32.6.

72. C. S. Lewis, "The Weight of Glory," in *The Weight of Glory and Other Addresses*
(New York: HarperCollins e-books, 2009), 26–48, offers a powerful argument
against thinking of charity as self-denial.

73. Aquinas, *Summa theologica,* I–II.96.3.

74. In fact, there are some good books that show the value of Aristotle as a source
for rethinking economics. In addition to Yuengert, *Approximating Prudence,*
see also Ricardo F. Crespo, *A Re-Assessment of Aristotle's Economic Thought*
(London: Routledge, 2014), and Ricardo F. Crespo, *Philosophy of the Economy:
An Aristotelian Approach* (Heidelberg: Springer Cham, 2013).

2. The Rational Choice Model and Its Limitations

1. Joan Robinson, *Economic Philosophy* (Garden City, NY: Doubleday, 1964).

2. But see Deirdre McCloskey, *The Bourgeois Virtues: Ethics for an Age of Commerce* (Chicago: University of Chicago Press, 2006).

3. *Heterodox economics* is the umbrella term for all economics that is not neoclassical. Varieties of heterodox economics include but are not limited to
Marxist, institutionalist, and feminist economics.

4. The assumption of unbounded or infinite desire for finite goods is so ubiquitous that it frequently informs analysis done by Christians who are perhaps
unaware of the theological problems introduced by positing such a desire.

5. Lionel Robbins, *An Essay on the Nature and Significance of Economic Science*
(London: Macmillan, 1932), is the source of the standard definition. It is not
the only one used historically, but since World War II, it has been the most
common definition, and most others orbit around it. See Roger E. Backhouse
and Steven G. Medema, "On the Definition of Economics," *Journal of Economic Perspectives* 23, no. 1 (Winter 2009): 221–233.

6. Before the financial crisis of 2008, a lot of the "hot" economics was of the sort
done by Steven D. Levitt and Stephen J. Dubner, *Freakonomics: A Rogue Economist Explores the Hidden Side of Everything* (New York: Harper Perennial,
2009), applying economic reasoning and tools to a wide variety of questions
concerning human behavior. See Gary Becker, *The Economic Approach to
Human Behavior* (Chicago: University of Chicago Press, 1976), for a more
scholarly exercise of that perspective.

7. Mary S. Morgan, *The World in the Model: How Economists Work and Think*
(Cambridge, UK: Cambridge University Press, 2012) offers a thorough account of the practice of model building in economics. Dani Rodrik, *Economics
Rules: The Rights and Wrongs of the Dismal Science* (New York: W. W. Norton,
2015), provides an economist's perspective on the practice of model building.

8. Adam Smith, who is typically regarded as the father of economic science, did
not use mathematics in his economic reasoning. Indeed, his economic thought
was a mixture of thick observation of the world and the sort of reductive
analysis that has since come to define the discipline. David Ricardo, who appeared in the generation following Smith's, was the first major economist to
rely heavily on the abstract reasoning of models. The shift from classical economics to neoclassical economics was accompanied by an increased reliance
on mathematical reasoning. Even so, the early neoclassical economist Alfred
Marshall, who developed the form of the supply-and-demand model most
commonly used, argued that economists should only use mathematics as a
discipline to their thought and that they should translate their findings into
prose and burn the mathematics they had used to arrive at their insights. It
is only since the mid-twentieth century that economists have insisted that
genuine economic reasoning be essentially a form of applied mathematics,
with translation into prose an optional matter. For an accessible overview of
the history of economic thought, see Robert Heilbroner, *The Worldly Philosophers: The Lives, Times and Ideas of the Great Economic Thinkers* (New York:
Touchstone, 1999).

9. The field of behavioral economics, which has blossomed over the past few decades, does conduct experiments in a laboratory setting and sometimes also
in the field, but there are only a limited number of questions that can be ad-

dressed in such a setting. The apparatus for testing theories with the use of data generated naturally is called econometrics, which is a form of statistics that primarily serves to study the correlations among multiple variables, so that the impact of one variable on another can be discerned while holding all other variables constant.

10. Andrew Yuengert, *Approximating Prudence: Aristotelian Practical Wisdom and Economic Models of Choice* (New York: Palgrave Macmillan, 2012), explores the constraints the emphasis on mathematical precision imposes on economic model-building.

11. In his best-selling introductory textbook, Gregory Mankiw, *Principles of Economics*, 4th ed. (Mason, OH: Thomson South-Western, 2007), titles his second chapter "Thinking Like an Economist."

12. Anne Krueger, Kenneth Arrow, Olivier Blanchard, Alan Blinder, Claudia Goldin, Edward Leamer, Robert Lucas, John Panzar, Rudolph Penner, Paul Schultz, Joseph Stiglitz, and Lawrence Summers, "Report of the Commission on Graduate Education in Economics," *Journal of Economic Literature* 29, no. 3 (September, 1991): 1035–1053.

13. The classic text is Milton Friedman, "The Methodology of Positive Economics," in *Essays in Positive Economics* (Chicago: University of Chicago Press, 1966), 3–43.

14. The central point here is that economists model human decision making as an exercise in maximizing a utility function subject to constraint rather than as optimizing a utility function that has a natural point of satiation. It is this feature of economic thought that gives rise to the notion that we always face trade-offs. There is always some good one would like more of, but because of constraints one can only get more of that desirable good by sacrificing some other good.

15. See David Kreps, *A Course in Microeconomic Theory* (Princeton, NJ: Princeton University Press, 1990), 17–70, for an example of the technical backdrop to all of this.

16. Paul Samuelson, "A Note on the Pure Theory of Consumer's Behaviour," *Economica*, n.s., 5, no. 17 (February 1938): 61–71.

17. As Samuelson, "A Note on the Pure Theory of Consumer's Behaviour," 62, writes, "I propose, therefore, that we start anew in direct attack upon the problem, dropping off the last vestiges of the utility analysis. *This does not preclude the introduction of utility by any who may care to do so, nor will it contradict the results attained by use of related constructs.* It is merely that the analysis can be carried on more directly, and from a different set of postulates" (emphasis added).

18. Richard Kraut, *What Is Good and Why: The Ethics of Well-Being* (Cambridge, MA: Harvard University Press, 2007), 14n19, associates the word *maximization* with the idea of assigning some quantitative measure to goods and

selecting the option with the highest quantitative value. However, he acknowledges that others use the term the way economists claim to, as choosing by ranking options without necessarily assigning quantitative values to the various choices. Kraut observes that in some sense it is trivially true that we choose the best, or at least the not-worse, option whenever we can. The question is whether the fact that economists map these rankings onto a quantitative measure and talk about maximizing does not, in fact, force them closer to the more content-laden assumption that people maximize some quantity of goodness when making choices.

19. The seminal article is Daniel Kahneman and Amos Tversky, "Prospect Theory: An Analysis of Decision under Risk," *Econometrica* 47, no. 2 (March 1979): 263–291. The new field of behavioral economics has the ability to do things like make sense of bubbles (something that's not easily done under a strict rational choice view).

20. The underlying approach for economists is to find a model of human behavior that can be treated mathematically and used to generate predictions.

21. Gary Becker, *A Treatise on the Family* (Cambridge, MA: Harvard University Press, 1993).

22. See Ted Bergstrom, "Love and Spaghetti: The Opportunity Cost of Virtue," *Journal of Economic Perspectives* 3, no. 2 (Spring 1989): 165–173, for a discussion of the puzzle.

23. A. M. C. Waterman, *Revolution, Economics, and Religion: Christian Political Economy, 1798–1833* (Cambridge, UK: Cambridge University Press, 1991), 205–207, reports that ironically the positive / normative distinction was first made by Anglican theologian / political economist Richard Whately, who wanted to prevent radicals from using the conclusions of political economy in support of their public policy positions (and to defend the study of political economy to the Church).

24. Andrew Yuengert, *The Boundaries of Technique: Ordering Positive and Normative Concerns in Economic Research* (Lanham, MD: Lexington Books, 2004), 1.

25. As discussed in Chapter 1, the failure to distinguish between means and ends most commonly manifests itself by noneconomists intervening in economic disputes about policy at the wrong level of discussion. They will read one side of the debate as having better values and argue for those values, when in fact the values are essentially agreed on and the argument is about how best to realize those values.

26. Friedman, "The Methodology of Positive Economics," 5. In his compilation of important works in economic philosophy, Daniel Hausman, *The Philosophy of Economics: An Anthology* (Cambridge, UK: Cambridge University Press, 1994), 180, describes Friedman's essay as "the most influential work on economic methodology of [the twentieth] century."

27. Yuengert, *The Boundaries of Technique*, 49.

28. Yuengert, *The Boundaries of Technique,* 57.
29. Yuengert, *The Boundaries of Technique,* 8
30. Yuengert, *Approximating Prudence.*
31. Joel Waldfogel, "The Deadweight Loss of Christmas," *American Economic Review* 83, no. 5 (December 1993): 1328–1336; Sara J. Solnick and David Hemenway, "The Deadweight Loss of Christmas: Comment," *American Economic Review* 86, no. 5 (December 1996): 1299–1305; Joel Waldfogel, "The Deadweight Loss of Christmas: Reply," *American Economic Review* 86, no. 5 (December 1996): 1306–1308; John A. List and Jason F. Shogren, "The Deadweight Loss of Christmas: Comment," *American Economic Review* 88, no. 5 (December 1998): 1350–1355; Sara J. Solnick and David Hemenway, "The Deadweight Loss of Christmas: Reply," *American Economic Review* 88, no. 5 (December 1998): 1356–1357; Joel Waldfogel, "The Deadweight Loss of Christmas: Reply," *American Economic Review* 88, no. 5 (December 1998): 1358–1360; Bradley J. Ruffle and Orit Tykocinski, "The Deadweight Loss of Christmas: Comment," *American Economic Review* 90, no. 1 (March 2000): 319–324; Sara J. Solnick and David Hemenway, "The Deadweight Loss of Christmas: Reply," *American Economic Review* 90, no. 1 (March 2000): 325–326. The concept of deadweight loss is explained more fully below.
32. For example, Kristine E. Principe and Joseph G. Eisenhauer, "Gift-Giving and Deadweight Loss," *Journal of Socio-Economics* 38, no. 2 (March 2009): 215–220, conclude that although there have been some moves in the direction of giving cash cards to reduce the deadweight loss, "there remains substantial deadweight loss associated with non-monetary gift-giving" and that "market-based solutions have not been successful in alleviating this market failure" (220).
33. Joel Waldfogel, "Gifts, Cash, and Stigma," *Economic Inquiry* 40, no. 1 (July 2002): 415–427.
34. The tax will successfully transfer money to the government. The deadweight loss from the tax is not premised on the idea that the government will not use that money well. It is that the manner of transferring the money to the government creates a wedge in the prices, which causes some beneficial transactions to not take place. The deadweight loss is a side effect of the tax.
35. A lot of effort goes into thinking about how to design tax policies that are as neutral as possible, but it is difficult because whatever it is that gets taxed will have a price distortion that alters behavior.
36. I am bracketing a large and standing problem with the measure of efficiency, which is that it takes the distribution of income as a given. If Bill Gates feels like paying $100,000 for the last sandwich available, and the starving poor man can only pay $1, it would be most "efficient" for Bill Gates to get that sandwich. This is the reasoning behind Larry Summers's controversial World Bank memo in which he argued that it would be efficient to transfer pollution to

poor countries. Economists recognize that there are multiple efficient equilibria corresponding to different distributions of income but relegate the question of which of these equilibria is to be preferred to the subject of normative economics.

37. John Kenneth Galbraith, *The Affluent Society* (Boston: Houghton Mifflin, 1958); Thorstein Veblen, *The Theory of the Leisure Class: An Economic Study of Institutions* (New York: Macmillan, 1912). Hazel Kyrk, *A Theory of Consumption* (Boston: Houghton Mifflin, 1923), has a good discussion that blends these and other related concerns.

38. John Elster, *Sour Grapes: Studies in the Subversion of Rationality* (Cambridge, UK: Cambridge University Press, 1985).

39. Tyler Cowen, "The Scope and Limits of Preference Sovereignty," *Economics and Philosophy* 9, no. 2 (October 1993): 253–269. Cowen also raises the question of whether the standard model can account for the value of being surprised in life.

40. Wesley Mitchell, *The Backward Art of Spending Money and Other Essays* (New York: A. M. Kelley, 1950).

41. Daniel M. Hausman and Michael S. McPherson, *Economic Analysis, Moral Philosophy, and Public Policy,* 2nd ed. (Cambridge, UK: Cambridge University Press, 2006), 97–156, devote an entire section of their book to the problem.

42. Daniel Kahneman and Alan B. Krueger, "Developments in the Measurement of Subjective Well-Being," *Journal of Economic Perspectives* 20, no. 1 (Winter 2006): 3–24.

43. Daniel Kahneman and Richard H. Thaler, "Anomalies: Utility Maximization and Experienced Utility," *Journal of Economic Perspectives* 20, no. 1 (Winter 2006): 221–234.

44. Subjective measures used include life-quality assessments that ask respondents about their overall satisfaction in life and time studies that ask respondents to pause several times a day to report on their activities and their effect. Bruno S. Frey, *Happiness: A Revolution in Economics* (Cambridge, MA: MIT Press, 2008), offers a good overview of the field.

45. Colin Camerer, "The Case for Mindful Economics," in *The Foundations of Positive and Normative Economics: A Handbook,* ed. Andrew Caplin and Andrew Schotter (Oxford, UK: Oxford University Press, 2008), 43–69.

46. Camerer, "The Case for Mindful Economics," 58.

47. Faruk Gul and Wolfgang Pesendorfer, "The Case for Mindless Economics," in Caplin and Schotter, *Foundations of Positive and Normative Economics: A Handbook,* 3–42.

48. Gul and Pesendorfer, "The Case for Mindless Economics," 5 (emphasis added).

49. Kahneman and Krueger, "Developments in the Measurement of Subjective Well-Being," tend to move in that direction. George Lowenstein and Emily Haisley, "The Economist as Therapist: Methodological Ramifications of 'Light'

Paternalism," in Caplin and Schotter, *Foundations of Positive and Normative Economics*, 210–248, take up the question of how to square light paternalism with the traditional split between positive and normative economics. As Joseph Persky, "Retrospectives: Consumer Sovereignty," *Journal of Economic Perspectives* 7, no. 1 (Winter 1993): 183–191, argues earlier in the twentieth century, William Hutt conceded that there were many reasons to question a tight connection between choice and well-being and argued instead for consumer sovereignty on the grounds of freedom.

50. Daniel Hausman, "Mindless or Mindful Economics: A Methodological Evaluation," in Caplin and Schotter, *Foundations of Positive and Normative Economics,* 143.

51. Hausman, "Mindless or Mindful Economics," 147.

52. Daniel M. Hausman and Michael S. McPherson, "Preference Satisfaction and Welfare Economics," *Economics and Philosophy* 25, no. 1 (March 2009): 1–25.

53. Lest I be misunderstood here, my own position is not that freedom of choice is not an important value to be preserved; it is rather that it is instrumental to the achievement of happiness in a manner other than the one that is implicit in Hausman and McPherson's position.

54. Amartya Sen, "Rational Fools: A Critique of the Behavior Foundations of Economic Theory," *Philosophy and Public Affairs* 6, no. 4 (Summer 1977): 317–344.

55. Sen, "Rational Fools," 326–327.

56. Other topics Sen mentions are public goods and the free-rider problem and worker commitment as an important component in raising productivity.

57. Amartya Sen, *Rationality and Freedom* (Cambridge, MA: Harvard University Press, 2002), 213–214.

58. Philip Pettit, "Construing Sen on Commitment," *Economics and Philosophy* 21, no. 1 (April 2005): 15–32; Daniel M. Hausman, "Sympathy, Commitment, and Preference," *Economics and Philosophy* 21, no. 1 (April 2005): 33–50.

59. Pettit, "Construing Sen on Commitment."

60. In the traditional formulation, two criminals are separately offered the following deal: If you confess, and your partner doesn't, you will go free, but your partner will spend ten years in jail. If you both confess, you both will spend two years in jail. If neither confesses, neither will go to jail. In economics the problem arises in situations like the question of whether oligopolies can cooperate with one another to form successful cartels, or whether they will inevitably cheat and thereby reduce profits all around, hence the framing above in terms of payoffs rather than reduced sentences.

61. The problem with the prisoner's dilemma is that it is an exception to the rule in economics that pursuit of private interest generally leads to better outcomes all around rather than worse outcomes all around.

62. The usual strategy is to assume that individuals have uncertainty about what the other would do, but that gives us the perverse conclusion that rational behavior requires that people operate out of relative ignorance.

63. Jeannette Brosig, "Identifying Cooperative Behavior: Some Experimental Results in a Prisoner's Dilemma Game," *Journal of Economic Behavior & Organization* 47, no. 3 (March 2002): 275–290.

64. The matrix in Table 2 is read as follows: If F, which reflects the direct value of cooperating, is greater than 1, cooperating would become the dominant strategy for both players, and the game would no longer be a prisoner's dilemma.

65. K. G. Binmore, *Game Theory and the Social Contract* (Cambridge, MA: Harvard University Press, 1984), 104.

66. Greg Mankiw, *Macroeconomics,* 5th ed. (New York: Worth Publishers, 2003), 42. The quote comes from *Mansfield Park* by Jane Austen. The line is spoken by Mary Crawford, who ends up being shunned by the protagonists of the novel owing to character flaws flowing from her overestimation of the value of wealth and status.

67. The basic tool here is the indifference curve, which shows the trade-offs between two goods that would leave a consumer equally well off. In the basic diagram there are an ever-ascending series of indifference curves, and the aim of utility maximization is to achieve the highest possible indifference curve given one's constraints. Increases in income shift out the "budget constraint" and allow consumers to achieve a higher level of utility.

68. John Maynard Keynes, "Economic Possibilities for Our Grandchildren," in *Essays in Persuasion* (New York: W. W. Norton, 1963), 358–373.

69. Tibor Scitovsky, "Are Men Rational or Economists Wrong?," in *Human Desire and Economic Satisfaction: Essays on the Frontiers of Economics* (New York: New York University Press, 1986), chap. 6. Scitovsky did important work in mainstream microeconomics before taking up the sorts of questions I raise about the overall rationality of the economic system.

70. Juliet B. Schor, *The Overworked American: The Unexpected Decline in Leisure* (New York: Basic Books, 1991); Juliet B. Schor, *The Overspent American: Upscaling, Downshifting, and the New Consumer* (New York: Basic Books, 1998).

71. Stephen Marglin, *The Dismal Science: How Thinking Like an Economist Undermines Community* (Cambridge, MA: Harvard University Press, 2010), 215–217. Marglin's claim that the meaning of scarcity has mutated with the advent of modernity is compatible with my own construal of Thomas's thought about consumption; see Chapter 5.

72. The retraining focused on public education, the main purpose of which was to inculcate the idea of punctuality and work schedules into the future working force. See E. P. Thompson, *The Making of the English Working Class* (New York: Pantheon Books, 1963).

73. Richard A. Easterlin, "Does Economic Growth Improve the Human Lot?," in *Nations and Households in Economic Growth: Essays in Honor of Moses Abramovitz,* ed. Paul A. David and Melvin W. Reder (New York: Academic Press, 1974), 89–125.

74. Angus Deaton, "Income, Health, and Well-Being around the World: Evidence from the Gallup World Poll," *Journal of Economic Perspectives* 22, no. 2 (Spring 2008): 53–72.

75. Carol Graham, Soumya Chattopadhyay, and Mario Picon, "The Easterlin and Other Paradoxes: Why Both Sides of the Debate May Be Correct," in *International Differences in Well-Being,* ed. Ed Diener, John F. Helliwell, and Daniel Kahneman (Oxford, UK: Oxford University Press, 2010), 247–290.

76. The argument that it is doubtful that unlimited economic growth is desirable should not be taken as an argument that it is doubtful that economic growth is a very good way of lifting large numbers of people out of dire poverty.

77. I add in the caveat of "all things considered" to avoid the confusion that the argument here is that we should work as hard as possible in order to maximize income. Leisure is a good, effort is usually seen as a cost. Both factor into the bundles of choices themselves. So the increase in income ceteris paribus is meant to get at basically an increase in productivity or any change that would allow us to expand our consumption without having to give up leisure (or would allow us to expand leisure without having to give up goods).

3. Happiness and the Distinctively Human Exercise of Practical Reason: The Metaphysical Backdrop

1. Thomas Aquinas, *Summa theologica,* trans. Fathers of the English Dominican Province (Allen, TX: Christian Classics, 1948), I–II, 1.

2. As Georg Wieland, "Happiness (Ia IIae, qq.1–5)," trans. Grant Kaplan, in *The Ethics of Aquinas,* ed. Stephen J. Pope (Washington, DC: Georgetown University Press, 2002), 57, argues, Aquinas's prologue says that insofar as man is made in the image of God "he is himself the principle of his actions, possessing, so to speak, a free will and control over his actions" (I.II, prologue). The qualifier "so to speak" (*quasi*) is a gesture toward the fact that no action can be done apart from God. As Wieland observes, in the *Summa contra Gentiles* Aquinas focuses more on God's role in creation. In this analysis I do not deal with the vexed question of how we understand our agency vis à vis God's agency. The distinctions I draw center on how our agency contrasts with the agency of nonrational creatures. The way we move ourselves in creation differs from the way other animals move themselves, however one thinks of God's role in moving creatures within creation.

3. Aquinas, *Summa theologica,* I–II, 1.1.

4. Aquinas, *Summa theologica,* I–II, 1.1.ad.3.

5. Aquinas, *Summa theologica,* I–II, 1.2.ob.1

6. Aquinas, *Summa theologica,* I–II, 1.2.

7. "Illa vero quae ratione carent, tendunt in finem per naturalem inclinationem, quasi ab alio mota, non autem a seipsis, *cum non cognoscant rationem finis,* et ideo *nihil in finem ordinare possunt,* sed solum in finem ab alio ordinantur" (Aquinas, *Summa theologica,* I–II, 1.2; emphasis added).

8. Aquinas, *Summa theologica,* I–II, 1.2.ad.1.

9. We might object that in the wake of Darwin we know better than to believe that there is purpose in nature. First, Thomas plainly thinks nature is ordered by God—and insofar as Thomas sees God as *not* a cause commensurate with other created causes, that ordering by God is compatible with an ordering within nature that follows from the action of natural selection on random mutations. God could direct the order in nature as easily through random causes as through nonrandom causes. See Ernan McMullin, "Evolution and Creation," in *Evolution and Creation,* ed. Ernan McMullin (Notre Dame, IN: University of Notre Dame Press, 1985), 1–58, for a good discussion of the compatibility of evolution with God's creation of the world. Second, even biologists have admitted that teleological language is necessary when talking about biological organisms in their own operations. Jean Porter, *Nature as Reason: A Thomistic Theory of the Natural Law* (Grand Rapids, MI: William B. Eerdmans Publishing, 2005), 82–124, offers an excellent discussion of this issue.

10. Alasdair MacIntyre, *Dependent Rational Animals: Why Human Beings Need the Virtues* (Chicago: Open Court, 1999).

11. MacIntyre, *Dependent Rational Animals,* 23, 47–48. MacIntyre also lauds dolphins on their ability to learn and teach, to investigate new objects inquisitively, and to cooperate in hunts. I am as skeptical of the implications MacIntyre draws from these behaviors as I am of the conclusions he draws from the fact that dolphins sometimes eat and sometimes play with their food. (Not that he's wrong, simply that he has not reported the underlying scientific studies clearly enough for one to really reflect on what's at stake in the observations.)

12. John H. Kagel, Raymond C. Battalio, Howard Rachlin, Leonard Green, Robert L. Basmann, and W. R. Klemm, "Experimental Studies of Consumer Demand Behavior Using Laboratory Animals," *Economic Inquiry* 13, no. 1 (March 1975): 22–38.

13. M. Keith Chen, with Venkat Lakshminarayanan and Laurie R. Santos, "How Basic Are Behavioral Biases? Evidence from Capuchin Monkey Trading Behavior," *Journal of Political Economy* 114, no. 3 (June 2006): 517–537.

14. The idea that humans may "satisfice" rather than optimize originated with Herbert Simon, *Administrative Behavior: A Study of Decision-Making Processes in Administrative Organization,* 1st ed. (New York: MacMillan, 1947).

More recently, there's been a proliferation of models assuming "bounded rationality." See, for example, Gerd Gigerenzer and Reinhard Selten, *Bounded Rationality* (Cambridge, MA: MIT Press, 2002).

15. Milton Friedman, "The Methodology of Positive Economics," in *Essays in Persuasion* (Chicago: University of Chicago Press, 1966), 19–20.

16. Aquinas, *Summa theologica,* I–II, 6.1.

17. Thomas Aquinas, *De veritate,* trans. Robert W. Schmidt, S.J. (Chicago: Henry Regnery Company, 1954), 24.2.

18. Aquinas, *De veritate,* 24.2.c.

19. Aquinas, *De veritate,* 24.2.ad.7.

20. Michael Sandel, *What Money Can't Buy: The Moral Limits of Markets* (New York: Farrar, Straus and Giroux, 2012), 118–119.

21. Robert Axelrod, in *The Evolution of Cooperation* (New York: Basic Books, 1984), summarizes the results.

22. The *locus classicus* on this argument is Israel Kirzner, *Competition and Entrepreneurship* (Chicago: University of Chicago Press, 1978).

23. Thomas Aquinas, *Summa contra Gentiles,* trans. James F. Anderson (Notre Dame, IN: University of Notre Dame Press, 1975), 3.112.1.

24. Aquinas, *Summa theologica,* I–II, 1.3.

25. Aquinas, *Summa theologica,* I–II, 1.3.ad.3.

26. Daniel Klein, "Does Economics Need an Infusion of Religious or Quasi-Religious Formulations? A Symposium Prologue," *Econ Journal Watch* 11, no. 2 (May 2014): 97–105, complains that economists are too prone to flattening the human experience across a number of dimensions. That is the essence of the critique I am drawing out here.

27. Aquinas, *Summa theologica,* I–II, 1.4.

28. Aquinas, *Summa theologica,* I–II, 1.4.

29. Aquinas, *Summa theologica,* I–II, 1.4.ob.2.

30. Aquinas, *Summa theologica,* I–II, 1.4.sc.

31. Aquinas, *Summa theologica,* I–II, 1.8.

32. Aquinas, *Summa theologica,* I–II, 1.4.ad.2.

33. Aquinas, *Summa theologica,* I–II, 1.4.

34. As Georg Wieland, "Happiness (Ia IIae, qq.1–5)," 58, puts it, "[without positing a final end,] the floodgates would be open for randomness and complete relativity."

35. Aquinas, *Summa theologica,* I–II, 2.

36. Aquinas, *Summa theologica,* I–II, 1.5.

37. Aquinas, *Summa theologica,* I–II, 1.5.sc.

38. Aquinas, *Summa theologica,* I–II, 1.6.

39. Aquinas, *Summa theologica,* I–II, 1.7.

40. I use the term *metaphysics* broadly to mean the set of answers one would give to foundational questions about the nature of the world in which we find

ourselves. Where did it come from? Does it have any meaning? What is good? And so on. Per this usage, everyone has a metaphysics of some sort since the way one answers these questions informs the way one thinks about things—even if one is unaware of the metaphysical assumptions one has made.

41. I have in mind something like Charles Taylor's concept of the "social imaginary." Charles Taylor, *Modern Social Imaginaries* (Durham, NC: Duke University Press, 2004).

42. Robert Sokolowski, *The God of Faith and Reason: Foundations of Christian Theology* (Washington, DC: Catholic University of America Press, 1982), likewise begins his account of Christian theology by stressing the unique concept of a Creator God. The analysis here reaches the same conclusions, though he works through St. Anselm's conception of God as "that than which nothing greater can be thought," whereas this account works through Aquinas's metaphysics of creation. See David Bentley Hart, *The Experience of God: Being, Consciousness, Bliss* (New Haven, CT: Yale University Press, 2013), for the argument that a philosophy grounded in the assumption that God created the world ex nihilo is both plausible and coherent.

43. The opening lines of Genesis 1 would seem to be a description of a demiurge, but the Judeo-Christian tradition evolved toward thinking of God as creating the world ex nihilo. For Aquinas the key text is in Exodus 3:14, where God says to Moses, "I am who I am."

44. Sokolowski, *The God of Faith and Reason*, 23. David Burrell, C.S.C., *Freedom and Creation in Three Traditions* (Notre Dame, IN: University of Notre Dame Press, 1993), argues that the distinction between God and creation is central to Jewish and Muslim thought as well.

45. Aquinas, *Summa theologica*, I, 2.3.

46. Denys Turner, *Faith, Reason, and the Existence of God* (Cambridge, UK: Cambridge University Press, 2004), suggests that the proofs are better understood as showing that we can push reason to its limits by finding well-formulated questions to which we know we can find no well-formulated answers, thereby opening up space for that which we understand as God.

47. Aquinas, *Summa theologica*, I, 3.4.

48. Or at least, he exists for now. At the time of this writing, he is twenty years old and is getting pretty feeble!

49. Aquinas, *Summa theologica*, I, 44.1.

50. Aquinas believed that the world did have a starting point, but unlike some of his contemporaries, he thought this was an article of faith, not something that could be philosophically demonstrated. Aquinas, *Summa theologica*, I, 46.2.

51. Aquinas, *Summa contra Gentiles*, III:1, 65.

52. Aquinas, *Summa theologica*, I, 3.7.

53. Aquinas, *Summa theologica,* I, 3.prologue. Questions 3 through 11 of the *prima pars* seem to be about positive statements about God—that is, that he is simple, that he is perfect, and so on. But as Thomas himself states in the prologue cited here, these are all questions that discuss how God is not, not how God is. Thus what Thomas means by "simplicity" is that God is not "composite." See David B. Burrell, C.S.C., *Aquinas: God and Action,* 3rd ed. (Eugene, OR: Wipf & Stock, 2016).

54. Aquinas, *Summa Theologica,* I, 3.3.ad.1; 13.1.ad.2. We could try to escape the problem of ascribing composition to God by using abstract rather than concrete nouns. Thus "God is goodness." But language fails there also since abstract nouns do not connote subsisting beings, and God is a subsisting being. Whichever way we go, our language falls short of the reality.

55. Aquinas, *Summa theologica,* I, 13.5.

56. William C. Placher, *The Domestication of Transcendence: How Modern Thinking about God Went Wrong* (Louisville, KY: Westminster John Knox Press, 1996), offers a good discussion of both the cause and consequences of the modern tendency to think of God using univocal language.

57. Robert Sokolowski, *The God of Faith and Reason,* works through Anselm's definition of God to arrive at the same set of conclusions I am discussing in this section.

58. Moses Maimonides, *The Guide to the Perplexed,* trans. Michael Friedländer, Kindle ed. (Santa Cruz, CA: Evinity Publishing, 2009).

59. Aquinas, *Summa theologica,* I, 3.prologue.

60. Aquinas, *Summa theologica,* I, 13.2.

61. Aquinas, *Summa theologica,* I, 13.2.

62. Aquinas, *Summa theologica,* I, 4.1.

63. Aquinas, *Summa theologica,* I, 13.2.

64. A generation after Aquinas, John Duns Scotus famously took issue with the doctrine of analogy, though he did so by taking on the version of that doctrine found in Henry of Ghent, not from Thomas himself. Mary Beth Ingham, "Re-Situating Scotist Thought," *Modern Theology* 21, no. 4 (October 2005): 611–612. Scotus insisted that we can only prove God's existence if our talk of God is univocal. The Radical Orthodoxy movement has argued that Scotus's move undermines our ability to appreciate God's transcendence. A good summary of the position can be found in Catherine Pickstock, "Duns Scotus: His Historical and Contemporary Significance," *Modern Theology* 21, no. 4 (October 2005): 543–574. Denys Turner, "On Denying the Right God: Aquinas on Atheism and Idolatry," *Modern Theology* 20, no. 1 (January 2004): 141–162, offers a good discussion of this issue, arguing that Scotus insists on univocity because he conceives the nature of the proofs differently from Thomas. On that reading, Scotus and Thomas are not at direct odds with each other on this issue.

65. Aquinas, *Summa theologica*, I, 13.5.
66. Aquinas, *Summa theologica*, I, 13.5.
67. Aquinas, *Summa theologica*, I, 13.6.
68. See Henk J. M. Schoot, *Christ the "Name" of God: Thomas Aquinas on Naming Christ* (Leuven: Peeters, 1993), for a good discussion of the importance of grammar for understanding Aquinas's theology.
69. Aquinas, *Summa theologica*, I, 44.4
70. Aquinas, *Summa theologica*, I, 12.2.
71. Aquinas, *Summa theologica*, I, 3.3.ad.2.
72. Aquinas, *Summa theologica*, I, 47.1
73. Aquinas, *Summa theologica*, I, 47.3.
74. Aquinas, *Summa theologica*, I, 4.1.
75. Aquinas, *Summa theologica*, I, 4.2.
76. Aquinas, *Summa theologica*, I, 6.1.ad.2.
77. Aquinas, *Summa theologica*, I, 6.3.

4. Happiness and the Distinctively Human Exercise of Practical Reason: Virtue and Prudence

1. Thomas Aquinas, *Summa theologica,* trans. Fathers of the English Dominican Province (Allen, TX: Christian Classics, 1948), I–II, 2.
2. Aquinas, *Summa theologica*, I–II, 2.1.
3. Aquinas, *Summa theologica*, I–II, 2.2; 2.3.
4. Aquinas, *Summa theologica*, I–II, 2.4.
5. Aquinas, *Summa theologica*, I–II, 2.5.
6. Aquinas, *Summa theologica*, I–II, 2.6.
7. Aquinas, *Summa theologica*, I–II, 2.7.
8. Aquinas, *Summa theologica*, I–II, 2.8; 2.9.
9. Aquinas, *Summa theologica*, I, 93.4
10. Aquinas, *Summa theologica*, I, 12.12; I–II, 109.
11. Aquinas, *Summa theologica*, I, 93.4.
12. Denis J. M. Bradley, *Aquinas on the Twofold Human Good: Reason and Happiness in Aquinas's Moral Science* (Washington, DC: Catholic University of America Press, 1997), gives an overview of the debate. Kevin Staley, "Happiness: The Natural End of Man?," *The Thomist* 53, no. 2 (1989): 215–234, argues for the analogical reading I suggest here.
13. Aquinas, *Summa theologica*, I–II, 3.2.ad.4.
14. Aquinas, *Summa theologica*, I–II, 3.6.
15. Aquinas, *Summa theologica*, I, 4.3.
16. Aquinas, *Summa theologica*, I, 93.2.
17. Aquinas, *Summa theologica*, I–II, prologue.

18. Aquinas, *Summa theologica,* I–II, 3.2.ad.4.

19. Aquinas, *Summa theologica,* I, 93.1.

20. Aquinas, *Summa theologica,* I, 93.4.

21. Aquinas, *Summa theologica,* I–II, 2.8; 3.4.

22. The discussion of the human capacity for self-direction and self-development should not be understood as claiming special agency vis à vis God. God's grace works through all of our choices and acts. See Joseph Wawrykow, *God's Grace and Human Action: "Merit" in the Theology of Thomas Aquinas* (Notre Dame, IN: University of Notre Dame Press, 1995), for a nuanced discussion of the multiple ways in which grace works in Aquinas's account. See Jennifer Herdt, *Putting on Virtue: The Legacy of the Splendid Vices* (Chicago: University of Chicago Press, 2008), for an account of how anxiety about God's agency vis à vis human agency has complicated Christian pursuit of virtue. Herdt thinks that Aquinas might navigate the tensions satisfactorily, though she ultimately pursues a more Erasmian approach to reclaiming the virtues for Christian moral theology. For my purposes, I hope it is sufficient to note that however we understand God's role in human affairs, Aquinas's claims about human self-direction can be fruitfully understood as a way of explaining what is distinctive about humans compared with nonrational creatures, and, more importantly, why we need a better account of practical reason than the one embedded in the rational choice model.

23. Aquinas, *Summa theologica,* I–II, 49, prologue. By contrast, our actions are also shaped by the "extrinsic principles" of law and grace (I–II, 90, prologue).

24. Aquinas, *Summa theologica,* I–II, 49.1,3,4.

25. Jonathan Haidt, *The Happiness Hypothesis: Finding Modern Truth in Ancient Wisdom* (New York: Basic Books, 2006), offers a survey of the findings of the modern social sciences that resonate with the view that habits play a crucial role in how we behave.

26. Aquinas, *Summa theologica,* I–II, 51.2,3; 52.1; 53.2.

27. Aquinas, *Summa theologica,* I–II, 51.4.

28. Aquinas, *Summa theologica,* I–II, 55.1.

29. Aquinas, *Summa theologica,* I–II, 55.2.

30. Aquinas, *Summa theologica,* I–II, 55.2.ad.3.

31. Aquinas, *Summa theologica,* I, 93.4.

32. Aquinas, *Summa theologica,* I–II, prologue.

33. Aquinas, *Summa theologica,* I–II, 55.3.

34. Aquinas, *Summa theologica,* I, 95.1.

35. M. F. Burnyeat, "Aristotle on Learning to be Good," in *Essays on Aristotle's Ethics,* ed. Amelie O. Rorty (Berkeley: University of California Press, 1980), 69–92.

36. The *locus classicus* for this literature is Thomas C. Schelling, "Egonomics, or the Art of Self-Management," *American Economic Review* 68, no. 2 (May 1978):

290–294. There is room here for fruitful engagement on the question of how we should think about this problem, and the role for incentives in nudging behavior, as discussed in Chapter 7.

37. Aquinas, *Summa theologica,* I–II, 58.3.

38. Aquinas, *Summa theologica,* I–II, 56.3.

39. Aquinas, *Summa theologica,* II–II.

40. Aquinas, *Summa theologica,* I–II, 62.1.

41. Aquinas, *Summa theologica,* II–II, 47.8.

42. Aquinas, *Summa theologica,* I–II, 65.1.

43. Jean Porter, *Nature as Reason* (Grand Rapids, MI: William B. Eerdmans Publishing, 2005), 141–230.

44. Porter, *Nature as Reason,* 221–223, makes it clear that she takes the paradigmatic form of the happy life to be the ordinary conceptions of human flourishing pursued by most people. That creates some tension, since Aquinas himself thinks that religious life, with its vows of poverty, chastity, and obedience, is a more perfect form of life. Aquinas likewise takes the theological and infused virtues as the more paradigmatic form of virtue (*Summa theologica,* I–II, 55.4; 62.1.ad.3). I am sympathetic to the claim of Christopher Franks, *He Became Poor: The Poverty of Christ and Aquinas's Economic Teachings* (Grand Rapids, MI: William B. Eerdmans Publishing, 2009), that we best understand Aquinas's teachings in light of the counsels, such as the counsel to poverty, and accordingly place more weight on the idea that a form of life is more perfect to the extent that it is more consciously structured around love of God. This difference enters into the arguments of Chapter 5, but it is a difference in emphasis more than anything else.

45. There is a long and lively discussion about how to integrate Aquinas's teachings on natural law and his teachings on virtue. In addition to Porter, *Nature as Reason,* see Daniel Mark Nelson, *The Priority of Prudence: Virtue and Natural Law in Aquinas and the Implications for Modern Ethics* (University Park: Pennsylvania State University Press, 1992), and Pamela Hall, *Narrative and the Natural Law: An Interpretation of Thomistic Ethics* (Notre Dame, IN: University of Notre Dame Press, 1994).

46. Aquinas, *Summa theologica,* I–II, 91.1,2.

47. Aquinas, *Summa theologica,* I–II, 91.3.

48. Aquinas, *Summa theologica,* I–II, 94.2.

49. Aquinas, *Summa theologica,* I–II, 4.5.

50. See Julia Annas, *The Morality of Happiness* (Oxford, UK: Oxford University Press, 1993), for a fulsome discussion of the ancient struggle to understand the relative roles of virtue and well-being in any account of human happiness.

51. Deirdre McCloskey, *The Bourgeois Virtues: Ethics for an Age of Commerce* (Chicago: University of Chicago Press, 2006).

52. Aquinas, *Summa theologica*, I–II, 57.5.

53. Aquinas, *Summa theologica*, I–II, 66.3.ad.3.

54. Aquinas, *Summa theologica*, II–II, 47.2.

55. James F. Keenan, S.J., "The Virtue of Prudence (IIa IIae, qq. 47–56)," in *The Ethics of Aquinas*, ed. Stephen J. Pope (Washington, DC: Georgetown University Press, 2002), 259.

56. Aquinas distinguishes between prudence proper and what he calls regnative prudence, or the prudence relating to our affairs in common. Nonetheless, they are different species within the same broad family of prudence (*Summa theologica*, II–II.47.11). Notice again that on Aquinas's account, prudence deals with all of our choices, not just those that are directed to our own self-concern.

57. Aquinas, *Summa theologica*, II–II, 49.1.

58. Aquinas, *Summa theologica*, II–II, 49.2.

59. Aquinas, *Summa theologica*, II–II, 49.3.

60. Aquinas, *Summa theologica*, II–II, 49.4.

61. Aquinas, *Summa theologica*, II–II, 49.5.

62. Aquinas, *Summa theologica*, II–II, 49.6.

63. Aquinas, *Summa theologica*, II–II, 49.8

64. Aquinas, *Summa theologica*, II–II, 49.7.

65. Aquinas, *Summa theologica*, I, 22.1.

66. Aquinas, *Summa theologica*, I, 22.1.ad.1.

67. Aquinas, *Summa theologica*, I–II, 91.2.

68. Andrew Yuengert, *Approximating Prudence: Aristotelian Practical Wisdom and Economic Models of Choice* (New York: Palgrave Macmillan, 2012).

69. Yuengert, *Approximating Prudence*, 159.

5. Economic Life as Ordered to Happiness

1. Thomas Aquinas, *Summa theologica*, trans. Fathers of the English Dominican Province (Allen, TX: Christian Classics, 1948), I–II, 2.1.

2. But see Armen A. Alchian, "Why Money?," *Journal of Money, Credit, and Banking* 9, no. 1, pt. 2 (February 1977), 133–140, who argues that barter is cumbersome not because it is difficult to find someone who has what you want and wants what you have but rather because imperfect information about goods creates a tendency for a well-known, easily evaluated commodity to emerge as a medium of exchange. The medium of exchange also typically functions as a unit of account, in that prices are most naturally quoted in terms of the medium of exchange and as a store of value, allowing individuals to sell in one time period and spend in another.

3. Aquinas, *Summa theologica*, I–II, 2.1. Aquinas does not include services in the term, though the approach taken in this book does.

4. Gary Becker, *A Treatise on the Family,* enlarged ed. (Cambridge, MA: Harvard University Press, 1991), 23–24.

5. Aquinas, *Summa theologica,* I–II, 4.7.

6. Aquinas, *Summa theologica,* I–II, 2.1.ad.3.

7. Some modern writers also criticize the widespread modern thought that more wealth is always desirable. See, for example, Juliet Schor, *The Overspent American: Upscaling, Downshifting, and the New Consumer* (New York: Basic Books, 1998); Robert Skidelsky and Edward Skidelsky, *How Much Is Enough? Money and the Good Life* (New York: Other Press, 2012).

8. Aquinas, *Summa theologica,* I–II, 4.7; II–II, 182.1

9. Christopher Franks, *He Became Poor: The Poverty of Christ and Aquinas's Economic Teachings* (Grand Rapids, MI: William B. Eerdmans Publishing, 2009).

10. Aquinas, *Summa theologica,* II–II, 32.6.

11. Aquinas, *Summa theologica,* I–II, 57.3.

12. Aquinas, *Summa theologica,* I–II, 57.3.ad.1.

13. Aquinas, *Summa theologica,* II–II, 117.4; II–II, 117.4.ad.2.

14. Aquinas, *Summa theologica,* II–II, 134.2.

15. Aquinas, *Summa theologica,* II–II, 134.1.ad.3.

16. Aquinas, *Summa theologica,* II–II, 134.2.ad.2.

17. Aquinas, *Summa theologica,* II–II, 134.3.ad.3.

18. Aquinas, *Summa theologica,* II–II, 134.2.ad.3.

19. Aquinas, *Summa theologica,* II–II, 118.3.ad.2.

20. Aquinas, *Summa theologica,* II–II, 119.1.

21. Aquinas, *Summa theologica,* II–II, 119.1.ad.3.

22. Aquinas, *Summa theologica,* II–II, 119.2.ad.2.

23. Aquinas, *Summa theologica,* II–II, 118.1.

24. Aquinas, *Summa theologica,* II–II, 118.1.ad.1.

25. Aquinas, *Summa theologica,* II–II, 118.1. Aquinas draws on Aristotle for the example of medicine.

26. Tibor Scitovsky, "Are Men Rational or Economists Wrong?," in *Human Desire and Economic Satisfaction: Essays on the Frontiers of Economics* (New York: New York University Press, 1986), chap. 6.

27. Aquinas, *Summa theologica,* II–II, 118.8. The "daughter" vices are treachery, fraud, falsehood, perjury, restlessness, violence, and insensibility to mercy.

28. Aquinas, *Summa theologica,* II–II, 118.7.

29. Aquinas, *Summa theologica,* II–II, 118.7.ad.1.

30. Aquinas, *Summa theologica,* II–II, 118.7.ad.2.

31. Aquinas, *Summa theologica,* I–II, 2.1.ad.2.

32. Aquinas, *Summa theologica,* I–II, 2.1.

33. Aquinas, *Summa theologica,* II–II, 77.

34. Aquinas, *Summa theologica,* II–II, 78.

35. Mark Blaug, *Economic Theory in Retrospect,* 5th ed. (Cambridge, UK: Cambridge University Press, 1997), 31–32.

36. Opinions range from that of John T. Noonan Jr., who finds the usury teachings of the Middle Ages to be inapplicable to the modern world, to Christopher Franks, who construes usury as a sin of presumption. Bernard Dempsey offers the most thorough engagement with economic thought and argues that modern capitalism entails a type of institutional usury. Brian M. McCall also argues that the scholastic teachings on usury have purchase on the modern economy. See Eugen von Böhm-Bawerk, who exhaustively surveys the various approaches to understanding interest for a sense of the complexity of the question. See John T. Noonan Jr., *The Scholastic Analysis of Usury* (Cambridge, MA: Harvard University Press, 1957); Franks, *He Became Poor;* Bernard Dempsey, *Interest and Usury* (Washington, DC: American Council on Public Affairs, 1943); Brian M. McCall, *The Church and the Usurers: Unprofitable Lending for the Modern Economy* (Ave Maria, FL: Sapientia Press of Ave Maria University, 2013); and Eugen von Böhm-Bawerk, *Capital and Interest,* vol. 1, *History and Critique of Interest Theories,* trans. George D. Huncke and Hans F. Sennholtz (South Holland, IL: Libertarian Press, 1959; orig. pub. 1884).

37. Karl Marx, *Capital,* vol. 1, in *The Marx Engels Reader,* 2nd ed., ed. Robert C. Tucker (New York: W. W. Norton, 1978), 319–329, refers to this phenomenon as commodity fetishism.

38. Pascal-Emmanuel Gobry, "The Real Reason Wells Fargo Employees Resorted to Fraud," *The Week,* October 3, 2016, http://theweek.com/articles/652186/real -reason-wells-fargo-employees-resorted-fraud.

39. Thomas Aquinas, *Summa contra Gentiles,* trans. James F. Anderson (Notre Dame, IN: University of Notre Dame Press, 1975) 3.131.2–4.

40. Aquinas, *Summa contra Gentiles,* 3.134.2–4.

41. John Ruskin, "Unto This Last," in *Unto This Last and Other Essays,* ed. Clive Wilmer (London, UK: Penguin Books, 1997), 167–179, argues that just as the essence of being a physician is to heal, the essence of being a merchant is to provision.

42. Aquinas, *Summa theologica,* II–II, 78.1.

43. John Paul II, *Laborem exercens* (1981), 9.

44. See Martijn Cremers, "What Corporate Governance Can Learn from Catholic Social Thought," *Journal of Business Ethics* 145, no. 4 (November 2017): 711–724, for a more complete discussion of the functions of a virtuous firm.

45. Friedrich Hayek, "The Use of Knowledge in Society," *American Economic Review* 35, no. 4 (September 1945): 519–530.

46. Aquinas, *Summa theologica,* I–II, 2.1.

47. Aquinas, *Summa theologica,* I–II, 2.1.ad.3.

48. Aquinas, *Summa theologica,* I–II, 2.1.ob.3.

49. Aquinas, *Summa theologica,* I–II, 2.1.ad.3.

50. Aquinas, *Summa theologica*, I–II, 30.4.
51. Thomas Aquinas, *Commentary on Aristotle's Politics*, trans. Richard J. Regan (Indianapolis, IN: Hackett Publishing, 2007), 48 (emphasis added).
52. Aquinas, *Commentary on Aristotle's Politics*, 52.
53. Aquinas, *Commentary on Aristotle's Politics*, 53.
54. Aquinas, *Commentary on Aristotle's Politics*, 57.
55. Aquinas, *Commentary on Aristotle's Politics*, 57–58.
56. Modern-day capitalism has elicited similar critiques. Marx, *Capital*, 329–336, discusses the transition from exchanges that begin and end with commodities ($C \rightarrow M \rightarrow C$) to exchanges that begin and end with money ($M \rightarrow C \rightarrow M$). Ruskin, "Unto This Last," 167–179, has an extended discussion of the way professions are altered when they shift from being focused on their respective arts to being focused on generating income.
57. Aquinas, *Summa theologica*, II–II, 77.4.
58. Consider the character of Frank Kennedy in Margaret Mitchell's *Gone with the Wind*.
59. Aquinas, *Summa theologica*, II–II, 77.4.
60. Scripture itself refers to disordered desire for material goods without reference to a disordered desire for money. See, for example, Luke 12:16–20:

> And he told them a parable saying, "The land of a rich man was very productive. And he began reasoning to himself, saying, 'What shall I do, since I have no place to store my crops?' Then he said, 'This is what I will do: I will tear down my barns and build larger ones, and there I will store all my grain and my goods. And I will say to my soul, "Soul, you have many goods laid up for many years to come; take your ease, eat, drink and be merry."' But God said to him, 'you fool! This very night your soul is required of you; and now who will own what you have prepared?'"

Similarly, Socrates begins his account of the just city by describing a harmonious city with moderate demands, but he suggests that the citizens would inevitably want luxuries, which will require an expansion of the city and a consequent difficulty in structuring social life justly (Plato, *Republic*, II, 372eff). Socrates's account of the transition makes no reference to the corrupting influence of commerce.

61. Aquinas, *Summa theologica*, I–II, 30.3.
62. Aquinas, *Summa theologica*, I–II, 30.4.
63. Aquinas, *Summa theologica*, I–II, 30.4.ad.2.
64. Aquinas, *Summa theologica*, I–II, 30.4.ad.3.
65. Aquinas, *Summa theologica*, I–II, 2.1.ad.3.
66. Aquinas, *Summa theologica*, I–II, 3.2.
67. Aquinas, *Summa theologica*, I–II, 3.3.

68. Aquinas, *Summa theologica,* I–II, 3.4; 3.5; 3.8.

69. Aquinas, *Summa theologica,* I–II, 4.4.

70. Aquinas, *Summa theologica,* I–II, 4.5–6.

71. Aquinas, *Summa theologica,* I–II, 4.7.

72. Aquinas, *Summa theologica,* I–II, 4.8.

73. Aquinas, *Summa theologica,* I–II, 3.2.ad.4; 3.6.

74. Aquinas, *Summa theologica,* I–II, 5.3.

75. Aquinas, *Summa theologica,* I, 12.11.

76. Aquinas, *Summa theologica,* I–II, 3.8. Our perfect happiness still falls short of God's own happiness. We can see his essence but will never be able to comprehend it (Aquinas, *Summa theologica,* I–II, 3.8.ad.2).

77. Aquinas, *Summa theologica,* I–II, 3.8; I, 12.12.

78. Aquinas, *Summa theologica,* I, 12.13; I, 12.13.ad.1.

79. Aquinas, *Summa theologica,* I–II, 3.2.

80. Aquinas, *Summa theologica,* I–II, 5.3.

81. Aquinas, *Summa theologica,* I–II, 3.2.ad.4.

82. Aquinas, *Summa theologica,* I–II, 4.7.

83. Aquinas, *Summa contra Gentiles,* III–II, 133.2.

84. Aquinas, *Summa theologica,* I–II, 3.6.

85. Aquinas, *Summa theologica,* I–II, 4.7.ob.1.

86. Aquinas, *Summa theologica,* I–II, 4.7.ad.1.

87. Aquinas, *Summa theologica,* I–II, 4.7.ob.2.

88. Aquinas, *Summa theologica,* I–II, 4.7.ad.2.

89. Michael Sandel, *What Money Can't Buy: The Moral Limits of Markets* (New York: Farrar, Straus and Giroux, 2012), 90–95.

90. Leon Kass, *The Hungry Soul: Eating and the Perfecting of Our Souls* (New York: Free Press, 1999), 230–232, further suggests that our increasingly utilitarian approach to food also disrupts the rich social meaning of dining together. The tendency toward abstraction that is part of our commercial and technological culture leads us to miss the complex connection between the real material goods that constitute our lives and the human practices that evolve around them.

91. Aquinas, *Summa theologica,* II–II, 118.7.

92. Aquinas, *Summa theologica,* II–II, 118.7.ad.2.

93. Kathryn Tanner, "Christianity and the New Spirit of Capitalism," Gifford Lectures, a series of six lectures delivered in Edinburgh in May 2016, http://www.ed.ac.uk/humanities-soc-sci/news-events/lectures/gifford-lectures/gifford-lectures-2015-2016/professor-tanner-christianity-and-capitalism. A monograph of the lecture series is forthcoming from Yale.

94. Pope Francis, *Laudato si* (2015), 106.

95. Natasha Dow Schüll, *Addiction by Design: Machine Gambling in Las Vegas* (Princeton, NJ: Princeton University Press, 2012).

96. George A. Akerlof and Robert J. Shiller, *Phishing for Phools: The Economics of Manipulation and Deception* (Princeton, NJ: Princeton University Press, 2015).

97. Tanner, "Christianity and the New Spirit of Capitalism."

98. Aquinas, *Summa theologica,* II–II, 77.4.

99. Tanner, "Christianity and the New Spirit of Capitalism."

100. Aquinas, *Summa theologica,* II–II, 118.8.

101. Robert J. Shiller, *Finance and the Good Society* (Princeton, NJ: Princeton University Press, 2012).

102. Charles P. Kindleberger, *Manias, Panics, and Crashes: A History of Financial Crises* (New York: Macmillan, 1978). Economists have often resisted the idea of speculative bubbles because speculative bubbles suggest that behavior can be systematically irrational, contra the assumptions of the rational choice model. But behavioral economics has broken down that resistance some, and there is now a more general willingness to admit the phenomenon, which is rather self-evident to anyone who is not committed to the thought that consumer behavior is generally rational. See Andrei Shleifer, *Inefficient Markets: An Introduction to Behavioral Finance* (Oxford, UK: Oxford University Press, 2000), for a comprehensive study of the contribution behavioral economics has made to our understanding of the sources of financial instability.

103. Carmen M. Reinhardt and Kenneth Rogoff, *This Time Is Different: Eight Centuries of Financial Folly* (Princeton, NJ: Princeton University Press, 2009).

6. From Liberality to Justice

1. David J. O'Brien and Thomas A. Shannon, eds., introduction to *Catholic Social Thought: The Documentary Heritage* (Maryknoll, NY: Orbis Books, 1992), 2–3.

2. There are multiple readings of Aquinas on private property. Christopher Franks, *He Became Poor* (Grand Rapids, MI: William B. Eerdmans Publishing, 2009), draws a strong contrast between Aquinas and John Locke, stressing the nonproprietary aspect of Aquinas's justification of private property. My own analysis arrives at similar conclusions by a different route. Anthony Parel, "Aquinas' Theory of Property," in *Theories of Property: Aristotle to the Present,* ed. Anthony Parel and Thomas Flanagan (Waterloo, ON: Wilfrid Laruier University Press, 1979), 89–114, embeds Aquinas's teachings on private property in his metaphysical and ethical theories and thus parallels my own analysis in many ways.

3. Thomas Aquinas, *Summa theologica,* trans. Fathers of the English Dominican Province (Allen, TX: Christian Classics, 1948), II–II, 66.

4. Aquinas, *Summa theologica,* II–II, 66.1.ob.1.

5. This does raise a question about whether genetic engineering is licit. Catholic social thought is not hostile to genetic engineering per se, though it is cautious. See Pontifical Council for Justice and Peace, *Compendium of the Social Doctrine of the Church* (Washington, DC: United States Conference of Catholic Bishops, 2004), 206–207.

6. Aquinas, *Summa theologica,* II–II, 66.2.ob.2.

7. Aquinas, *Summa theologica,* II–II, 66.2.

8. I am indebted to Jean Porter for this point.

9. Thomas Aquinas, *Summa contra Gentiles,* trans. James F. Anderson (Notre Dame, IN: University of Notre Dame Press, 1975), III.131.2,3; 134.2,3.

10. Aquinas, *Summa contra Gentiles,* III.131.4; 134.4.

11. Aquinas, *Summa theologica,* II–II, 26.4.

12. Aquinas, *Summa theologica,* II–II, 26.2.

13. Aquinas, *Summa theologica,* II–II, 26.4.

14. Aquinas, *Summa theologica,* II–II, 32.6.

15. Aquinas, *Summa theologica,* II–II, 57.3.

16. Aquinas, *Summa theologica,* II–II, 25.7.

17. John Locke, *Second Treatise of Government,* ed. C. B. Macpherson (Indianapolis, IN: Hackett Publishing, 1980), chap. 5.

18. C. B. MacPherson, *The Political Theory of Possessive Individualism: Hobbes to Locke* (Oxford, UK: Oxford University Press, 1962).

19. B. Andrew Lustig, "Natural Law, Property, and Justice: The General Justification of Property in John Locke," *Journal of Religious Ethics* 19, no. 1 (Spring 1991): 119–148, offers a good survey of the debate on MacPherson's interpretation of Locke.

20. In Mary Hirschfeld, "How a Thomistic Moral Framework Can Take Social Causality Seriously," in *Distant Markets, Distant Harms: Economic Complicity and Christian Ethics,* ed. Daniel Finn (Oxford, UK: Oxford University Press, 2014), 146–169, I argue that other features of economic thought, notably the division of labor identified as a source of prosperity, can be used to create a more balanced picture of economic life as a matter of both individual effort and social cooperation. The aim is to nudge us toward a conception of humans as individuals but also as essentially political animals, which I take to be a reflection of Aquinas's view of the matter.

21. Aquinas, *Summa theologica,* II–II, 57.3.

22. The tradition of Catholic social thought has at least one strand, most notably found in Pope Leo XIII, *Rerum novarum* (1891), 7, and repeated in Pope John Paul II, *Laborem exercens* (1981), 12, and Pope John Paul II, *Centesimus annus* (1991), 31, which does argue that the property right originates in our labor. The right to property so grounded is still subordinated to the common destination of all goods. As we read in Pope Paul VI, *Populorum progressio* (1967), 59, "Private property, in fact, regardless of the concrete forms of the regulations

and juridical norms relative to it, is in its essence only an instrument for respecting the principle of the universal destination of goods; in the final analysis, therefore, it is not an end but a means." Aquinas's doctrine is distinct from Catholic social thought in this regard. As Manfred Spieker writes, in "The Universal Destination of Goods: The Ethics of Property in the Theory of a Christian Society," *Journal of Markets and Morality* 8, no. 20 (Fall 2005): 335, "Work as the principle of legitimacy of individual property is not found in Thomas."

23. Aquinas, *Summa theologica,* II–II, 66.2.

24. Aquinas, *Summa theologica,* II–II, 66.7 (emphasis added).

25. Aquinas, *Summa theologica,* II–II, 66.7.

26. Aquinas, *Summa theologica,* II–II, 66.2.ad.3.

27. There is more to say about Aquinas's nuanced understanding of private property and the way it mediates between humans as individuals and humans as members of a society. See Hirschfeld, "How a Thomistic Moral Framework Can Take Social Causality Seriously," for more reflections on how this balance might be struck between the individual and society when it comes to economic questions.

28. Although Aquinas does not treat private property rights as absolute, he is willing to tolerate imperfect institutions if it would be even more destabilizing to overthrow them. As Anthony Parel, "Aquinas's Theory on Property," 107–108, argues, Aquinas is mindful of cultural possibilities and does not expect or even desire that institutions be designed according to the metaphysical or ethical considerations taken up here. What is meant is a sketch of the ideals against which we should judge our institutions and policies, as we plod along in the realm of what is culturally or politically possible. If it is the case that, for example, excessively high tax rates would destabilize the economy because too many people are formed by a Lockean view of property and only would work if motivated by the prospect of excessive monetary gain, we ought not to impose them even if we might believe that higher tax rates would be a way of socially redistributing wealth from those who have too much to those who have not enough. Aquinas's system of thought is not innately liberal or conservative in its tendencies. He is a pragmatist.

29. Ian Parker, "The Gift," *New Yorker,* August 2, 2004, 54–63, recounts the story of Zell Kravinsky, who felt so compelled to alleviate the suffering of others that in addition to giving away vast portions of his own wealth he went on to donate a kidney to a stranger in need. Peter Singer, "Famine, Affluence, and Morality," *Philosophy & Public Affairs* 1, no. 1 (1972): 229–243, offers a utilitarian basis for such a stance toward giving: if the marginal cost to you is less than the marginal benefit to others, it is not clear that one in good conscience could refrain from giving. Such extreme stances do not seem fully humane, and I would argue that the root error is thinking that we as individuals

are responsible for global outcomes. I would argue that Aquinas is able to resist such moves because he respects human finitude. We are and ought to be responsive to others, but we are not provident for the world as a whole— only the sphere of it that we engage, and only in due measure. Onora O'Neill, "Ending World Hunger," in *World Hunger and Morality*, 2nd ed., ed. William Aiken and Hugh LaFollette (Upper Saddle River, NJ: Prentice Hall, 1996), 94–112, offers a reading of Kant that likewise respects human finitude and grounds morality in what humans can do rather than in some imagined responsibility for global outcomes.

30. Even with respect to the first sense, Aquinas makes some exceptions. If we were confronted with a choice of maintaining our own life or the life of someone who was more important to the community, we might sacrifice ourselves for the greater good. Aquinas, *Summa theologica*, II–II, 32.6.

31. Aquinas, *Summa theologica*, I–II, 32.6.

32. Aquinas, *Summa theologica*, II–II, 118.1,4.

33. Aquinas, *Summa theologica*, II–II, 66.2.ad.3.

34. Douglass C. North and Robert Paul Thomas, *The Rise of the Western World: A New Economic History* (Cambridge, UK: Cambridge University Press, 1973), 33–70.

35. North and Thomas, *The Rise of the Western World*, 48. Aquinas was writing during a period of expansion that pressed agricultural production to the limits, setting the stage for the demographic disaster of the fourteenth century, including the calamity of the Black Plague at midcentury.

36. Stephen Marglin, *The Dismal Science: How Thinking Like an Economist Undermines Community* (Cambridge, MA: Harvard University Press, 2008).

37. Kelly S. Johnson, *The Fear of Beggars: Stewardship and Poverty in Christian Ethics* (Grand Rapids, MI: William B. Eerdmans Publishing, 2007), 1–70, has an interesting discussion of the voluntary poverty movement as a reaction to the sense of economic dislocation brought on by the rising merchant class. See also Lester Little, *Religious Poverty and the Profit Economy in Medieval Europe* (Ithaca, NY: Cornell University Press, 1983).

38. Aquinas, *Summa theologica*, II–II, 77.4.ob.1.

39. Aquinas, *Summa theologica*, II–II, 77.4.

40. Adam Smith, *Theory of Moral Sentiments*, in *The Essential Adam Smith*, ed. Robert L. Heilbroner (New York: W. W. Norton, 1986), 78–79.

41. Amartya Sen, *The Standard of Living* (Cambridge, UK: Cambridge University Press, 1985). Douglas A. Hicks, "Inequality, Globalization, and Leadership: Keeping Up with the Joneses across National Boundaries," *Annual of the Society of Christian Ethics* 21 (November 2001): 63–80, analyzes the problem in the context of globalization.

42. Hazel Kyrk, *A Theory of Consumption* (Boston: Houghton Mifflin, 1923). Frances M Magrabi, Young Sook Chung, Sanghee Sohn Cha, and Se-Jeong

Yang, *The Economics of Household Consumption* (New York: Praeger, 1991), cite Kyrk as a central figure in the discipline of home economics, though Kyrk held a joint appointment in the Economics Department at the University of Chicago.

43. Kyrk cites vacations as an example, arguing that many vacations entail "roughing it" and are regarded as pleasurable precisely because one is less encumbered by goods. That example might have somewhat less traction today.

44. The material in this subsection is drawn from Mary Hirschfeld, "From a Theological Frame to a Secular Frame: How Historical Context Shapes Our Understanding of the Principles of Catholic Social Thought," in *The True Wealth of Nations: Catholic Social Thought and Economic Life,* ed. Daniel K. Finn (Oxford, UK: Oxford University Press, 2010), 188–190.

45. Margaret Reid, *The Economics of Household Production* (New York: J. Wiley and Sons, 1934), offers invaluable reflections on the special quality of household labor that set it out as virtuous activity rather than something that is merely instrumental to other ends.

46. Have a look in our basements, overstuffed closets, or garages to see the detritus of a life of ill-considered choices about consumption. (I plead guilty to having such basements and closets!)

47. Jean Porter, *The Recovery of Virtue: The Relevance of Aquinas for Christian Ethics* (Louisville, KY: Westminster John Knox Press, 1990), 156–162.

48. Juliet B. Schor, *The Overspent American: Why We Want What We Don't Need* (New York: Harper, 1998), likewise points to the importance of finding small communities to support the effort to achieve a more rational standard of living.

49. Benedict XVI, *Deus caritas est* (2005), 28.b.

50. Benedict XVI, *Deus caritas est,* 26.

51. Paul VI, *Quadragesimo anno* (1931), 4, worries that the wealthy are "content to abandon to charity alone the full care of relieving the unfortunate, as though it were the task of charity to make amends for the open violation of justice, a violation not merely tolerated but sanctioned at times by legislators."

52. Daniel C. Maguire, "The Primacy of Justice in Moral Theology," *Horizons* 10, no. 1 (Spring 1983): 72–85.

53. Maguire, "The Primacy of Justice in Moral Theology," 73.

54. Maguire, "The Primacy of Justice in Moral Theology," 75–78.

55. Maguire uses the term *charity,* but I take him to mean only almsgiving and not the virtue of charity, which, of course, is much broader than the practice of almsgiving. For Aquinas, charity is "the mother and the root of all the virtues, inasmuch as it is the form of them all" (Aquinas, *Summa theologica,* I–II, 62.4; see also, II–II, 23.8), and I do not believe Maguire would quarrel with that view.

56. Stephen J. Pope, "Aquinas on Almsgiving, Justice, and Charity: An Interpretation and Reassessment," *Heythrop Journal* 32, no. 2 (April 1991): 167–191, likewise observes that Aquinas views the question of almsgiving as a matter of both charity and justice.

57. If individuals have utility functions that continue to treat extra consumption as beneficial, the economic analysis that suggests that policies aimed at achieving equity tend to erode incentives to produce and thus lead to a decline in efficiency would need to be taken seriously.

58. Bruce D. Meyer and James X. Sullivan, "Consumption, Income, and Material Well-Being after Welfare Reform" (Working Paper 11976, National Bureau of Economic Research, Cambridge, MA, January, 2006), document the rising income inequality in the United States but observe that consumption inequality has not risen as much owing to the efficacy of existing social programs.

59. "Working for the Few: Political Capture and Economic Inequality," Oxfam Briefing Paper, January 20, 2014.

60. The Occupy Wall Street movement is the most prominent example of this concern.

61. Charlie Camosy raised this point during a question-and-answer session following my presentation of the paper "Retrieving a Medieval Scholastic for Reflection on the Financial Crisis: Aquinas on the Proper Function of Artificial Wealth" (presented at the meetings of the Society of Christian Ethics, Seattle, January 2014).

62. Luigi Zingales, *A Capitalism for the People: Recapturing the Lost Genius of American Prosperity* (New York: Basic Books, 2012). As Zingales observes, "Not surprisingly, seven out of the ten richest counties in the United States now are in the suburbs of Washington, D.C." (90).

63. See the essays in *Income Distribution and High-Quality Growth,* ed. Vito Tanzi and Ke-Young Chu (Cambridge, MA: MIT Press, 1997), for a range of opinions on the relationship between income distribution and economic growth.

64. "Rich Enclaves Are Not as Generous as the Wealthy Living Elsewhere," *Chronicle of Philanthropy,* August 19, 2012, https://www.philanthropy.com/article /Rich-Enclaves-Are-Not-as/156255.

65. Robert D. Putnam, "The Crumbling American Dream," *New York Times,* August 3, 2013.

66. In "The Inequality That Matters," *American Interest,* January 1, 2011, Tyler Cowen observes that there are some, and perhaps even many, who sacrifice higher earnings in favor of pursing intrinsically satisfying careers or to spend more time with family and friends. He calls them "threshold earners" and observes that their presence in the population will cause increased income inequality in a society, since they focus on earning enough and therefore tend

to be left behind as others pursue the disordered dream of ever more wealth. Such choices should be honored, since they reflect choices to order instrumental goods properly to higher goals.

67. Joan Robinson, *Economic Philosophy* (Garden City, NY: Doubleday, 1964), 46.
68. Aquinas, *Summa theologica,* II–II, 61.2.

7. Toward a Humane Economy

1. Juliet B. Schor, *The Overspent American: Upscaling, Downshifting, and the New Consumer* (New York: Basic Books, 1998).
2. Kathryn Tanner, "Christianity and the New Spirit of Capitalism," Gifford Lectures, a series of six lectures delivered in Edinburgh in May 2016, http://www .ed.ac.uk/humanities-soc-sci/news-events/lectures/gifford-lectures/gifford -lectures-2015-2016/professor-tanner-christianity-and-capitalism. A monograph of the lecture series is forthcoming from Yale.
3. This is not to say that there are no benefits to be derived from the economic growth we have enjoyed to date. Some of the goods we have available to us because of our affluence genuinely support human flourishing. The claim is simply that a portion of our wealth, possibly a large portion of our wealth, is wasted insofar as it is not well ordered to genuine human flourishing.
4. In the wake of the financial crisis of 2008, there is good reason to ask whether economic analysis of macroeconomic issues is as valuable as more narrowly focused policy analysis. Although I personally do not think the complexity of a dynamic economic system is amenable to the sort of mathematical modeling economists employ, there are no better alternatives, and some of their insights can be helpful.
5. Thomas Aquinas, *Summa theologica,* trans. Fathers of the English Dominican Province (Allen, TX: Christian Classics, 1948), I–II, 96.2.
6. Aquinas, *Summa theologica,* I–II, 95.3.
7. Aquinas, *Summa theologica,* I–II, 96.2. Though note that in a community of people who are more advanced in the cultivation of virtue, it would be reasonable to outlaw a greater range of vices. Some cultures, for example, might flourish under prohibition, whereas others might not do so well with such legislation. It is beyond the scope of this book to discuss Aquinas's understanding of the relationship between law and virtue. But briefly, law can provide necessary communal support to the project of cultivating virtue, although true virtue consists in freely chosen acts and thus cannot be legislated directly.
8. I am overstating the case for economics here. Although economists do work to produce objective analysis, they are not immune from the human tendency to read evidence in a way that supports their preexisting biases. See Anthony

Randazzo and Jonathan Haidt, "The Moral Narratives of Economists," *Econ Journal Watch* 12, no. 1 (January 2015): 49–57.

9. Gary S. Becker, *The Economic Approach to Human Behavior* (Chicago: University of Chicago Press, 1976), 5, 14.

10. Becker, *The Economic Approach to Human Behavior,* 10.

11. Becker, *The Economic Approach to Human Behavior,* 10. On bribing a spouse to stay in the marriage, see Gary S. Becker, *A Treatise on the Family* (Cambridge, MA: Harvard University Press, 1993), 331–335.

12. Becker has done considerable work on the economics of marriage and the family and claims to have a good deal of empirical support for his theories—in part because modern notions of marriage are not so far from the economic model and in part because it is an artifact of the weakness of empirical techniques in economics.

13. Insurance works by pooling risk. Let's say there are ten houses, one of which will burn down on average every year. If all ten home owners buy insurance, their premiums should be 10 percent of the cost of replacing a home (plus a bit more to cover the expenses of the insurer in running the program). If there were a law that said you could buy insurance for your home after it burnt down, there would be no incentive to buy the insurance. When your home does burn down, your insurer would basically have to charge you the cost of replacing the home for your insurance policy. In health care, if you can get coverage after you have gotten sick, the insurers are going to have mostly sick people getting insurance. If the percentage of sick people in their coverage pool rises, their costs will rise, and insurance premiums will rise accordingly.

14. Congressional Budget Office, "Estimates for the Insurance Coverage Provisions of the Affordable Care Act Updated for the Recent Supreme Court Decision," July 28, 2012.

15. A notable example can be found in Gerardo Sanchis Muñoz, "Public Service, Public Goods, and the Common Good: Argentina as a Case Study," in *Empirical Foundations of the Common Good: What Theology Can Learn from Social Science,* ed. Daniel K. Finn (Oxford, UK: Oxford University Press, 2017), 142–169. Sanchis argues that the widespread adoption of the economic approach to human behavior in Argentina had a deleterious impact on social norms, which, in turn, undermined economic performance.

16. Samuel Bowles, *The Moral Economy: Why Good Incentives Are No Substitute for Good Citizens* (New Haven, CT: Yale University Press, 2016).

17. Andrew Yuengert, *The Boundaries of Technique* (Lanham, MD: Lexington Books, 2004), 71. Yuengert likewise considers the practice of economists from a Thomistic framework and identifies two proximate goals for economists: publication of articles and policy prescription.

18. Daniel Hausman, introduction to *The Philosophy of Economics: An Anthology,* ed. Daniel Hausman (Cambridge, UK: Cambridge University Press, 1984), 6.

19. Joseph Dorfman, *The Economic Mind in American Civilization*, vol. 5, *1918–1933* (New York, NY: Viking Press, 1959). See his chapter on the home economics movement. When I presented my work on consumption economics to economic seminars, I was invariably met with the challenge that the inquiry seemed fruitless since such research could only issue in paternalistic regulations, and such regulations were repugnant.

20. Mary L. Hirschfeld, "Methodological Stance and Consumption Theory: A Lesson in Feminist Methodology," *History of Political Economy* 29, supp. no. 1, ed. John B. Davis (1997): 191–211. In that paper I present an alternative approach I dubbed the conversational stance, which I discovered in the work of Hazel Kyrk, *A Theory of Consumption* (Boston: Houghton Mifflin, 1923). See also Margaret Reid, *The Economics of Household Production* (New York, NY: J. Wiley & Sons, 1934). Kyrk's writings on the question of whether we are consuming wisely puzzled me until I realized that she is writing to home economics students. She was talking about the things one might consider in developing a wise approach to consumption, which would not yield up any sort of policy prescriptions but made sense when understood as being addressed to individuals who would go on to manage households. In other words, Kyrk did not see her task as being limited to a description of what people were doing (as a prelude to controlling them). She thought it worthwhile to talk to the agents themselves about what they were doing and to offer them suggestions on how they might do it better.

21. Aquinas, *Summa theologica,* I, prologue.

22. Mark D. Jordan, "The *Summa*'s Reform of Moral Teaching and Its Failures," in *Contemplating Aquinas: On the Varieties of Interpretation,* ed. Fergus Kerr, O.P. (Notre Dame, IN: University of Notre Dame Press, 2003), 41–54. Jordan goes on to observe that Thomas's intent was almost immediately thwarted, in that the *Secunda secundae,* which is Thomas's catalogue of virtues and vices, was most widely copied and tended to circulate apart from the work as a whole.

23. I am leaving aside a consideration of the fact that Aquinas believes that in the wake of the Fall humans cannot achieve their end, not even their natural end, apart from God's grace (Aquinas, *Summa theologica,* I–II, 109). God's causal actions in the world are not to be understood as causes alongside natural causes. God operates through natural causes, and it would take us deep into territory that is not germane to this book to try to sort out the extent to which Aquinas means that God's grace assists us in realizing our natural abilities in ways that would look to external observers like a Pelagian attainment of our natural end through our own efforts.

24. John R. Carter and Michael D. Irons, "Are Economists Different, and If So Why?," *Journal of Economic Perspectives* 5, no. 2 (Spring 1991): 171–177.

25. The aim is so central it even becomes the title of a textbook: Paul Heynes, *The Economic Way of Thinking,* 11th ed. (Upper Saddle River, NJ: Prentice Hall, 2005).

26. Greg Mankiw, *Principles of Economics,* 4th ed. (Mason, OH: South-Western, 2007), 5–6.
27. Mankiw is a bit of an exception on this. He waits until chapter 2 to make the distinction between positive and normative economics.
28. The discrepancy between what economists assume humans do and what they assume students need to be taught is not limited to the concept of opportunity cost. When the subject of firm behavior is broached, students need to be taught that sunk costs do not matter for decision making at the margin. In macroeconomics students need to be taught that it is real, not nominal, interest rates that are relevant for decision making, and so on.
29. Mankiw, *Principles of Economics,* 6 (emphasis in the original).
30. Thomas Schelling, "Egonomics, or the Art of Self-Management," *American Economic Review* 68, no. 2 (May 1978): 290–294, is one good example.
31. Andre de Palma, Gordon M. Myers, and Yorgos Y. Papageorgiou, "Rational Choice under an Imperfect Ability to Choose," *American Economic Review* 84, no. 3 (June 1994): 419–440, for example, addresses the problem as one of insufficient information-processing capacity that can be addressed through modeling agents as incrementally changing consumption patterns in search of a local (but not a global) optimum. As discussed below, the emphasis on incremental decisions marginalizes the Thomistic view that choice has a great deal to do with ordering diverse goods into a coherent whole.
32. Life-cycle models, overlapping generations models, any model of investment are examples of intertemporal models.
33. Finn E. Kydland and Edward C. Prescott, "Rules Rather than Discretion: The Inconsistency of Optimal Plans," *Journal of Political Economy* 85, no. 3 (June 1977): 473–492, is the key article here.
34. James Wetzel, *Augustine and the Limits of Virtue* (Cambridge, UK: Cambridge University Press, 2008), has an interesting discussion of the project of integrating one's self across time.
35. The opera ticket example comes out of my own experience. At the time I encountered the problem I had only been trained as an economist, and so I "rationally" decided to stay home. The problem is that I noticed that this habit of habitually disregarding sunk costs made me more cavalier about prior commitments I had made. Thinking at the margin encourages one to think about how one feels in the moment, which leads one to systematically refuse to incur short-term discomforts in the quest for long-run goods. The self I am today would be better off if I had heard that opera. The comfort of sinking into an easy chair instead passed away long ago.
36. Tibor Scitovsky, "Are Men Rational or Economists Wrong?," in *Human Desire and Economic Satisfaction: Essays on the Frontiers of Economics* (New York: New York University Press, 1986), chap. 6.
37. There are exceptions to this. Carol Graham, *The Pursuit of Happiness: An Economy of Well-Being* (Washington, DC: Brookings Institution Press, 2011),

has moved in the direction of thinking of happiness in more Aristotelian terms.

38. Amartya Sen, *Development as Freedom* (New York: Knopf, 1999); Martha Nussbaum, "Nature, Functioning, and Capability: Aristotle on Political Distribution," *Oxford Studies in Ancient Philosophy* 6, supplementary volume (1988): 145–184. "Human Functioning and Social Justice: In Defense of Aristotelian Essentialism," *Political Theory* 20, no. 2 (1992): 202–246.

39. Paul VI, "Pastoral Constitution on the Church in the Modern World—*Gaudium et Spes*" (1965), 26, http://www.vatican.va/archive/hist_councils/ii_vatican_council/documents/vat-ii_cons_19651207_gaudium-et-spes_en.html.

40. Bowles, *The Moral Economy.*

41. Terrence McCoy, "The Creepiness Factor: How Obama and Romney Are Getting to Know You," *Atlantic Monthly,* April 10, 2012.

42. Kyrk, *A Theory of Consumption*, and Reid, *The Economics of Household Production*, are two good examples. Frances M. Magrabi, Young Sook Chung, Sanghee Sohn Cha, and Se-Jeong Yang, *The Economics of Household Consumption* (New York: Praeger, 1991), offers an overview of this school of thought.

43. Dorfman, *The Economic Mind in American Civilization.*

Acknowledgments

The journey toward the completion of this book has been long and would not have been possible without the help of family, friends, and colleagues. Too many have played a role in shaping my thought or supporting me through this process to acknowledge by name, but there are several who have played such key roles in my life that they need to be mentioned.

My intellectual journey properly started during my graduate studies at Harvard University. One of course learns much from one's professors, and my two dissertation advisers, Jeffrey G. Williamson and Lawrence Summers, taught me much. But my real awakening came from conversations with Deborah Weiss and Tyler Cowen, who jointly nudged me out of the habit of unthinkingly adopting the conventional wisdom of my peers. From them I learned the wisdom of conservative or libertarian thought even if I never fully embraced it.

While at Harvard I began to feel that something was missing from economics. I was fortunate in securing a position in the Economics Department at Occidental College, where my senior colleagues Jim Halstead, Robby Moore, Woody Studenmund, and Jim Whitney generously gave me room to pursue those concerns in both the sort of teaching I was able to do and the sort of research that they accepted from me. My first major exploration was in the field of feminist economics, an inquiry launched as a result of conversations with my dear friend and colleague Jane Rossetti. In particular, Jane encouraged me to write a paper about Hazel Kyrk and the early home economists. Although that was meant to be a project in feminist economics, what I learned from Kyrk was that no account of economic life is complete without an adequate theory of consumption, and that is the thread that carries through to this project.

My unexpected conversion to Catholicism interrupted that line of inquiry, however. I am often asked who played a role in my conversion, and I usually reply that my conversion was something like Paul's being knocked off of a horse. But that is not entirely true. My extended conversations with Tyler Cowen in the months leading up to my conversion and the first few years thereafter about the relative merits of theism and atheism profoundly shaped my understanding of the proper relationship between faith and reason. It is because of Tyler that I am a convinced Thomist, though that outcome would undoubtedly horrify him.

Becoming Catholic was the most intellectually exhilarating experience in my life. I entered into the Master of Theological Studies program at the University of Notre Dame without really knowing the caliber of the program there. To my great joy, I found an embarrassment of riches. In my first semester, I studied with David Burrell, whose spirit haunts this book even if he is not once mentioned by name. I had my first of many courses with Jennifer Herdt, whose generous spirit and capacious mind inspire me more than she could possibly know, and with Gerald McKenny, with whom I spent many treasured hours in conversations ranging over a multitude of topics. Over the next few years I had the privilege of studying Augustine with John Cavadini, scripture with Gary Anderson and Brian Daley, Aquinas with Joseph Wawrykow, and systematic theology with Cyril O'Regan. Any one of these individuals would make a graduate program worthwhile, and I remain grateful to have been able to study with all of them.

The faculty at Notre Dame inspired me to want to do pure theology, and I remain sorry that my path moved in other directions. The shift back toward a blend of economics and theology would partly be the fault of my dissertation director, about whom more below. But it is also partly the fault of Dan Finn, whom I met at the Society of Christian Ethics meetings. Dan drew me into the True Wealth project operating out of the Institute for Advanced Catholic Studies at the University of Southern California. It was in writing a paper for the first conference sponsored by that group that I found I did have something to say about how theology and economics might be brought into conversation. But more importantly, Dan has been unstintingly supportive over the past several years. I have learned much from him and value his friendship enormously. Through Dan I have met a number of individuals working in the intersection of economics and theology. Foremost among them are Albino Barrera and Andy Yuengert, both of whom have been steadily encouraging. Thomas Levergood invited me to join the annual meetings between theologians and economists sponsored by Lumen Christi. Those conversations have served to remind me of how economists think and the concerns they would bring to a project such as mine. I am particularly grateful to Joseph Kaboski for valuable conversations.

The book was long in development for a variety of reasons. I am therefore extremely grateful to both the Charlotte W. Newcombe Foundation for generous financial support in my sixth year at Notre Dame and to the Institute for Advanced Studies at Notre Dame for both financial support and the chance to participate as a graduate student fellow. I am especially indebted to Vittorio Hösle and Francesco Berto for helpful conversations. Over the years my work has appeared in the *Journal of the Society of Christian Ethics* and the *Journal of Catholic Social Thought*. I am grateful to both for the opportunity to initially explore and develop my positions on some topics, which are freshly reexamined in Chapters 5 and 6.

My time at Notre Dame would not have been as fruitful as it was were it not for my fellow students. I learned much both in class and out from Elizabeth Agnew, Carter Aikin, Steve Battin, Tom Bushlack, Victor Carmona, Adam Clark, Doug Finn, Gloria Wasserman Frost, James Helmer, David Lantigua, John Martin, John Perry, and many others. I am especially grateful to my erstwhile roommates Hannah Hemphill Barrett and Ellen Concannon Scully for their friendship and fantastic conversations. I could not have survived the program without the special friendship of Deonna Neal and Daria Lucas Spezzano, neither of whom can really know how essential they were and are to me. Although he and I did not overlap in our studies at Notre Dame, Father Michael Sherwin has also been an invaluable fellow traveler. Josephine Dickinson offered unflagging encouragement my last few years at Notre Dame, and I owe her a great deal.

The past six years I have been in the Humanities Department at Villanova, which might well be a Platonic ideal. My colleagues in the department—Kevin Hughes, Jesse Couenhoven, Margaret Grubiak, Gene McCarraher, Anna Moreland, David and Jeanne Schindler, Mark Shiffman, Thomas Smith, Mike and Helena Tomko, and James Wilson—inspire me both as teachers and as scholars. In addition, my parish priest, Father David Ousley, was an indispensible companion as I navigated the last painful year of this project. His counsel and prayers helped me across the finish line.

Above all I am grateful to Jean Porter, my dissertation director. In addition to insisting that I play my cards as an economist-turned-theologian, she has challenged me consistently with her bracing intellectual rigor. Yet at the same time I could not have asked for a more generous or supportive adviser. The last several years have been difficult for me, and Jean has been warm and patient throughout. She never gave up on me, though Lord knows she had good reason to. Although we disagree about much, we share a love of Thomas, and at the end of the day, what more is required?

Family, of course, is everything. I don't have a lot of family, but the family I have is wonderful. I cannot imagine my life without the love of my aunt Jan and uncle Bob, who are like second parents to me. My brother Stuart and his children, Eli, Anya, and Caleb, bring me great joy. My cousins Terri and Carol have always made me feel like a part of their immediate families. All of their love has meant a lot, especially since losing my mother and my father. I dedicated the dissertation on which this book is based to her memory and closed with a special thanks to my father: "It has been a long road, and he has been unstinting in his support. I am more grateful to him than I can say." Sadly, my father did not live to see the book in its final form. And so I dedicate this book to him.

Index